D0371680

DISCARDED

The Science of Addiction

A Norton Professional Book

32⁰⁰

The Science of Addiction

From Neurobiology to Treatment

Carlton K. Erickson, Ph.D

RC
564
E67
2007

W. W. Norton & Company
New York • London

EL CAMINO COLLEGE
LIBRARY

Copyright © 2007 by Carlton K. Erickson

All rights reserved
Printed in the United States of America
First Edition

For information about permission to reproduce selections from this book, write to Permissions, W. W. Norton & Company, Inc., 500 Fifth Avenue, New York, NY 10110

Production Manager: Leeann Graham
Manufacturing by Quebecor World, Fairfield Graphics

Library of Congress Cataloging-in-Publication Data

Erickson, Carlton K.
The science of addiction: from neurobiology to treatment / Carlton K. Erickson.
p. cm.
"A Norton professional book."
Includes bibliographical references and index.
ISBN-13: 978-0-393-70463-1
ISBN-10: 0-393-70463-7
1. Substance abuse—Physiological aspects. 2. Substance abuse—Treatment. I. Title.

RC564.E67 2006
616.86—dc22 2006047156

W. W. Norton & Company, Inc., 500 Fifth Avenue, New York, N.Y. 10110
www.wwnorton.com

W. W. Norton & Company Ltd., Castle House, 75/76 Wells St., London WIT 3QT

5 7 9 0 8 6 4

Dedication

Anyone with a successful family knows that hard work, frequent travel, and periods of serenity happen only because of the sacrifices of a loving spouse and children. To my most supportive and beautiful wife, Eunice, and the children, their spouses, and our grandchildren: Steig (Sheri and Emma); Dirk (Jennifer); Annika Bennett (Bill, Hunter and Luke); and Hans (Mandy and Hayden)—this book is dedicated to you.

Contents

Abbreviations

A.A. – Alcoholics Anonymous
ADH – Alcohol dehydrogenase
ADHD – Attention deficit hyperactivity disorder
ALDH – Aldehyde dehydrogenase
BAC – Blood alcohol concentration
BU – Beverage unit
CB – Cannabinoid receptor
CBT – Cognitive behavioral therapy
CNS – Central nervous system
COGA – Collaborative Study on the Genetics of Alcoholism
CRF – Corticotropin releasing factor
CT – Computerized tomography
DA - Dopamine
DAT – Dopamine transporter
DNA – Deoxyribonucleic acid
DRD2 – Dopamine receptor (type) D2
DSM-IV – *Diagnostic and Statistical Manual of Mental Disorders,* Fourth Edition
DTs – Delirium tremens
DUDs – Drug-use disorders
DUI – Driving under the influence
DWI – Driving while intoxicated
ERP – Event-related potential
FAE – Fetal alcohol effects
FAS – Fetal alcohol syndrome
FASD – Fetal alcohol spectrum disorder
GABA – Gamma aminobutyric acid
GHB – Gamma hydroxybutyrate
GLU – Glutamate

5-HT – Serotonin
ICD-10 – *International Classification of Diseases,* Tenth Revision
LSD – Lysergic acid diethylamide
MAO – Monamine oxidase
MDMA – Methylenedioxy methamphetamine
MDS – Mesolimbic dopamine system
MET – Motivational enhancement therapy
MI – Motivational interviewing
M.M. – Moderation management
MRI – Magnetic resonance imaging (fMRI = functional MRI)
mRNA – Messenger ribonucleic acid
N.A. – Narcotics Anonymous
NAcc – Nucleus accumbens
NIAAA – National Institute on Alcohol Abuse and Alcoholism
NIDA – National Institute on Drug Abuse
NMDA – N-methyl-D-aspartate
OCD – Obsessive compulsive disorder
OPD – Other psychiatric disorders
PCM – Primary-care management
PET – positron emission tomography
PNS – Peripheral nervous system
PTSD – Posttraumatic stress disorder
QTL – Quantitative trait locus
RAS – Reticular activating system
RM – Recovery management
rRNA – Ribosomal ribonucleic acid
RVE – Research validity estimate
SERT – Serotonin transporter
SIDS – Sudden infant death syndrome
SPECT – Single photon emission computerized tomography
SSRIs – Selective serotonin reuptake inhibitors
TBW – Total body water
TC – Therapeutic community
tRNA – Transfer ribonucleic acid
THC – Tetrahydrocannabinol
THIQs (TIQs) – Tetrahydroisoquinolines
TSF – Twelve-step facilitation
VTA – Ventral tegmental area

Preface

THE MOST EXCITING NEWS about the "science of addiction" is that neuroscience is playing a ground-breaking role in helping us clarify the exact causes of compulsive alcohol and other drug use. Neuroscience research on "addiction" involves an understanding of how drugs act on individual nerve cells as well as on large groups of nerve cells in the central nervous system. Research is also helping us clarify what "addiction" is, what it is not, and how it can be better treated. Unlike earlier alcoholism and addiction research, neurobiological research on addicting drugs is unique in that it interacts with so many other important areas: social work, psychology, sociology, medicine, pharmacology, physiology, genetics, brain imaging, epidemiology, and treatment research. Thus, this book covers, in order: (1) changes in the terminology and conceptualization of "addiction" that are emerging based on new neuroscience, genetic, and clinical findings, and that help us understand why one type of drug problem is a chronic medical brain disease; (2) the basics of neuroscience; (3) the neuroanatomy and function of brain reward sites; (4) the genetics of alcohol and other drug dependence; (5) the basic pharmacology of stimulants and depressants; (6) the basic pharmacology of alcohol; (7) the basic pharmacology of other drugs; (8) current and emerging treatments for chemical dependence and how neuroscience helps us understand the way they work; (9) how to evaluate the validity of science in this area and how to read and interpret new research findings; and (10) future research trends and important questions that addiction science should answer. The book closes with two appendices that provide supplemental information on alcohol (Appendix A) and other drugs (Appendix B).

The scientific conclusions that appear in this book are mine, and the story they tell is the result of over 30 years of addiction science research. Much of this research has substantiated the anecdotal reports told by those in recovery from the disease. When science agrees with real-life experience, and vice versa, the story is strengthened. Certainly, the story will change subtlety as the scientific evidence grows, and other scientists may draw somewhat different conclusions from those presented in this book. Some may suggest that I have misinterpreted the results of some scientific studies; others may say that I have missed key recent publications. Any omission of important research is unintentional: My goal is to accurately and articulately represent a cross-section of the scientific areas discussed in the text. The fact is that we have not yet solved the causes of drug problems, nor do we have all the answers to cure people. Thus, scientific conclusions are always open to challenge. The biggest challenge is for all of us to educate policy makers and to advocate for more alcohol and other drug research funding to find the final answers. No person's conclusions about the causes and best treatments for "addictions" are stronger than the weight of their scientific data, and more scientific data are urgently needed in this area!

Who This Book Can Help

Abuse of alcohol and illicit drugs affects millions of people on a daily basis (Hanson & Li, 2003). Over 8 million U.S. individuals meet the diagnostic criteria for alcohol dependence and another 5.6 million meet the criteria for alcohol abuse (Grant, Hasin, Chou, Stinson, & Dawson, 2004). In 2001, there were about 66.5 million tobacco smokers and 16 million illicit drug users (Grant et al., 2004). The U.S. economic cost of such abuse was estimated to be more than $484 billion per year, including $185 billion due to alcohol overuse, $138 billion due to smoking, and about $161 billion due to illicit drugs. Finally, of the more than 2 million U.S. deaths per year, around 1 in 4 is due to alcohol, tobacco, or illicit drug use.

Preface

This book attempts to help the almost 21.6 million Americans and millions more worldwide who abuse or are dependent on drugs (Volkow & Li, 2005b), by teaching their caregivers (or them) about the latest "addiction science" research. Through better definitions for drug-related health conditions and a better understanding of drug action on the brain and of how treatment works, the consequences of drug use will decline. This book is about helping addiction professionals understand the foundations and applications of neuroscience so that they will be better able to empathize with their patients and apply such science to principles of treatment. Experience and a few studies (see Lawson, Wilcox, Littlefield, Pituch, & Erickson, 2004) have shown that when professionals learn the proper scientific and clinical terminology, they tend to incorporate it into their everyday language and professional care environment. Thus, the value of this book is great to those who read it with a goal of learning something new.

Note from the author: Although I work at the College of Pharmacy at the University of Texas at Austin and hold an endowed professorship originally funded by a pharmaceutical company, I have no vested interest in pharmaceutical products and do not receive compensation from the pharmaceutical industry or any other industries associated with alcohol or other drug products.

Acknowledgments

MANY PEOPLE HAVE SUGGESTED, usually after an extremely long and tiring 6-hour workshop, that I write a book about the neuroscience of addiction. But nothing can be more motivating than an invitation by a publisher. I am thus extremely grateful to Deborah Malmud, Michael McGandy, and the staff at W. W. Norton for inviting me to submit a book proposal, as well as for their expert editing during the writing process. Deborah was extremely helpful and responsive to frequent emails, especially during the early writing of the manuscript. Michael has been a guiding light and provided most of the editing suggestions during the latter stages of manuscript preparation. Our copy editor, Casey Ruble, provided detailed editing with her extra hard work and insight. A third editor at Norton, Kristen Holt-Browning, skillfully pulled the entire manuscript together at the end.

Perhaps the unique nature of this book will show through in that I not only know some science, but also quite a bit about alcoholism and other drug addiction, treatment, and recovery. One doesn't have to have cancer to be a cancer researcher, and my interest in this topic is purely academic. However, it is hard to be involved in addiction science without becoming emotionally connected to those who are suffering. For helping me understand the disease and putting it in context with the latest science, I am forever grateful to John T. O'Neill, a friend with whom I've discussed this topic almost daily for over 25 years. His teaching, mentoring, intelligence, humor, and inspiration have made me the educator I am today. To other friends in the 12-step programs who have shared openly and often, especially Hank M. and Mike R., I am truly blessed. I also thank John Schwarzlose, president of the Betty Ford Center, who invited me to participate in a Professionals in Residence program at that internationally known treatment center, and who continues to support the science of addiction through the center's monthly newsletter, *Findings*, for which I have the privilege of serving as science editor. I am perhaps most indebted to the many people in recovery I have met over the years for their open sharing, challenging questions, and willingness to tell me when the science didn't seem to connect with their experience. When lecturing, whether to students or to treatment professionals, I always learn from the probing questions. I believe that more scientific hypotheses can be generated by insightful questions or comments from learners who look at things differently than I do. From my students in recovery, I have learned about many issues that still need much more research. Finally, I need to state that in my experience scientists who design experiments while looking only at published literature are narrowly focused indeed. Scientists who put their studies into context with real-life people and outcomes have a greater insight into the real truth. This is something I have tried to emulate.

I've noticed that there is a lot of finger-pointing when people are concerned that the latest science on addiction is not getting into the hands of the people who need it. The scientists blame the treatment professionals for not taking the time to read the latest scientific literature or to attend educational science lectures. The treatment professionals tell the scientists that they are boring and use confusing jargon, and the government tries to get the two sides together. I feel fortunate that, like some of my colleagues, I have the interest, love to take the time, and apparently have the ability to be one of the scientific spokespeople who feel comfortable helping counselors, treatment and other health professionals, attorneys, and administrators become excited about addiction science and medicine. To the folks at the National Institute on Drug Abuse and the National Institute on Alcohol Abuse and Alcoholism, I am thankful for early contracts and grants that helped me become a critical scientist and later to become interested in transforming myself into an addiction science educator. This early funding helped our team at the Addiction Science Research and Education Center in the College of Pharmacy at the University of Texas at Austin develop an ongoing collaboration focusing on basic pharmacology and neuroscience, on how people learn, how best to change their beliefs, and how to change their professional behavior to better help their patients. Thanks to our interdisciplinary research team: Rich Wilcox, Ken Lawson, John Littlefield, Keenan Pituch, Joe Miller, and Mary Velasquez. Special appreciation to my colleague Rich Wilcox, whose energy has produced several collaborative manuscripts, and the dean, Steve Leslie, who is himself a prominent alcohol researcher. Most importantly, Dean Leslie has supported my search for international understanding about these devastating diseases and has tolerated and even encouraged my frequent travels. My colleague John Brick, with whom I've written other books, is a much-appreciated friend who continues to confirm and encourage my work. My friend Stephanie Jones, who provided some of the reference materials, is to be commended for her enthusiasm in helping with the manuscript. Finally, I am most indebted to my colleague Peter Pociluyko. Peter is that rare individual who wanted to help by reading every word of the manuscript (at least twice), making insightful comments and changes, and confirming why certain material is important to the professionals in the field. I have never met such a giving, trusting, caring, supportive, and faithful colleague. Any success that this book might have is in large part due to his help. To him, I am humbly indebted.

There are a number of people who helped review the raw material for the appendices at the end of the book. They are all members of the federally funded Addiction Technology Transfer Centers (ATTCs): Mary Beth Johnson, director of the national office of the ATTCs (in Kansas City, Missouri); Pat Stilen and Jan Wrolstad (Mid-America ATTC); Wendy Hausotter (Northwest Frontier ATTC), Richard Spence and Phil Orrick (Gulf Coast ATTC); and Michael Flaherty, Holly Hagle, Heidi Norman, Melva Hogan, Joyce Boisell, Chris Hagle, and Iburia Scott-Johnson (Institute for Research, Education and Training in the Addictions, IRETA, and the Northeast ATTC).

Technically, I couldn't have pulled this book together if it weren't for three employees in the College of Pharmacy at the university. Debbie Brand, administrative associate in the Division of Pharmacology/ Toxicology, compiled the bibliography in her usual meticulous way. A student, Heidi Lau, cheerfully checked the accuracy and completeness of the references. Belinda Lehmkuhle in our Learning Resources Center drew and adapted most of the figures and tables, and her artistry also lives on in the website of our Center.

Let us continue to keep in our prayers those who have suffered and lost their lives to alcoholism and other drug addiction. Perhaps the information in this book can prevent countless others from suffering the same fate.

Permissions

The following publishers and individuals have kindly provided copyright permission for the indicated figures and tables. Tables and figures not listed are original artwork or materials developed by the author and individuals mentioned in the acknowledgments.

Table 1.3 – Adapted with permission from the *Diagnostic and Statistical Manual of Mental Disorders, Fourth Edition, Text Revision* Copyright 2000. American Psychiatric Association.

Figures 2.3, 3.2 – Adapted with permission from Cami, J. & Farre, M. (2003). *New England Journal of Medicine, 349*, 975–986. Copyright 2003. Massachusetts Medical Society. All rights reserved.

Figure 3.3 – Reprinted with permission from Koob, G. F. (2003). *Alcoholism: Clinical & Experimental Research*, *27*, 232–243. Copyright 2003. Lippincott, Williams & Wilkins.

Figure 3.4 – Reprinted with permission from Koob, G.F. & LeMoal, M. (1997). *Science 278*, 52–58. Copyright 1997. American Association for the Advancement of Science.

Figure 3.5 – Adapted with permission from Kalivas, P.W. & Volkow, N.D. (2005). *American Journal of Psychiatry, 162*, 1403–1413. Copyright 2005. American Psychiatric Association.

Figures 4.1, 4.2 – Adapted from Dick, D.M. & Faroud, T. (2002). *Alcohol Research & Health*, *26*, 172–174.

Table 4.1 – Adapted with permission from Mayer, P. and Hollt, V. (2005). *Current Opinion in Pharmacology,* *5*, 4–8. Copyright 2005. Elsevier.

Figures 10.1, 10.2 – Courtesy of A. Pfefferbaum, Stanford University.

The Science of Addiction

CHAPTER 1

Terminology and Characterization of "Addiction"

I ADMIT UP FRONT THAT I DON'T LIKE THE WORD "addiction." I'm not alone in this, as attempts have been made in the medical and clinical communities to change the terminology. Any book with the word "addiction" in the title is going to be suspect with regard to its credibility, opinions, and breadth. "Addiction" is, however, a prevailing public health interest. Everyone knows someone who is "addicted" to something. Nevertheless, there are good reasons why researchers like me do not like the word.

First, the word "addiction" is unscientific. You won't find it mentioned in the best diagnostic manual on mental disorders. Another manual on classification of mental and behavioral disorders refers readers to "dependence syndrome" when they look up "addiction." Although there are scientific journals with "addiction" in the title, most of the articles in these journals pertain to various forms of drug problems, and only in a few cases are the so-called process or behavioral "addictions" (e.g., gambling) mentioned. (This should tell us how little we know scientifically about "process addictions," although there are several recent exciting studies on compulsive gambling disorder.) "Addiction" is a wonderful word when someone wants to talk about behaviors getting out of hand, but it is imprecise (thus my use of quotation marks around it). If *addiction* means "compulsive, out-of-control use of a dangerous drug," is this the same as a person's being "addicted" to a cell phone? Scientists cannot work or live with imprecision.

Second, the word is too broad, too vague, and too misunderstood. People flippantly state that they are "addicted" to coffee, sugar, other people, computer games, shopping, tanning booths, or knitting. There is no doubt that over-involvement in any of these activities can sometimes mess up a person's life, but such widespread use of the term reveals just how ill-defined it is. The fact is that alcohol "addiction" is much worse than lingerie "addiction," cocaine "addiction" is far worse than Internet "addiction," and heroin "addiction" can in no way compare to chocolate "addiction" in terms of poor quality of life. In an attempt to help people with "addictions," some investigators have tried to understand Internet "addiction" by developing a theory that Internet overusers have brain chemistry changes associated with the need for being "online"—yet there is little science behind such a theory. Other studies showing that the opioid antagonist naloxone blocks the euphoria from gambling "addiction" have been published. But they are not helpful, because euphoria is not involved in "addiction" (see Chapter 3) and one study is unlikely to prove anything compared to multiple confirmatory studies (see Chapter 9). In fact, because we cannot directly measure brain chemistry changes in humans (see Chapter 10), it may be impossible with today's science to fully test such a hypothesis, which makes it mere speculation.

Third, any treatment professional in this field realizes that "addiction" to chemicals is extremely stigmatized, even more so than mental illness. Such stigmatization (along with social prejudice and discrimination against addicts, misunderstanding about what "addiction" is and what it is not, and anger against those "druggies" who scare and hurt us) has led to (a) mind-boggling inertia against more research, (b) frustratingly inadequate treatment for those who need it, and (c) relatively ineffective prevention measures. How much better our world would be if we knew how to treat "addictions" better, and if the mystery of "addiction" could be solved through more research.

I have observed that the term *alcohol dependence* is in much wider use than the term *alcoholism* in the alcohol scientific literature, whereas the term *addiction* is still more prevalent than *drug dependence* or *chemical dependence* in the "other drug" scientific literature. Some people prefer the term "addiction" over "dependence" to avoid confusion with the term "physical dependence," which relates to withdrawal from drugs (Volkow & Li, 2005a; O'Brien, Volkow, & Li, 2006).

So where does this lack of agreed-upon terminology leave us? First, the term *chemical dependence* is the term I prefer and is the closest in meaning to the term *addiction* as used by scientists. Popular use of the term *addiction*, however, is incorrect scientifically and clinically. Similarly, the term *alcohol dependence* is the term preferred by scientists like me and is closest in meaning to the term *alcoholism* used by non-scientists. Popular use of the term *alcoholism* is, however, very broad and based upon Alcoholics Anonymous programs. Throughout this book, I will use the more scientific terms "chemical dependence" and "drug abuse" whenever possible. However, there will be situations when citing the work of others that I will use the word *addiction* in a scientific context when it is not clear whether the authors are referring to the disease state or to the global set of problems popularly known as *addiction*. Lest this be confusing, this is *most* important: the terms *drug abuse* (not a brain disease) and *chemical dependence* (the brain disease) are the preferred terms for scientific studies and clinical differentiation of people with drug problems.

Equally problematic are the phrases *substance abuse*, *drug abuse*, and *alcohol abuse*. These terms are technically incorrect; no one "abuses" alcohol in the same manner that someone abuses a child or spouse. The word *abuse* is also problematic for other reasons, such as the fact that it tends to be a catch-all term for anyone with a drug problem (see Myth #1, Chapter 9).

In spite of the use of *substance abuse* in the diagnostic texts described later, I use the term *drug abuse* throughout this text, since the word *substance* is scientifically imprecise. *Drug abuse* is not a perfect term, but it is an established phrase in the field. (*Drug misuse*, used in British journals, is far better because it more clearly places the responsibility for drug use on the person.)

"Addiction," A Vague Term

The popular term *addiction* is a common part of every person's vocabulary. How often do we hear, "I love that so much, I'm addicted to it" or "I guess I'm hopelessly addicted to it." *Addiction* used in this way is colloquial and not scientific.

Have you ever noticed people's tendency to describe drug problems with a single word that conveys their (usually negative) impression of what's happening? People who drink a lot and lose their normal behavioral characteristics are often described as "drunks" or "alcoholics." People who smoke marijuana are referred to as "pot heads." People who use illegal drugs such as heroin are called "addicts." And don't forget "dope fiends," "acid heads," and "junkies." These pejorative phrases indicate that drug users are not "like us," that the drug problem is their fault and that they should be punished. Such people are "bad," "crazy," or "stupid," and need only get "good," "sane," or "educated" to stop their drug use.

To overcome such pejorative misperceptions, it is critical to understand how bad the problem is. Following are three practical examples of how "addiction" and other drug-use problems are misinterpreted:

- Newspapers frequently run stories about mothers who have abused their children by using drugs during pregnancy. The headlines of these stories read something like this: "Mother Held Responsible for Crack-Addicted Baby." Whether you agree that drug-using mothers should be punished or not, there is no scientific evidence for babies being born "addicted." Yes, babies can go through withdrawal at birth, but as we will see later in the criteria for chemical dependence, withdrawal is not the same as "addiction." Furthermore, we have no scientific evidence that babies born of drug-using mothers have a greater likelihood of becoming "addicted" later in life. (Yes, they may be more likely to use drugs later in life, but that is not "addiction.")
- In a recent field newsletter, the following title appeared: "New Website Offers Help to Smokeless Tobacco Users." The article itself stated that "individuals who are addicted to nicotine in smokeless tobacco" now have access to a new website where they can receive help. Who is the website intended for, users or addicts? Are all users "addicts"?
- Here's another from the same newsletter: "New Study Shows Hope for Treating Inhalant Abuse." The article then described that the new drug "vigabatrin may block the addictive effects of toluene." Is "inhalant *abuse*" the same as "*addictive* effects of toluene"?

Beyond the everyday examples cited above, the scientific literature is filled with examples of scientists and philosophers trying to cope with the meaning of the word *addiction*. Some argue that in everyday use the term has weight related to the moral and medical aspects of drug use (Stepney, 1996). A more philosophical handling of *addiction* involves concepts of "self" (Gray, 2005) and "addiction" as an ideology (Luik, 1996). Campbell (2003, p. 673) acknowledged that "acts of will or volition (by addicts) are usually not accepted as diseases, because volition is an act of choice or free will." He suggested that addicts have a volitional disorder (a problem with decision-making or making a conscious choice) based on cognitive impairment caused by impaired memory access, but no data are cited to support this conclusion.

In the pain management area of medicine, there has been a large gap in the understanding of "addiction." To address this, a working group jointly created by the American Society of Addiction Medicine, the American Pain Society, and the American Academy of Pain Medicine developed a definition that attempts to bridge the gap between pain specialists and addiction specialists, cited by Portenoy, Lussier, Kirsh, & Passik (2005):

"Addiction is a primary, chronic, neurobiologic disease, with genetic, psychosocial, and environmental factors. . . It is characterized by behaviors that include one or more of the following: impaired control over drug use, compulsive use, continued use despite harm, and craving." (Savage, Joranson, & Covington, 2003, p. 662)

One author (Pociluyko, personal communication) has long defined *addiction* as a "biopsychosocial disorder characterized by compulsive use of the drug (behavioral); obsession and preoccupation with the drug (psychological); loss of control while using more than intended, despite conscious efforts to control use (biological); high risk or frequent episodes of relapse after abstinence (biological, social, and psychological); plus serious consequences due to use (social) and continued use despite the consequences."

Much of the confusion regarding "addiction" is due to the umbrella-like nature of the term: it lumps all drug-use problems together. It also fails to acknowledge the critical difference between conscious *drug abuse* ("bad judgment" use of drugs, not a disease) and pathological *chemical dependence* (impaired control over drug use, a brain disease). Discussions about "addiction" would be so much clearer if the distinction between these two drug-use states were more well known and used in everyday clinical and scientific language, as it is in the more recent neurobiological and treatment literature (see Koob, Ahmed, Boutrel, Chen, Kenny et al., 2004; Dackis, Kampman, Lynch, Pettinati, & O'Brien, 2005; McNeese & DiNitto, 2005). If only everyone could visit a treatment center and interview chemically dependent people. Such a visit can be very enlightening, revealing that people with the disease have a loss of control over their drug use. Even when their willpower in other areas of life is unquestioned, they struggle enormously to stop using drugs. "Addicted" is not a strong-enough term to describe such individuals.

"Addiction" As a Brain Disease

Why is calling "addiction" a disease so controversial? Why is it important what we call it? How can people who care accurately describe "a maladaptive pattern of drug use leading to impairment or distress?" What exactly do we call such a disruptive pattern of drug use?

In the 1960s the highly influential American Medical Association declared *alcoholism* (the most popular of the "addictions") to be a disease (White, Kurtz, & Acker, 2001), but this was challenged by the United States Supreme Court (1988), when it found, in a disputed decision, alcoholism to be "willful misconduct." There have been a number of literary skirmishes that often relied on emotion or incomplete science rather than on "weight of the evidence" research (see Fingarette, 1970; Wallace, 1990). I believe the problem lies in a major terminology misunderstanding. Properly sorting out and discussing the terminology will allow people to better understand the research described in this book and why we can now use the word *disease* with confidence.

To many people who are bothered by the behavior of *drunks* or *dope-fiends*, saying that such people have a *disease* is tantamount to releasing them from the responsibility for their behavior; thus, it is difficult for such people to admit that any drug user can have a disease. For those people who live with alcohol or other drug users who exhibit aggressive behavior, and hurt or intimidate others, there may be more sympathy for the drug user, but still, "I'm not going to let him off by saying he can't help it." Thus, the word *disease* is controversial for those who feel that people should be punished for their destructive behavior.

A few scientists have used the word *disorder*, or even hedged and used the word *illness* (McLellan, Lewis, O'Brien, & Kleber, 2000). But *illness* is simply a synonym for *disease*. The word *syndrome* has also been suggested (Odegaard, Peller, & Shaffer, 2005), as a compromise to the controversial labeling of "addiction" as a disease. With respect to *alcoholism*, many scientists still talk about the *medical model* or the *disease concept*, but these are old terms that should be abandoned. The genetic and neurobiological research described in this book now clearly identifies the pathology, symptoms, and treatment principles that identify *chemical dependence* as a bonafide *medical disease* with the same general characteristics of other pathologies over which individuals have little/no control. Nevertheless, because of pervasive misunderstanding about the popular term *addiction*, and the emotion associated with the idea of a drug-induced brain *disease*, there may never be public consensus about such labeling.

I believe that much of the confusion regarding whether people who drink or take drugs too much are responsible for their own actions has stemmed from scientists' inability to properly educate the public, and the public's failure to understand that not everyone who drinks or drugs too much is an "addict." Clarification of the difference between conscious (volitional) drug *abuse* and pathological drug *dependence* allows professionals to understand that although all people should take responsibility for their actions while drinking or drugging, some cannot help their excessive drug use any more than a cancer patient can overcome a malignant tumor.

Excellent scientific research in the areas of genetics, neurobiology, and pharmacology in the past 20 years now clearly shows that chemical dependence is a chronic, medical brain disease, driven significantly by genetic vulnerability (Leshner, 1997). The site of the disease lies in the mesolimbic dopamine system, or "pleasure pathway," or "reward system."

A Brain Disease is More Understandable If People Know Where the Problem Occurs

Understanding that there is a specific brain area involved is just as important in identifying the disease as it is in diagnosing and treating it. Furthermore, it helps alleviate embarrassment, shame, guilt, fear, and denial commonly experienced by patients. Once they can understand that there is a brain area that is not working properly, and that the condition is not their fault, then it is to their benefit to seek treatment. This recognition is critical in saving the lives of victims of this disease, especially if the diagnosis is made early.

To help patients visualize this brain area, have them place two fingers in the shape of a V in the middle of the forehead, and place the index finger of the other hand above the right or left ear. The mesolimbic dopamine system is located where the finger-pointing lines cross in the middle of the brain (Figure 1.1).

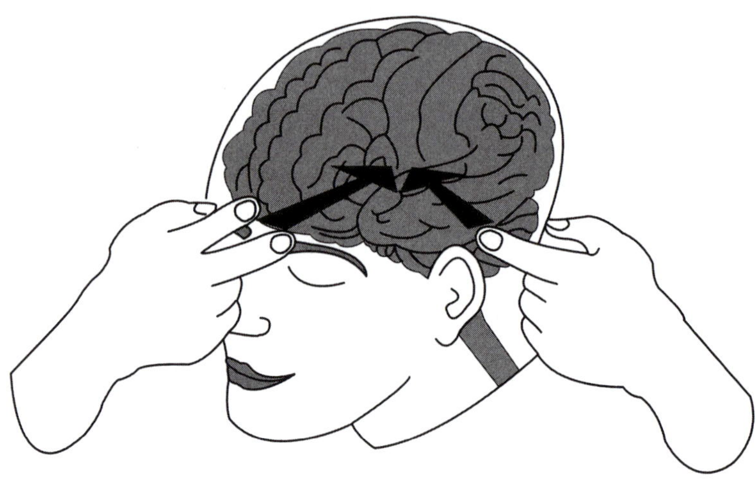

Figure 1.1

How to Locate the Mesolimbic Dopamine System

Proof of Disease

Because there are no agreed-upon medical criteria that establish a medical disease definition, the "proof" that something is a disease is based upon weight-of-the-evidence and consensus. As noted earlier, the American

Medical Association declared alcoholism to be a disease in 1967 (White et. al., 2001) and reaffirmed the definition in 1965. But with a condition so misunderstood and stigmatized, the idea that a disease process (not under the control of the individual) is related to the cause of problem drinking or drugging is foreign to and even rejected by many people.

At least two significant clinical papers that assume the neurobiological proof of brain involvement in "addiction" have directly tackled the similarities between chemical dependence and other well-understood diseases. Lewis (1991) compared several vital characteristics of different diseases (coronary heart disease, essential hypertension, diabetes mellitus, gout, cancer, syphilis, rheumatoid arthritis, schizophrenia, and alcoholism). The characteristics were (1) clear biological basis, (2) unique, identifiable signs and symptoms, (3) predictable course and outcome, and (4) inability to control the cause of the disease. He concluded that "any attempt to define disease so as to exclude alcoholism also excludes many conditions about which there is no debate concerning their medical significance" (p. 264).

McLellan and colleagues (2000) made similar comparisons between chemical (including alcohol) dependence, type II diabetes mellitus, hypertension, and asthma. They pointed out that "genetic heritability, personal choice, and environmental factors are comparably involved in the cause and course of all of these disorders" (p. 1689). We also know from family and marital dynamics that such factors can play a role in the onset and course of a disease. For example, there appears to be a link between severe asthma and family affective disorders, posttraumatic stress disorder, antisocial personality disorder, and drug abuse (Wamboldt, Weintraub, Krafchick, & Wamboldt, 1996). More subtly, there also appears to be a link between frequency of use of asthma medications by asthmatic children and the level of stress in the family environment (Sawyer & Fardy, 2003).

In the McLellan and colleagues (2000) study, the authors provided strong evidence that with chemical dependence, compliance with treatment was as good or better than compliance with treatment of the other three diseases (see Chapter 8). This means not only that treatment for chemical dependence works, but also that patients who relapse are just as likely to return to treatment as sufferers of the other three diseases. This is another indication that patients with chemical dependence disease can be responsible for their own recovery. Finally, the article concludes that "drug dependence should be insured, treated, and evaluated like other chronic illnesses" (p. 189).

It is usually not fruitful to try to force someone who has an emotional or financial interest in viewing "addiction" as volitional to believe that it is a medical disease. (For example, if your father has a drinking problem and abused you as a child, you are going to be less likely to "let him get away" with calling his problem a disease. Likewise, insurance companies will be reluctant to accept "addiction" as a disease because doing so would mean paying for the treatment of drug problems.) In the history of medicine, consensus about whether a condition is a disease usually revolves around finding the precise causes of the disease, thereby allowing it to be compared with other established diseases. This has occurred in the cases of type I diabetes (in which pancreas cells fail to produce insulin), in epilepsy (where the focus of the disease in the brain can be identified), in polio (where the infection is caused by a virus), and in cancer (where causes of out-of-control cell growth are becoming known). These and other diseases were formerly stigmatized because of the fear of "catching" the disease or because the affected person's behavior was unusual or unexpected.

A comparison of several diseases is provided in Table 1.1. When standard medical characteristics are compared across diseases, we see that chemical dependence fares very well. (Remember that we are not talking about intentional drug *abuse*.) It is important for people who are trying to make a decision about the consequences of problem drinking or drugging to study this table and recognize that there is really no reason to not call chemical dependence a chronic, relapsing, medical brain disease. This illness deserves the same attention and help for its victims as other physical diseases that are fully validated and accepted by the medical profession and the public.

Another way of comparing medical disorders is by disorder types (Table 1.2). Medical problems can be designated as a "disease" (more serious, associated with pathology) or a "condition" (less serious, controlled by lifestyle factors). Notice how chemical dependence nicely fits the disease criteria. Few people question whether heart disease, diabetes, and some types of overeating are diseases.

Table 1.1
A Comparison of Several Diseases and Chemical Dependence

Medical Characteristic	**Type 2 Diabetes**	**Hyper-tension**	**Attention Deficit Hyper-activity Disorder**	**Parkinson's Disease**	**Chemical Dependence**
Signs/ Symptoms	Y	Y	Y	Y	Y
Diagnostic Tests Available	Y	Y	Y	Y	Y
Severity Progression	Y	Y	N	Y	Y
Treatable	Y	Y	Y	Y	Y
Environmental Component	Y	Y	Y	Y	Y
Pathophysiology	Y	Y	Y	Y	Y
Precursor condition*	Y	Y	Y	Y	Y
Pain or suffering	Some	Minor	Some	Y	Y
Life-Threatening	Y	Y	N	Y	Y
Medications for Treatment	Y	Y	Y	Y	Y
Genetic vulnerability	Y	Y	Y	Y	Y
Impact on family	Y	Y	Y	Y	Y
Chronic nature	Y	Y	Y	Y	Y
**Curable over lifetime	N	N	Sometimes	N	N

**Denotes a condition preceding the disease, such as obesity for Type-II Diabetes, obesity for hypertension, neonatal hypoxia for ADHD, schizophrenia medication for Parkinson's disease, and drug abuse for chemical dependence. Y= Yes, N= No*

***Relates to whether the disease resolves naturally over time.*

Table 1.2
Causes of Disorder Types

Medical Disorder	**Disease**	**Condition**
Heart Disease	Genetics Birth defects	Diet Lack of exercise Stress
Diabetes	(Type 1) Genetics Unknown factors Virus?	(Types 2, 3) Genetics Diet Lack of exercise Pregnancy
Overeating	(Morbid obesity) Metabolism (thyroid) Brain chemistry (hypo-thalamus)	(Overweight) Diet Exercise (lack)
Chemical Use	(Chemical Dependence) Genetics Brain chemistry Unknown factors	(Drug Abuse) Drug use Environment

Stigma and Discrimination

The reluctance to define *addiction* as a disease stems partly from a desire to hold drug users accountable for their actions. Individuals who have been emotionally, physically, or financially affected by other people's drinking or drugging may be loath to "let them off" by saying they couldn't help it. The sentiment that "if they hadn't taken that first drink or continued to use drugs, they wouldn't be in this position" is common among those individuals. But this claim ignores the fact that not everyone who drinks or drugs becomes an "addict." In addition, drugs used by "addicts" produce aggressiveness, passiveness, excessive happiness, or weirdness, leading nonaddicts such as family members to see only the drug effects and how the addict's behavior hurts or intimidates others. It is typical human nature to dismiss behavior that one doesn't understand or to hold people who hurt others responsible for what they have done. Furthermore, there is an element of revenge in not wanting to help addicts who have hurt people.

Negative stereotypes of alcoholics' being the "bums under the bridge" and addicts being criminals also persist. Several years ago, one responder to an invitation to hear Betty Ford speak at a fund-raising banquet for alcohol research wrote (anonymously) across the reply card "I'll never give a penny to help those d--n drunks." Such stigma, prejudice, anger, and misunderstanding have killed many people with "addiction," and our nation's limited desire and resources to treat such people compound the problem.

Additionally, the "addiction" field's long history of being quiet, or anonymous, about those who have gained recovery, particularly through 12-step programs such as Alcoholics Anonymous (A.A.) has contributed to the widespread misunderstanding of "addiction." There are good reasons why this position of anonymity is maintained (White, 1998), but shrouding recovery in secrecy inhibits others from understanding it. For example, one of the overriding misconceptions about alcoholics and other drug "addicts" is that the addiction is a behavioral problem. The effectiveness of 12-step behavioral- or group therapy treatment further leads people to assume that the disorder is a behavioral problem. However, "addiction" is much more complex: It is not solely a behavioral problem, nor is it purely a biological, genetic, or physiological problem. Any approach that tries to understand "addiction" from a purist or unitary view misses other key components.

Placing an emphasis on the new scientific facts illustrating that chemical dependence (not just heavy drinking or drugging, defined later) is a brain disease should help reduce stigma and discrimination over time, if the history of stigma reduction with other medical diseases such as leprosy, epilepsy, and AIDS is any indication. By educating people with good research findings, we can begin to debunk the myth that addiction is a "you did it to yourself" problem or a moral problem not deserving of medical attention. Of course, changing people's beliefs and accommodating and applying new information are complex issues, which are treated in more detail in the specialized education literature (see Sorensen & Guydish, 1991).

Why is it so important to talk about whether "addiction" is a disease or not? The answer is that treatment for a condition (and the money to fund treatment) is greatly affected by whether policy makers know what they're giving money for (Dackis & O'Brien, 2005). Treatment itself, as will be seen in later chapters, is also affected by whether caregivers believe they are treating a "self-induced problem" or a medical disease. It all begins with whether "addicts" are sick people or not.

Two Drug Problems: Abuse and Dependence

Whether "addicts" are sick people or not depends upon the diagnosis. Obviously, all drug users are not sick. There are drug users who never have any significant drug-related problems. Diagnostic criteria described below allow clinicians to differentiate between people with drug-related problems who can stop using when they wish, and people who have the disease of chemical dependence. The people with the latter diagnosis have a brain disease associated with a dysregulation of the mesolimbic dopamine system and generally cannot stop using drugs without intensive intervention into their drug use problems. Drug *abusers* generally can stop using drugs when they decide to, or when the adversity associated with their drug use outweighs perceived benefits of the drugs.

Diagnostic criteria in addiction medicine can be found in the latest edition of the *Diagnostic and Statistical Manual of Mental Disorders* (Fourth Edition, Text Revision, *DSM-IV-TR*; American Psychiatric Association, 2000). In this manual, the word *addiction* is never used. Instead, two major drug problems are described as shown in Table 1.3.

According to these criteria, drug *abuse* is intentional, "conscious," or voluntary. Drug *dependence* is pathological and unintended. Criteria similar to these can be found in the tenth edition of the *International Classification of Diseases and Other Health Problems* manual (ICD-10, World Health Organization, 1992).

Although *tolerance* is one criterion for drug dependence, it does not in itself constitute "addiction." Tolerance is a reduced response to a drug's action. It can be inborn, in which an individual initially fails to respond to usual doses of a drug, or it can be acquired as a person uses a drug. Most drugs produce some degree of acquired tolerance, which leads to a need for higher and higher doses of the drug to produce the initial effect. Tolerance occurs in the liver (where enzymes become more active in breaking down the drug) or in the target tissues, such as the

Table 1.3
Criteria for Drug Abuse and Dependence*

Chemical (Drug) *Abuse*

I. A maladaptive pattern of drug use leading to impairment or distress, presenting as one or more of the following in a 12-month period:
   1. recurrent use leading to failure to fulfill major obligations
   2. recurrent use which is physically hazardous
   3. recurrent drug-related legal problems
   4. continued use despite social or interpersonal problems

II. The symptoms have never met the criteria for chemical dependence.

Chemical (Drug) *Dependence*

I. A maladaptive pattern of drug use, leading to impairment or distress, presenting as three or more of the following in a 12-month period:
   1. tolerance to the drug's actions
   2. withdrawal
   3. drug is used more than intended
   4. there is an inability to control drug use
   5. effort is expended to obtain the drug
   6. important activities are replaced by drug use
   7. drug use continues despite knowledge of a persistent physical or psychological problem

II. Two types of dependence can occur:
   A) with physiological dependence (including either items 1 or 2), or
   B) without physiological dependence (including neither items 1 nor 2).

*Adapted with permission from the *Diagnostic and Statistical Manual of Mental Disorders, Fourth Edition, Text Revision* (Copyright 2000). American Psychiatric Association.

brain (where the tissues somehow become less sensitive to the drug's effects).

If a person becomes tolerant to a drug, it does not necessarily mean that he or she is "addicted." Rather, chemical dependence comprises an array of symptoms that are related to "the inability to stop using the drug without help." Tolerance is only one of the dependence symptoms.

Physiological (physical) dependence occurs when a person uses a drug on a regular basis over time. Gradually, the person's body adapts to the presence of the drug, so that without the drug, the person cannot function normally. When drug use is abruptly stopped in a physically dependent individual, the person goes through "withdrawal," where signs and symptoms opposite to the drug's original effects on the body are seen. Like tolerance, physical withdrawal is *not* the same as dependence and is only one of the criteria for chemical dependence.

What causes withdrawal? Physical withdrawal (seen most often when the use of depressant drugs such as opioids, benzodiazepines, alcohol, and nicotine is stopped) is a "rebound hyperexcitability." When such drugs are used in high amounts over a long period of time, the body's functions are depressed (made less active), and the body adapts to the presence of the drug over time. When the person stops using the drug, the body attempts to normalize itself and mechanisms kick in to restore the normal state. This "normalization" process pushes bodily systems to become more active and in so doing causes a state of hyperexcitability until normal function is restored. An opposite type of withdrawal is mental "hyperdepression," which follows cessation from central nervous system stimulants such as cocaine. A person undergoing hyperdepression does not have the clear dramatic withdrawal signs of a person going through withdrawal from central nervous system depressants. However, they are uncomfortable with symptoms of mental depression, excessive sleepiness, anhedonia (the inability to experience pleasure), and drug craving.

Drug Abuse

Drug abuse is described as the intentional (conscious) overuse of drugs in cases of poor judgment, self-medication, overcelebration, and other situations where drug use can be harmful or illegal. The drug abuse criteria, however subjective and difficult to quantify, are extremely important in helping professionals understand that not all drug users are addicts, that this form of drug use is under the control of the user, and that the consequences of such use can still be tragic. (Once again, drug abuse is a serious disorder that causes huge socioeconomic costs to society, but it is not the same as drug *dependence*.)

Notice that according to the *DSM-IV* criteria for drug abuse, a person must have at least one of the four criteria within a 12-month period to "qualify." (The most accurate diagnosis is carried out by a trained assessment professional; self-diagnosis is not possible, as bias can affect the results.) Someone who is diagnosed as an "abuser" is more effectively described as someone who is using drugs too much, too often, for too long a period of time, with some adverse consequences—often due to environmental influences that encourage excessive drug use. However, stopping the use of drugs in such cases is rather easy—people can stop when they perceive continued danger from drug use, or when their life situation changes, or when they "just decide to stop cold turkey." A perfect example of a drug abuser is the college binge-drinking student, who might drink and drive, engage in risky sexual behavior, or do poorly in class. Most such students have an alcohol *abuse* problem, for they can stop (or cut down) when they graduate, leave the university environment, get a job, have a family, and increase their responsibilities. (However, they may return to periodic or routine use of the drug, such as commonly occurs with alcohol.) It is estimated that only 10–15% of college students will become dependent on alcohol sometime during their lives.

If drug abuse is not assessed and abusers go into treatment, they will usually do well. Abusers often find that intensive counseling and abstinence work well for them. They are probably the ones who go to several 12-step meetings, find sobriety, and no longer care to drink or drug for the rest of their lives. They may even "go back" to moderate or controlled drinking (Walitzer & Connors, 1999). Unlike people dependent on drugs, drug abusers will often respond to less intensive measures: education about what drugs do and don't do, coercive pleas from a spouse to stop drinking/using, punishment (embarrassment over a driving-while-intoxicated conviction), "maturing out of the habit," or traumatic life events (e.g., physical or psychological trauma) that shift the focus of attention from drugs to repairing a life. (Chemically dependent people usually do not respond to such interventions and may even drink or drug more intensely when drug abuse "treatments" such as education or sanctions are implemented.)

Chemical Dependence

Chemical dependence is compulsive, pathological, impaired control over drug use, leading to an inability to stop using drugs in spite of adverse consequences. Researchers have identified the exact brain area that is affected in the chemically dependent person. It's called the mesolimbic dopamine system and is covered in detail in Chapter 3.

Notice that according to the *DSM-IV* criteria for chemical dependence, a person must have three or more of the seven criteria within a 12-month period in order to "qualify." If a person only shows one or two physiological signs, such as withdrawal or tolerance, this is insufficient to warrant the diagnosis. The last five criteria in the *DSM-IV-TR* dependence list are psychological/environmental criteria, suggesting "impaired control" over drug use. A person could have withdrawal, tolerance, and one of these other criteria to be considered "dependent." Or the person could have three of the five final criteria (with no withdrawal or tolerance) to be considered "dependent." The proper use of these criteria, through oral or written assessment probes, especially in conjunction with other assessment measures (drinking or drugging history, family history, or other non-*DSM-IV* assessment tools), can be most accurate in making a diagnosis. The simple observation of "too much drinking or drugging" is insufficient to make a diagnosis. In addition, it is critical for "addiction" professionals to understand that withdrawal signs alone are no longer satisfactory for making a proper diagnosis. Generally, central nervous system stimulant drugs (cocaine, amphetamines, LSD) do not produce noticeable physical withdrawal signs, yet these are dependence-producing drugs. Conversely, anyone who shows some withdrawal signs or reports that increased doses are necessary to get the original effect of the drug (tolerance) may or may not be dependent, depending on the presence of other factors. Even people on powerful pain medications, steroids, antidepressants, antihypertensives, and other drugs can experience severe rebound withdrawal when quitting abruptly, but this does not indicate dependence on these medications.

Thus, chemical dependence is not a "too much, too often, withdrawal" disease; it's an "I can't stop using without help disease." In other words, one cannot diagnose "addiction" by looking at the amount and frequency of drug use, or whether tolerance or withdrawal has occurred. Professional assessment of the individual by qualified diagnosticians is necessary for accurate diagnosis.

The appropriate rehabilitation of a chemically dependent person should involve formal "treatment," which may include detoxification ("detox"), abstinence, counseling, education, proper nutrition, exercise, anticraving medications (if available), and other measures to stabilize emotional and psychological status. (I will discuss treatment options in detail in Chapter 8.)

Severity of Drug Problems

Many people are surprised to hear that chemical dependence has different degrees of severity. Figure 1.2 illustrates the relationships between drug abuse and drug dependence severity as they relate to drug-seeking behavior. Notice that there are mild, moderate, and severe forms of both drug abuse and drug dependence. These differences in severity are never usually discussed, as many people believe that you either abuse drugs or you don't and that drug dependence is something you either have or don't have. But long-term outcomes of treatment illustrate that some people follow treatment very successfully (they find treatment and its outcome easy), while others are so severely dependent that they die intoxicated or overdosed. There are many stories of drug-dependent people who are treated multiple times, who have run out of money for treatment after several failed efforts, and who "work the steps" as hard as anyone and still cannot stay clean and sober.

Figure 1.2

Drug Abuse	Drug Dependence		Drug-Seeking
Mild			Little/None
Moderate			Some
Severe	Mild	"ADDICTION"	A Lot
	Moderate		Even More
	Severe		All the Time

The Unique Definition of *Alcoholic*

One of the most common "addictions" is "alcoholism." It is a special case because of the wide availability of alcohol and its impact on public health (see Chapter 6 for a detailed discussion on alcohol). "Alcoholism" is as poorly understood as "addiction," as the word itself is used differently among those who attend 12-step meetings and among scientists who study it. As described later, not all heavy alcohol use is "addiction" or "alcoholism," and not all "addiction" or "alcoholism" is due to heavy alcohol use.

So, who is an "alcoholic"? Although the scientific definition of an "alcoholic" is someone who is "addicted to alcohol" or "alcohol dependent" (NIAAA, Frequently Asked Questions, 2006a), members of A.A. use a broader definition. In their eyes, anyone who has a drinking problem and who wants to stop is welcomed into their group and then declares, "I'm an alcoholic." There is no formal distinction between "abusers" and "dependents" in community A.A. meetings. This may be one of the reasons that A.A. members are not unanimous in their belief that alcohol dependence is a disease, as some members are alcohol abusers and others are dependent (the numbers are not known). Nevertheless, a proper diagnosis is not important when people are trying to find a way to stop drinking. If successful, they are much better off than before they worked the fellowship program (twelve-step programs are discussed in more detail in Chapter 8).

Because of the shame, guilt, fear, remorse, and self-directed anger inherent in thinking about going to A.A. meetings or into formal treatment, "alcoholics" are often said to be in denial about having a problem. Thus, intervention by concerned family members or friends is often necessary to motivate a person with a drinking problem to seek treatment. Sometimes people will acknowledge that they have a problem and begin attending 12-step meetings with very little resistance. Clinical experience suggests that when people, properly diagnosed as alcohol dependent, understand they have a chronic brain disease and it is not their fault, treatment is more easily accepted. Helpful assessment methods for alcohol problems have recently been reviewed (Allen & Wilson, 2005).

Case Study: George

George was 29, employed, and had been living on his own since age 17. He had a prior driving-while-intoxicated offense and recently had been involved in a car accident in which he struck another driver head-on and killed her. He ended up serving 6 months in jail for vehicular manslaughter. His blood alcohol concentrations at the time of the first and second arrests were 0.13% and 0.24%, respectively.

George's facial affect was very flat and blunted, and he spoke in a monotone. He showed little emotion yet there was no evidence of depression. Although he expressed some remorse for the death of the

> other driver, his emotional response seemed superficial and shallow. His remarks and thinking process appeared very egocentric and he was concerned about being in control, being able to do as he pleased, and being able to live his own life. His own drinking was somewhat sporadic and often occurred on weekends, although occasionally he drank during the week.
>
> He had a history of frequent marijuana use and fights, some of which occurred when he was under the influence of alcohol. Alcohol seemed to increase his risk of becoming argumentative, decrease his tolerance for stress, or cause him to react aggressively when even a mild joke was made about him. Drinking also seemed to cause him to become provocative and challenge others to a fight.
>
> George reported a family history of alcoholism. However, he showed no evidence of loss of control over his alcohol use and no evidence of withdrawal. He did show tolerance to alcohol but did not drink compulsively. In fact, he appeared to drink to excess by choice.

Professional assessment concluded that George met the criteria for antisocial personality disorder and alcohol abuse. An untrained counselor might have diagnosed him as "alcoholic," and he would certainly qualify as one if he were to attend A.A. and work the steps. However, according to *DSM-IV* criteria, he would be an alcohol abuser who would benefit from A.A. meetings, group counseling, or individual counseling. The prognosis for George is not clear, because he probably would fall into the "severe" subcategory of alcohol abuse as described in Figure 1.2. His commitment to treatment would probably be the determining factor in his eventual quality of life.

Proper Diagnosis of Drug Disorders

The diagnostic criteria of *DSM-IV* and *ICD-10* are quite subjective, relying on the assessment tools and experience of the counselor. A common flaw is to simply ask questions of the person being assessed. These questions usually refer to the *DSM-IV* criteria, and often only a "yes" or "no" answer is requested. For more accurate outcomes, it is best to use a battery of tests in conjunction with the *DSM-IV* criteria. In addition, complete drinking/drugging histories as well as family drinking/drugging backgrounds can aid in a proper diagnosis of chemical dependence. Finally, the Addiction Severity Index (ASI; McLellan,

Luborsky, O'Brien, & Woody, 1980) is an excellent measure of disruption of various life events related to "addiction."

The *DSM-V* is projected to be published in 2011. There is some speculation that it will focus more on a dimensional approach to diagnosis (i.e., looking at disorders on a continuum) instead of the current categorical approach (placing disorders into one diagnostic category or another). Such a change would allow for incorporating the new evidence on biology of disorders, provide more individualized assessments, and perhaps enhance treatment specificity (Jackim, 2005). Such changes would be welcomed by many people, but whether enough research is available for the *DSM* monographs and criteria to change so dramatically is still unclear. In the meantime, the *DSM-IV* is becoming widely accepted by practitioners, and its utility is becoming more established. An emerging opinion is that the validity of *DSM-IV* alcohol dependence is higher than the validity of *DSM-IV* alcohol abuse (Grant, Harford, Muthen, Yi, Hasin, et al., 2006). ("Validity" in this sense refers to the correlation between the published criteria and their consistency and reproducibility in clinical and general populations.) Weaknesses of the criteria are related to their subjectivity, inconsistent use among practitioners, anecdotal poor validity in untrained face-to-face and telephone question-and-answer surveys, and anecdotal lack of validity in adolescent diagnoses. The best and most valid results will probably come from trained assessment professionals in interview situations.

Some people believe that once a person is "addicted" to a drug, the "addiction" will spread to the use of other drugs. That person is said to have an "addictive personality." This phrase actually has two additional meanings: (1) a personality trait in young people that predicts who may be at high risk for "addiction" later in life, and (2) a set of behavioral characteristics common among all "addicts" taking drugs. In the latter case, some people have suggested that addicts behave in a similar manner under the influence of drugs, or that they have a natural tendency to become addicted to many drugs or activities. Scientists have never identified the "addictive personality," regardless of how it is defined, although some studies have suggested that antisocial personality disorder and conduct disorder may be related to a later onset of alcohol dependence (Cloninger, Sigvardsson, Gilligan, von Knorring, Reich, et al.,1988).

A Promise of Better Diagnoses

No longer can we equate "addiction" to using a drug "too much, too often, for too long." Nor can we say that a person who undergoes withdrawal from drugs is chemically dependent ("addicted"). Nor can we worry that the frequency of hangovers or blackouts during drug use is a risk factor for later chemical dependence, or an effective diagnostic criterion for alcohol or other drug dependence. The precision of our diagnostic testing will become less subjective over time as new information is learned about the genes for chemical dependence and about brain functioning before and during the onset of disease symptoms.

Based upon new work in genetics and brain imaging, we can expect in the future to have more objective means of corroborating a diagnosis based upon self-report and subjective psychosocial criteria. If chemical dependence is a brain disease, then genes for vulnerability to the disease should be identifiable even in utero (during pregnancy) and brain imaging should be able to identify brain areas that are dysfunctional and related to out-of-control drug-seeking and overuse (Farah, 2002).

The Character of Chemical Dependence

It is extremely useful to compare chemical dependence disease with other established diseases. One characteristic of medical diseases, such as leukemia, diabetes, infectious diseases, and heart disease, is their ability to occur early or late in life. As Cloninger and colleagues (1988) have recognized, there is an early onset (before age 25) type of alcoholism (type II) and a later onset type of alcoholism (type I). These have different genetic characteristics, gender representation, degree of severity, and personality associations.

Erickson (2003) has identified other onset characteristics of chemical dependence:

Early onset. Some epidemiological studies suggest that adolescents are at higher risk for alcohol dependence, especially when they begin drinking at an early age (Grant & Dawson, 1997). Developmental motivation studies tend to support this (Chambers, Taylor, & Potenza, 2003). Other epidemiological studies indicate that a significant number of cocaine users become dependent in the first year of using (Wagner &

Anthony, 2002). There may be similar early-onset associations with nicotine, methamphetamine, and other dependence-producing drugs that have not yet been characterized.

"Instant" onset. Rarely mentioned in scientific literature (except Erickson, 2003) are anecdotal reports, especially from people in recovery, that some people become "instantly addicted" to alcohol or cocaine with the first use of the drug. People report that they "feel normal" for the first time in their lives when they use the drug and they know they are "addicted." Such reports might be nothing more than a false understanding of what "addiction" is, such as the belief that the feeling of infatuation associated with the drug-induced euphoria constitutes addiction. Therefore, whether these self-reports are true is still undetermined. The reports in the recovering community are so plentiful, however, that they deserve to be studied. There is also epidemiological evidence that chemical dependence occurs without preceding drug abuse (Hasin, Hatzenberger, Smith, & Grant, 2005), which indicates that abuse and dependence are two different drug overuse conditions. Such studies, of course, also need replication and expansion.

Late onset. Cloninger and colleagues (1988) have identified a late-onset form of alcohol dependence, defined as occurrence of the disease after the age of 25. With other chemical dependence, early and late onset ages have not been identified. There are anecdotal instances where the onset of "addiction" (such as alcohol dependence) may be delayed until the geriatric years (Oslin, Slaymaker, Blow, Owen, & Colleran, 2005).

Absence of onset. Some people do not "have what it takes" to become dependent. They may not be genetically vulnerable or, for whatever reason, never experience the disease in their lives. This is not surprising, as all people are not vulnerable to every disease. Even when people drink or drug heavily, only a third or fewer ever become dependent (Table 1.4). Other users are forever drug abusers, or social drinkers or nonproblem users of drugs, or stop using drugs altogether at some point in their lives. If they stop without treatment, this may be an indication that they did not have the disease (recall people who eat a lot of food but never become obese).

Dependence Liability

Dependence liability relates to the likelihood that a person will become dependent if he or she uses a drug. Some drugs, such as caffeine, antidepressants (e.g., the tricyclic antidepressants, monamine oxidase inhibitors, and serotonin reuptake inhibitors), antipsychotic medications (e.g., Zyprexa, Geodon), and newer anti-seizure medications (Neurontin, Topamax), do not have dependence liability. These drugs may affect feelings or produce a positive mood but do not appear to act on the mesolimbic dopamine system. Although we often hear about caffeine "addiction," this is mostly a misnomer propagated by the belief that withdrawal is the main measure of "addiction" (Wilson & Kuhn, 2005; see Chapter 5).

Other drugs, however, do have dependence liability. As Table 1.4 illustrates, epidemiologic studies indicate that of those people who use different drugs, a certain percentage (depending upon the drug) will become dependent (Anthony, Warner, & Kessler, 1994).

Table 1.4
Estimated Prevalence of Dependence Among 15- to 54-year-old Users (1990–1992)*

Drug	**Percentage of Users Who Become Dependent**
Nicotine	32%
Heroin	23%
Cocaine	17%
Alcohol	15%
Stimulants	11%
Cannabis	9%
"Sedatives"	9%
Psychedelics	5%
Inhalants	4%

*Data drawn from Anthony, Warner, & Kessler (1994)

Note that in Chapter 3 I discuss chemical dependence as a disease in which compulsive use of the drug is the symptom of the disease, not how drugs produce chemical dependence. In some individuals, the genetic tendency to become dependent—the disease—is triggered by the use of the drug. Thus, some drugs "have what it takes" to produce chemical dependence, and this only occurs in individuals who "have what it takes" to have the disease. However, for a given individual, the dependence liability will range from very low to very high, depending on factors such as family history, genetic vulnerability, quantity and frequency of drug use, and perhaps environmental factors that are as yet unknown. If one looks at a number of factors that can affect whether a person uses a drug, why they use it, the drug's availability, how "reinforcing" (positively rewarding) the drug is in animal models, the intensity of withdrawal, and multiple pharmacological factors, a somewhat different list can be made than that in Table 1.4.

Based upon methodology in Erickson, Javors, & Morgan (1990), Table 1.5 lists the dependence liability of various drugs and drug groups. However, this highly subjective listing is only an indication of the thinking of some pharmacologists and will undoubtedly change due to new research and clinical observation.

Table 1.5
Dependence Liability of Various Drugs/Drug Groups*

Highest	**Lower**
heroin, many opioid agonists	buprenorphine, codeine
nicotine	benzodiazepines
cocaine/crack	marijuana
alcohol	hallucinogens (e.g., LSD)
amphetamines	PCP, ketamine, inhalants

*Subjective dependence liability associated with drug use, based upon many pharmacological and epidemiological factors. Data drawn from Erickson, Javors, & Morgan (1990).

In Table 1.5, nicotine, heroin, and cocaine are the drugs with the highest dependence liability, based upon the accumulated research in 1990. My impression is that alcohol is only slightly behind those drugs, with amphetamines being slightly behind alcohol in liability. The right-hand column shows some opioid drugs such as codeine as having higher liability than benzodiazepines, followed by marijuana, LSD, PCP and ketamine, and inhalants. The problem with this column is that there is much less research on the dependence liability factors with these drugs, meaning that the drugs could possibly be presented in a different order. The dependence liability listings in Table 1.5 are somewhat subjective, since they represent a consensus of three editors who examined existing research on the drug classes listed (Erickson et al., 1990, p. 3). Goldstein and Kalant (1990) listed the pharmacological "relative risk of addiction" for many of the same drugs on the following scale, with 1 being the highest risk:

1 – cocaine, amphetamines
2 – nicotine, opiates
3 – alcohol, benzodiazepines, barbiturates
4 – cannabis
5 – hallucinogens, caffeine

A second problem with the list in Table 1.5 is that it does not include all drugs, as very little is known about the dependence liability of drugs such as propoxyphene (Darvon), tramadol, dextromethorphan, meprobamate, mescaline, and hydrocodone (Vicodin, Lortab) or oxycodone (Percocet, OxyContin). Often, we know more about the abuse liability of these drugs than their dependence liability. It is also likely that individual drugs within drug classes might have different dependence liabilities than other drugs in the same class (for example, based upon anecdotal reports, Xanax may have a higher dependence liability than Valium in the benzodiazepine class). In contrast, Ridenour, Maldonado-Molina, Compton, Spitznagel, and Cottler (2005) predicted the "addictive liability" of drugs by measuring the "length of time between onset of abuse and dependence" (LOTAD), with a shorter LOTAD being indicative of greater "addictive liability" (Ridenour, Maldonado-Molina, Compton, Spitznagel, & Cottler, 2005).

The concepts of cross-tolerance and cross-dependence (usually among drugs in the same class) are assumed to be present in Table 1.5. Thus, when a person becomes tolerant to one benzodiazepine (e.g., Xanax), that person will automatically be tolerant to other benzodiazepines. It is also possible for a person to be cross-tolerant to drugs of different classes. (For example, benzodiazepine use sometimes leads to alcohol tolerance.) The term cross-dependence is not generally used by pharmacologists, but in the "addiction" field, the term relates to whether a person dependent on one drug will also be dependent on other drugs. Reports suggest that such cross-dependence occurs between alcohol and cocaine, alcohol and nicotine, alcohol and benzodiazepines, and heroin and cocaine. Of course, just because two or more drugs are used at the same time doesn't mean that the person is dependent on all of them. In some clinical practices, multiple dependence diagnoses are commonly sought for insurance purposes; in others, just a simple recording of multiple drug use is sufficient.

Dependence Versus Reliance

Some people fervently believe that any drug that produces withdrawal symptoms is "addicting." For example, we often hear that depressed patients are "addicted" to antidepressants because withdrawal signs are seen upon cessation of therapy, and that some people "need" to stay on antidepressants for the rest of their lives. However, antidepressants have several characteristics that prevent them from producing dependence as defined by *DSM-IV* criteria:

- They have a long onset of action, so people are less likely to seek them out for any type of mood alteration.
- They anecdotally provide a "noisy, blunted, unpleasant" state, including drowsiness and other side effects that reduce their use or abuse.
- They have never been shown to have an effect on the mesolimbic dopamine system, the "dependence" area of the brain.
- Unlike with dependence-producing drugs, patients often forget to take antidepressant medication.
- Unlike with dependence-producing drugs, many depressed patients do not want to depend on "pills" to feel better and want to know when they can be taken off the medication.

Many drugs are overused, misused, and abused. But in the context of chemical dependence, there are now strict criteria related to the disease. Thus, when drugs are prescribed for medical purposes and are used as directed, they are not considered to be "abused." Certainly prescription medications (particularly those used to treat pain, narcolepsy, attention deficit hyperactivity disorder, depression, and anxiety) can be abused, but there is little evidence to indicate that larger numbers of users become dependent than when drugs are used recreationally. In fact, there is evidence that therapeutic use of prescription medications is associated with a lower risk of dependence of the same drugs (Biederman, Wilens, Mick, Spencer, & Faraore, 1999; Robbins, 2002).

When people use properly-prescribed medications for long periods of time or for a lifetime, it may be best to state that such people are "reliant" on medications to reduce the symptoms of their disease (J. O'Neill, personal communication). Thus, diabetic patients are reliant on insulin, depressed patients are reliant on antidepressants, attention-deficit hyperactivity disorder (ADHD) patients are reliant on amphetamines—for the purpose of living longer and more comfortably. Whether some of these patients also meet *DSM-IV* dependence criteria with such medications will never be known in such cases, as there is often no need to remove them from medications that are required for medical purposes. If they do decide to stop using the medications and core symptoms do not return, they can live very comfortably without the medications. In other words, medically reliant patients do not have the disease of chemical dependence as it manifests in those who cannot stop using drugs that are producing harm.

Now that experts have described two major types of drug problems, is it possible for society to begin describing drug users in ways that are not pejorative? Is drug overuse always a "sin," a "willpower problem," or "addiction"? Is it possible that some drug users have a disease over which they have no control? If so, could we replace terms such as "addicts," "drunks," and "alcoholics" with "alcohol or drug-dependent individuals"?

Gambling and Impulse-Control Disorders

Chemical dependence disease shares some of the same characteristics as impulse-control and obsessive compulsive disorders. With respect to nonchemical problems, clinicians and the public are eager to label behavior as "addiction"—to gambling, sex, food, exercise, and so on.

None of these is considered a pathology in the *DSM-IV* except gambling, and compulsive gambling or gambling "problems" are formally labeled "pathological gambling" in the *DSM-IV* (found under Impulse-Control Disorders Not Elsewhere Classified). This disorder is rather common, estimated to affect 1–2% of the population, or 4–6% of gamblers, with young gamblers being at higher risk for the disease. A few studies have suggested that the causes of pathological gambling are involved with overactivity (Hollander, Pallanti, Allen, Sood, & Rossi, 2005) or underactivity (Reuter, Raedler, Rose, Hand, Glascher, et al., 2005) of brain areas, including the mesolimbic reward system.

Pathological gambling has been described as a chronic and progressive mental illness. It is characterized by persistent and recurrent maladaptive patterns of gambling behavior, and it is associated with impaired functioning, reduced quality of life, and high rates of bankruptcy, divorce, and incarceration. Recent community-based longitudinal studies have pointed out the transitory nature of gambling-related problems, however, and a recent article indicates that *DSM-IV*-assessed pathological gamblers do not always follow a chronic and persisting course (Slutske, 2006). Slutske pointed out that more than a third of pathological gamblers do not experience any gambling-related problems in a followup year, and that they "recover," most without formal treatment. Although Gamblers Anonymous groups generally promote gambling abstinence, it may be that even the most seriously affected gamblers can regain control of their gambling over time. For those with persistent symptoms, medications are available. Naltrexone, augmentation of naltrexone with an antidepressant, and lithium (for gamblers with bipolar disease) have been reported to be helpful (Grant & Kim, 2002). More recently, low-dose nalmefene (in clinical studies in the U.S.) has been shown to be effective while providing less liver toxicity than naltrexone in high doses (Grant, Harford, Muthen, Yi, Hasin, et al., 2006). It is interesting that pharmacotherapies used to treat other chemical dependencies and psychiatric disorders are useful in treating pathological gambling. This suggests that there are central nervous system neurochemical dysregulations that may be common to all of these brain disorders (Papgeorgiou, Rabavilas, Liappas, & Stefanis, 2003; Tamminga & Nestler, 2006).

Recommendations

The public and the media have used and will continue to use the word *addiction* to describe situations where drugs, gambling, and other disorders are negatively affecting people's lives. As long as this continues, it will be difficult (in my opinion) for the public and policy makers to relate the word *addiction* to *disease*. Treatment professionals can at least recognize that "addiction" is not a highly accurate scientific term, that it is a broad descriptor for many conditions, and that it has limited usefulness when making a diagnosis or trying to treat a client or patient. Proper use of the terms *chemical* (or *drug*) *abuse* and *chemical* (or *drug*) *dependence* not only increases accuracy of diagnosis and treatment, but also elevates the treatment field to a higher level, more closely aligned to contemporary psychiatry and medicine. It also fosters the understanding that chemical dependence is a chronic, medical brain disease. This is the key to greater acceptance and understanding about drug problems by the public and policy makers, who obviously do not yet fully understand "addictive" disease.

Chapter 2

Basics of Brain Science

ONE WAY TO THINK ABOUT ALCOHOLICS ANONYMOUS (A.A.), Narcotics Anonymous (N.A.), and other 12-step programs is that they aim to foster a return to physical health (step 1), establish a foundation for psychological and behavioral health (step 2), and lay the foundation for spiritual recovery or health (step 3). People wishing to join A.A. must have a desire to stop drinking and are asked to admit that they are powerless over alcohol (step 1). For the millions of A.A. members, this means admitting to themselves and others the truth about what has happened to them physically, mentally, and spiritually. By way of the 12 steps, they come to recognize that alcohol and other mood-altering drugs have "hijacked" their thinking and caused them to act in ways that violate their core values. The resulting emotional consequences (shame, fear, guilt, self-directed anger) are manifested as defensive behavior (hostility, rage, false charm, even disguised defenses like overachievement). It also means acknowledging that the delusion that surrounds their disease is blocking them from seeing how alcohol and other drugs had become the focus of their lives to the point of forsaking anyone or anything else (steps 3, 4, 5).

It is most helpful for recovering people and those who treat them to fully understand that powerlessness is not a mental or moral weakness, but rather a disease involving brain chemistry and in most cases a genetic vulnerability. Alcohol and other drugs alter the delicate workings of the human nervous system all the way down to the cellular level, changing the way that these cells communicate with each other. This not only produces the temporary situation of "intoxication," but also, in some people, more permanent changes leading to a chemical dependence that makes it almost impossible to stop using alcohol or drugs without help (i.e., powerlessness).

Alcohol and other drugs produce their effects by changing the activity of the nervous system. Treatment professionals who want to understand the causes and physical changes produced by long-term drug use should familiarize themselves with the following basic parts and operations of the nervous system.

The Nervous System

The nervous system is the body's control and communication network. In humans, this system:

- Senses changes both in and outside the body (the *sensory* function),
- Interprets and explains the changes (the *integrative* function),
- Responds to the interpretation by making muscles interact and glands secrete hormones or other chemicals into the circulatory system (the *motor* function)

The nervous system itself is divided into: (1) the *central nervous system* (*CNS*), which includes the brain and spinal cord and acts as a "control center," and (2) the *peripheral nervous system* (*PNS*), which includes all other nerve elements. These two systems connect the brain and spinal cord to muscles and glands. Within the CNS, nerve cells communicate with each other to allow feeling, thinking, learning, and behaving. Whereas the "brain" is the physical organ in which such phenomena occur (Figure 2.1), the "mind" is the seat of consciousness and higher functions, such as cognition, reasoning, willing, and emotion.

Nerve Cells (Neurons)

The body is made up of many billions of cells. Cells are the basic unit of all living things. Even single-celled organisms such as bacteria can

Figure 2.1
Important Areas of the Brain

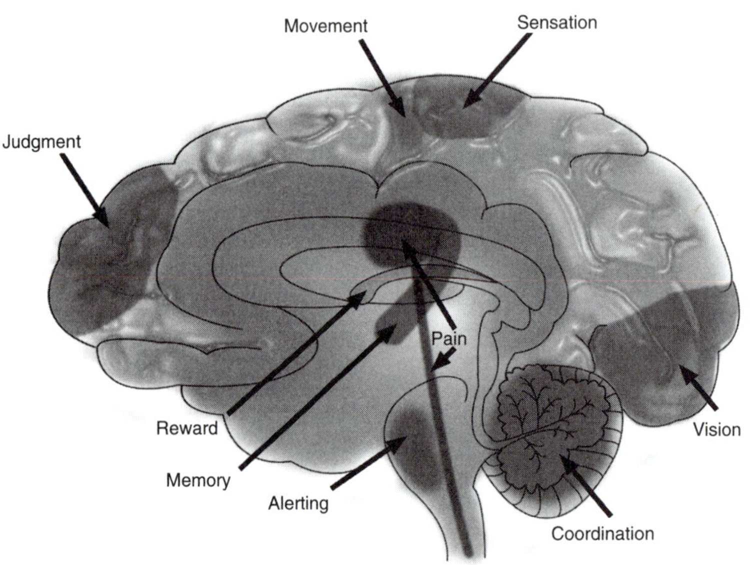

perform the basic functions needed to sustain life. These basic functions include gathering energy from food, reproducing, and producing waste material.

Nearly all cells include three parts:

- An outer wall called a *membrane*
- A *nucleus* that contains essential chemicals
- A body of clear fluid called the *cytoplasm*

Plants, animals, and humans are multicellular creatures. Cells specialize in certain functions. For example, some cells become part of muscle tissue and help us move. Other cells make up organs, tissues such as blood, and glands, veins, arteries, bone, and the nervous system.

To serve its three functions, the nervous system includes vast circuits of delicate cells that are elaborately interconnected. In fact, the brain, spinal cord, and nerves throughout the body contain special kinds of cells called *neurons*, and the brain also contains *glia*. Neurons are active cells that carry nerve signals; glia are supportive and nutritional cells of the brain. Neurons are specialized, and their specific function is to allow our brains to learn, reason, remember, and experience emotions. Through the activity of neurons, the body responds and adjusts to changes in the environment. These changes, called *stimuli*, set off impulses in our sense organs: the eye, ear, organs of taste and smell, and sensory receptors located in the skin, joints, muscles, and other parts of the body. Every time something is felt or thought—including the effects of a drug—millions of neurons are "firing" messages to and from one another. Those messages consist of chemicals and electrical impulses.

Neurotransmitters

Each neuron may have thousands of branches that connect to other neurons. The branches are called *dendrites* or *axons*. *Dendrites* carry messages toward the cell body; *axons* carry messages away from the cell body. Axons extend for as long as 4 feet in humans. In some animals, they are even longer.

In the past, scientists thought that axons and dendrites simply ran through the body continuously, like wires. Then they discovered a space between each axon and dendrite. They called this space a *synaptic cleft*. The synaptic cleft is the space between the axon of one neuron and the dendrites of the next neuron in a nerve pathway (Figure 2.2). That gap is extremely small—about one-millionth of an inch. The larger area involving the synaptic cleft, the presynaptic area on the transmitting side, and the postsynaptic area on the receiving side is known as a *synapse*.

Researchers originally thought that electrical impulses jumped these gaps, like electricity jumps across the gap in a spark plug. Now we know this is not true. Chemicals—not electrical impulses—travel across the gaps. These chemicals are known as *neurotransmitters*. Today we know the identity of more than 60 neurotransmitters (although hundreds will perhaps be identified in the future). The neurons in the body synthesize neurotransmitters. The chemical building blocks for neurotransmitters (mostly amino acids) come from the foods we eat.

Neurons store neurotransmitters. The storage areas, called *vesicles*, are located close to the ending of each axon. Neurons synthesize some neurotransmitters right in the vesicle. Other neurotransmitters are

Figure 2.2
Synapses Between Nerve Cells

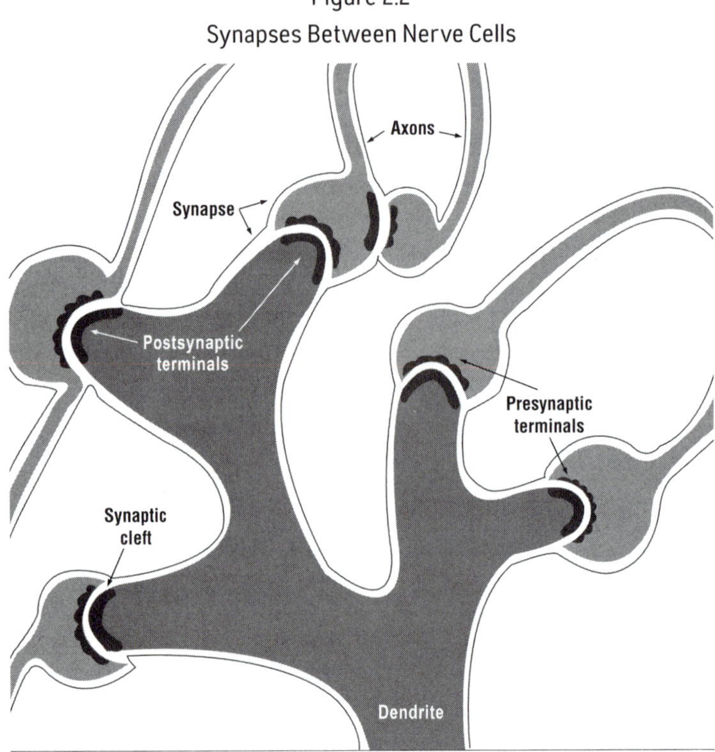

synthesized in the body of the cell and are transported down to the vesicle. Most drugs involved in chemical dependence mimic neurotransmitters or change their effects. To understand how these drugs work, we must review what we know about neurotransmitters and how they act as chemical "messengers."

Neurotransmitters are sometimes called *first messengers*. The chemical responses inside the receiving neuron produce chemicals called *second messengers*. Second messengers pass along the original message from the neurotransmitter, after the neurotransmitter travels from the *presynaptic terminal* of the sending neuron to the *postsynaptic terminal* of the receiving neuron.

Neurotransmitter Criteria

Neurotransmitters are *molecules*—groups of atoms, joined by a chemical bond, that act as a unit. In order to be called a neurotransmitter, a molecule must meet three criteria:

- The molecule must be present in the brain and distributed unevenly. That is, the molecule must be spread out among different types of neurons and across regions of the brain that have different functions.
- The enzymes that help to create the neurotransmitter must be present in the brain. These enzymes must also be present in areas where the neurotransmitter is found.
- Directly injecting a neurotransmitter into a part of the brain known to contain certain neurons must imitate the effects of electrically stimulating the same neurons.

Neurotransmitter Functions and Receptors

In some ways, neurons act like computers. They receive messages, process those messages, and send out the results as new messages to other cells. In the case of neurons, the messages consist of chemicals. Each chemical message can get translated across a cell membrane and enter the cell. Once inside the cell, those chemicals can be processed—broken down or changed into other chemicals. Chemicals can also leave the cell and function as the cell's output.

The name for the constant exchange of chemical messages between neurons is *neurotransmission.* Neurotransmission involves three basic steps:

- *The release of neurotransmitters.* A resting neuron has a negative charge inside its membrane. That is, there are more negative ions inside the axon than outside the axon. (*Ions* are chemicals with an electric charge.) In contrast, the fluid outside the axon has a positive charge. Because the outside and inside of the axon have different charges, the axon is said to be *polarized.*

  When a neuron is excited (it *fires*), several events take place to create an electrical impulse. Sodium ions, which have a positive charge, enter the axon. This *depolarizes* the axon—that is, changes the electrical charge inside the axon from negative to positive. This change starts at one end of the axon and continues all the way to the other end. In response to this electrical impulse (called an *action potential*), the vesicles swarm to the very edge of the axon and release neurotransmitters into the synaptic cleft.

As the neurotransmitters are released, potassium ions flow out of the axon. Potassium ions have a positive charge, so their absence restores the negative charge inside the axon. The neuron is again polarized and at rest, waiting to fire another impulse.

- *Connection to a receptor.* Neurotransmitters drift across the synaptic cleft until they touch the dendrites of the next neuron. On each dendrite, neurotransmitters find molecules that are genetically designed to receive them. These molecules are called *receptors* (Figure 2.3). A receptor is actually a type of protein that serves as the point of attachment for a neurotransmitter. Neurotransmitters recognize specific receptors and connect to them, a process called *binding*. (The neuron that originally released the neurotransmitter is the "sending" neuron; the neuron that binds the neurotransmitter is the "receiving" neuron.) The neurotransmitter or drug binds to the receptor (near the channel). The receptor undergoes a conformational change, which opens the gate and allows ions to flow into the cell. This causes depolarization (excitation) or polarization (inhibition) of the membrane and the activation of certain proteins.

  Each receptor accepts only certain neurotransmitters, much like a security door accepts only a certain passcard. After the binding process, receptors release the neurotransmitters. At that point, several

Figure 2.3

A Gated Ion Channel (Receptor) of the Type Affected by Dopamine*

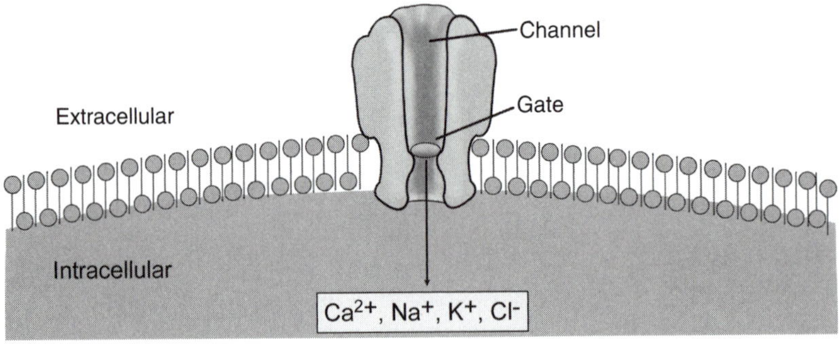

Adapted with permission from Cami, J. & Farre, M. (2003). *New England Journal of Medicine, 349*, 975–986. Copyright 2003. Massachusetts Medical Society. All rights reserved.

things can happen. Some neurotransmitters are destroyed by enzymes. In other cases, proteins transport neurotransmitters back into the axon from which they originally came, a process called *reuptake*. Reuptake allows neurons to use the same neurotransmitters over again—a kind of "recycling." Reuptake is also known as *active transport*, and the enzymes that actively move neurotransmitters from outside the cell to inside the cell are called *transporters*.

- *Binding to change function*. Binding causes a set of chemical reactions within the receiving neuron. The chemical responses inside the receiving neuron produce second messengers. Second messengers pass along the original message from the neurotransmitter, sometimes modified depending on the type of neurotransmitter and receptors involved. Those reactions either increase or decrease the chance that another impulse will be fired in the system. In this way, the original impulse from the sending neuron is conducted to the next neuron—and through the rest of the neurons in a nerve pathway. Eventually, the impulse reaches its final destination, such as a muscle, gland, or organ. The result is a change in the way we think, feel, or behave.

Dopamine: A Model Neurotransmitter

The most prominent neurotransmitter involved in the pleasurable and addictive effects of drugs is *dopamine* (DA). Many of the concepts and processes that apply to DA apply to other neurotransmitters as well. It is logical to talk about DA as a "model neurotransmitter system." Figure 2.4 shows a dopamine (DA) synapse. Sites of drug action include synthesis (1) from tyrosine through dihydroxyphenylalanine (DOPA) to DA, (2) vesicular uptake, (3) transmitter release into the synaptic space, (4) receptor binding, (5) cellular uptake (transport), and (6) transmitter metabolism into homovanillic acid (HVA). In general, each of the sites offers a potential target for drug action, as described in the sections below.

As a neurotransmitter, DA is structurally similar to *epinephrine* and *norepinephrine*. DA affects brain processes that control movement, motivation, emotional response, and the ability to experience pleasure and pain. Regulation of DA plays a crucial role in our mental and physical health. Neurons containing the neurotransmitter DA are clustered in

Figure 2.4
Sites of Drug Action for Dopamine

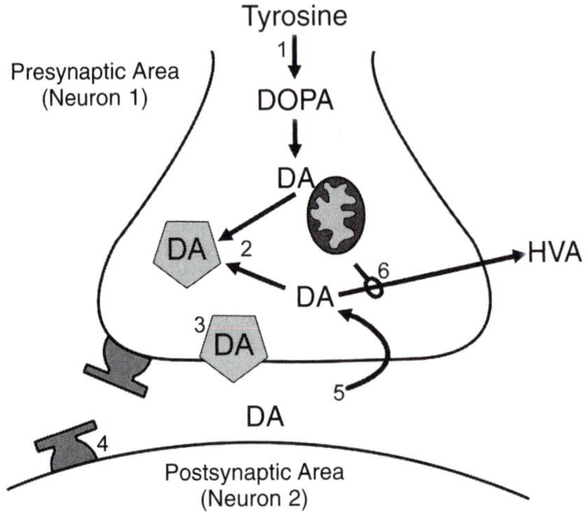

the midbrain in an area called the *substantia nigra*, which is a specialized area of the *basal ganglia*. In Parkinson's disease, the DA-transmitting neurons in this area die. As a result, certain areas in the brain contain almost no DA. One of the drugs used to reduce the tremors and muscle rigidity of Parkinson's is L-DOPA, a drug that can be converted in the brain to DA.

Parkinson's disease is analogous to chemical dependence in that *dysregulation* of neurotransmitter function (i.e., the neurotransmitter system isn't working properly) relates to the basic cause of the disease.

Dopamine Actions

Agonists are chemicals that bind to receptors in place of neurotransmitters and directly activate those receptors. Some drugs are known as *DA agonists*. Some DA agonists have been used to treat Parkinson's disease. These drugs stimulate DA receptors even in someone without DA neurons.

In contrast to agonists, *antagonists* are chemicals that bind but can't stimulate receptors. DA antagonists can prevent or reverse the actions of DA by keeping DA from binding to receptors. DA antagonists are traditionally used to treat people with schizophrenia and related mental disorders. A person with the disorder of schizophrenia is thought to have an overactive DA system. DA antagonists can help regulate this system by reducing DA activity.

Drugs such as cocaine and amphetamine produce their effects by altering the release or reuptake of neurotransmitters. Cocaine, for example, keeps DA around longer by blocking certain *autoreceptors* known as *DA transporters* (*DATs*), and prevents the neuron's uptake process from operating. Amphetamines, in contrast, increase DA in the synaptic cleft by increasing the release of DA. Drugs like cocaine and amphetamine are called *indirect*-acting because they depend on the activity of neurons for their effects. In contrast, some drugs bypass neurotransmitters altogether and act directly on receptors. Such drugs are called *direct*-acting.

Use of direct- and indirect-acting drugs can lead to very different results in treating the same disease. Because people with Parkinson's disease lose DA-containing neurons, the body produces more DA receptors on other neurons to partially compensate for the loss. Indirect agonists are not very effective in treating the disease because they depend on the presence of DA neurons. In contrast, direct agonists are effective because they stimulate DA receptors even when DA neurons are missing.

It's interesting that amphetamine and cocaine affect behavior and heart function in similar ways. This is because both drugs increase the amount of DA in the synaptic cleft. However, cocaine achieves this action by preventing DA reuptake, whereas amphetamine helps to release more DA. In other words, these drugs have similar effects, but through entirely different processes.

Sensitization and Desensitization

One important aspect of chemical dependence is how cells adapt to previous drug exposure (Erickson & Wilcox, 2001). For example, long-term treatment with DA antagonists increases the number of DA receptors. This happens as the nervous system tries to make up for less stimulation of the receptors by DA itself. In addition, the receptors themselves become more sensitive to DA. Both are examples of the same process that has been called *up-regulation* or *sensitization*. Sensitization is involved in at least one of the theories concerning how chemical dependence occurs (see Chapter 3).

An opposite effect occurs after DA or DA agonists repeatedly stimulate DA receptors. Here, overstimulation decreases the number of receptors, and the remaining receptors become less sensitive to DA. This process is called *down-regulation* or *desensitization*. Desensitization is also known as neuronal *tolerance*, where exposure to a drug causes less response than previously. Tolerance and sensitization reflect the actions of the nervous system to maintain *homeostasis*—a small range of cell activity in spite of major changes in receptor stimulation. The nervous system attempts to keep the body in this state of equilibrium, even when foreign chemicals are present.

Sensitization and desensitization do not only occur after long-term understimulation or overstimulation of DA receptors. In fact, both sensitization and desensitization can occur after only a single exposure to a drug, sometimes within a few minutes. In some cases, rapid desensitization is called *tachyphylaxis* (an example is the very rapid tolerance seen when a person takes doses of LSD one after the other).

Other Neurotransmitters

It is important to understand that all drugs, including psychoactive ones such as alcohol and heroin, work on existing neurochemical pathways in the CNS; that is, they do not create new pathways. The specificity of drug action comes from each drug's action on certain neurotransmitters and receptors, as well as from how and where the drugs distribute throughout the nervous system after ingestion or other forms of administration.

Dopamine was described earlier as a major player in chemical dependence. Several other neurotransmitters are also important and deserve attention. They include serotonin, norepinephrine, acetylcholine, endorphins, endocannabinoids, glutamate, and gamma aminobutyric acid (GABA).

Serotonin

Serotonin plays a major role in emotional disorders such as depression, suicide, impulsive behavior, and aggression. Neurons using serotonin as a neurotransmitter are found throughout the brain, but especially in the brain stem. Serotonin is normally involved in temperature regulation, sensory perception, and mood control. The psychedelic drug LSD acts on serotonin receptors; so do some antidepressant drugs. Prozac and other selective serotonin reuptake inhibitors (SSRIs) used to treat severe depression prevent the normal reuptake of serotonin. As a result, there is more serotonin floating around to bind to receptors and trigger impulses in the receiving neurons. This leads to increased stimulation of serotonin neurons in depressed people.

Norepinephrine

Norepinephrine is a neurotransmitter that does double-duty as a hormone. (*Hormones* are chemicals in the blood that regulate many body functions, including growth, digestion, and fluid balance.) As a neurotransmitter, norepinephrine helps to regulate arousal to the environment, dreaming, and moods. As a hormone, norepinephrine acts to increase blood pressure, constrict blood vessels, and increase heart rate—responses that occur when we feel stress.

Acetylcholine

Acetylcholine excites neurons in the brain and many other parts of the body, including muscles, tissues, and glands. Acetylcholine is released where nerves meet muscles and is therefore responsible for muscle contraction. One of the receptors in the brain that is activated by acetylcholine is the nicotinic receptor, which is also affected by the dependence-producing drug nicotine.

Endorphins

There is a group of endorphins (including beta-endorphin, enkephalins, and dynorphins) that are involved in pain regulation in the brain and spinal cord, and with sensations of dreaminess and calm. These endorphins are known to be released during stress, relaxation, and pain. Drugs affecting the endorphin system include opioid drugs such as morphine, heroin, and other powerful pain-relieving analgesic drugs.

Endocannabinoids

The discovery of receptors throughout the brain for tetra-hydrocannabinol (THC), the active ingredient in marijuana, provided a major boost to understanding how *endocannabinoids* might work in the brain. Endocannabinoids (naturally occurring cannabis-like chemicals) appear to activate the CNS receptors known as CB1 receptors. They are postulated to be involved in mood, pain control, and perhaps neurological function. Endocannabinoid antagonists (such as rimonabant) have been developed to aid in treating people with nicotine dependence and obesity.

Glutamate and GABA

Certain amino acids also act as neurotransmitters, including glutamate and GABA. Glutamate strongly excites neurons, whereas GABA strongly inhibits neurons. Glutamate and GABA are unique in several ways. For example, the number of synapses using glutamate and GABA is much greater than those using all other types of neurotransmitters combined. Also, glutamate and GABA neurons are found in many brain regions. As a result, glutamate and GABA work all over the brain whereas other neurotransmitters do not. Finally, glutamate has important functions in the body in addition to its role as a neurotransmitter. For example, it is needed by metabolism to break down food and make energy-rich molecules in cells. Drugs that act through an effect on GABA include benzodiazepines (e.g., Xanax and Valium); alcohol acts through an effect on glutamate.

The fact that GABA and glutamate occur so widely throughout the brain makes it understandable why they are involved in chemical dependence. This fact also makes it difficult to treat chemical dependence with a single drug: Because GABA and glutamate are so widely present, a drug that affects both could produce a host of side effects as well.

Importance of Receptors in Drug Action

Receptors for neurotransmitters and drugs exist throughout the entire body, not just in the CNS. Thus hormones such as epinephrine, when released from the adrenal gland, can have effects on the *PNS* (outside the brain and spinal cord) to affect heart rate, sweating, and so on. Such effects can be either *specific* (e.g., an effect on the heart rate) or *general* (e.g., an effect on blood pressure).

Before changing a neuron's activity, which then leads to a change in body function or behavior, a drug must physically interact with a receptor (as described earlier with neurotransmitters). Years of research in pharmacology have revealed that drugs must somehow interact with receptors to do their job. Receptors are the major targets for most clinically used drugs, as well as drugs of abuse. Furthermore, the dysregulation of neurotransmitter systems implicated in the cause of chemical dependence now appears to be related mostly to receptor malformation or malfunction.

Drugs and neurotransmitters are now known to activate the same receptors. Table 2.1 lists neuronal receptors that are involved in drug actions. (The "endogenous ligand" in the right-hand column is the natural chemical in the brain that uses the receptor for communication purposes.) Notice that every drug or drug class (except ethanol) has a specific receptor that it activates to produce a pharmacological response.

Table 2.1
Drug Receptors

Drug	**Receptor Identified?**	**Cloned?**	**Endogenous Ligand**
Opioids	Yes: mu, delta, kappa	Yes	Endorphins
Cocaine	Yes: DA transporter	Yes	Dopamine
Prozac	Yes: SER transporter	Yes	Serotonin
Nicotine	Yes: nicotinic ACh	Yes	Acetylcholine
Cannabis	Yes: cannabinoid	Yes	Endocannabinoids
Benzodiazepine	Yes (but opinions differ)	Yes	Opinions differ
Ethanol (alcohol)	No	NA	None

One of the major discoveries of neuropharmacology is that naturally occurring chemicals (endogenous ligands) occur in the brain. These ligands use the same receptors as drugs taken for recreational and therapeutic purposes, and most of them are neurotransmitters. Thus, the discovery of endorphins (naturally occurring morphinelike chemicals) and more recently, endocannabinoids (naturally occurring marijuanalike chemicals) has opened up an exciting entry into the understanding of how emotions might vary hour by hour or day by day through the natural (or environmentally induced) oscillations of such brain chemicals. In addition, such brain chemicals allow opportunities for manipulation by new medications to correct brain diseases involving neurochemicals.

Receptor Structure and Response

A receptor must have a high degree of specificity—that is, a strong ability to attach to a specific drug or neurotransmitter. Though specificity must be high, it does not have to be total. A tiny change in the chemical structure of a drug may greatly alter how much a cell responds to the drug. For example, amphetamine and methamphetamine are both powerful stimulants of the CNS. Chemically they differ only slightly. Both act on the same receptor in the brain. Yet methamphetamine is much more potent: at equal doses of both drugs, methamphetamine stimulates behavior far more than amphetamine.

One way to classify receptors, then, is through differences in their ability to bind drugs. We can also classify receptors based on the sequence of their amino acid components. The three-dimensional structure of a receptor determines its binding ability for neurotransmitters or drugs. In turn, the sequence of amino acids determines the structure of the receptor—the "lock" into which the neurotransmitter or drug ("key") fits.

Today we know the amino acid sequences for a large number of receptors. This has made it possible to group receptors into different families. In turn, we can further divide each family of receptors into subtypes. This helps us understand why medications that apparently have the same mechanism of action (such as SSRIs) have different efficacies and side effects in different people. For example, all SSRI antidepressant medications have the basic serotonin mechanism of action, but the reason they have different side effects and effectiveness in different patients is probably due to the presence of different serotonin receptor subtypes and how each medication interacts with those receptor subtypes. Table 2.2 lists the known receptor subtypes for each neurotransmitter involved in chemical dependence.

Table 2.2
Chemical Dependence Neurotransmitters and Their Receptor Subtypes

Neurotransmitter	Number of Receptor Subtypes
acetylcholine	two (muscarinic and nicotinic)
dopamine	five
serotonin	fifteen
GABA	two (A and B)
endorphins	four (mu, kappa, sigma, NOFQ)
glutamate	sixteen
endocannabinoid	two (CB1, CB2)

With respect to medications to treat chemical dependence, if we could develop drugs that bind selectively to specific receptor subtypes, we should be able to produce a specific clinical action with minimal side effects.

Helping Patients Understand Neurotransmission

People with drug-use problems and their families are usually eager for information about how drugs work in the brain. They are thus interested in where drugs work, and that education begins at the cellular level.

If clients want to know how nerve cells talk to each other, begin by showing them the cartoon in Figure 2.5, which illustrates how neurotransmission occurs between two neurons.

Figure 2.5

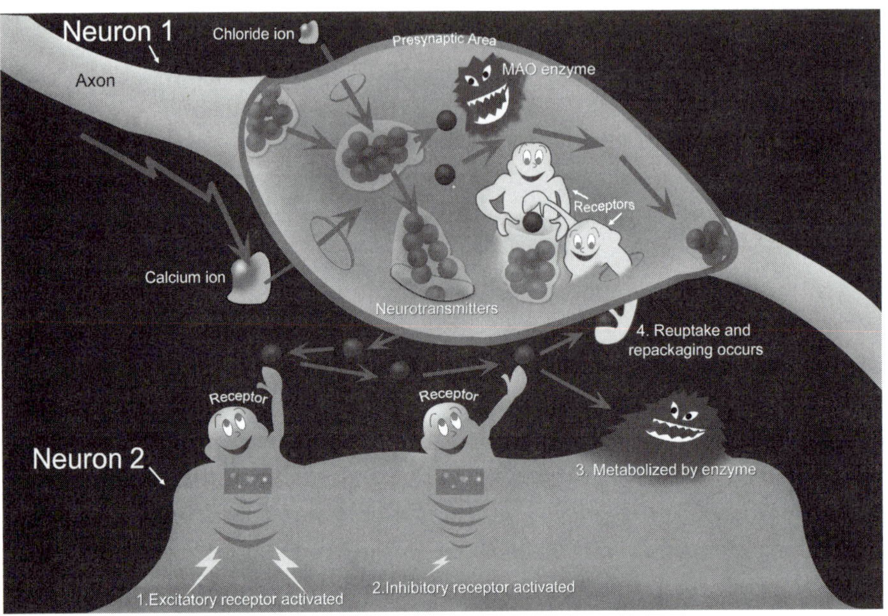

You can explain the figure as follows:

There are billions of cells in the brain. The figure depicts two nerve cells (neurons) and their important components. Neuron #1 is on the top; neuron #2 is on the bottom.

The large portion of neuron #1 is the working part of the cell, also known as the presynaptic area. *The presynaptic area is at the end of a sending fiber called an* axon, *which begins outside the boundaries of the picture in a cell body called the* soma. *Inside the soma are enzymes that manufacture chemicals called neurotransmitters.*

These neurotransmitters pass down the axon under the influence of a small electrical current called an action potential. *The neurotransmitters are packaged in what look like cellophane envelopes called* vesicles. *These vesicles release their contents (neurotransmitters) into the space between the two cells (the* synaptic cleft*), under the influence of small concentrations of calcium ions.*

Once in the synaptic cleft, one of four things can happen to the neurotransmitters. They can (1) activate an excitatory receptor (the "ghost" on the left), causing neuron #2 to be more likely to fire, (2) activate an inhibitory receptor (the ghost in the middle), causing neuron #2 to be less likely to fire, (3) be "gobbled up" (metabolized) by a "monster" enzyme (at the right), or (4) be taken back up into neuron #1 (reuptake), repackaged, and sent down the nerve cell for use later on.

Inside neuron #1 is another monster enzyme, known as monamine oxidase (MAO). MAO gobbles up the neurotransmitter molecules that accidentally leak out of the vesicles. Outside and above the nerve membrane is a small molecule known as chloride ion, which is necessary for the proper integrity of the vesicle membrane.

Under each of the receptor "ghosts" is a small rectangle containing globules of chemicals known as G proteins. These are the beginning of a chemical and electrical cascade of events that make neuron #2 more likely to fire (excitation) or less likely to fire (inhibition) and that carry the message of neuron #1 to the next nervous system component.

Receptors can be found both in the presynaptic nerve cell (for example, the reuptake site), and on the postsynaptic nerve cell. When neurotransmitter receptor function is "within normal limits," everything is fine in a person's brain. These "normal limits" are probably different for each person, and if we could somehow measure them they would be very complex. We assume that when a person is not feeling well, is behaving strangely, or is thinking abnormally, the neurotransmitter receptors are not functioning normally in a particular brain area. Further studies such as brain imaging will help us measure normal and abnormal neurotransmitter receptor functioning in specific brain areas.

*Portions of this chapter, including Figure 2.4, have been adapted from three booklets titled *Understanding Addiction* published by the Addiction Science Research and Education Center, University of Texas, written by Wilcox, R. E., Gonzales, R. A., & Erickson, C. K., and edited by D. Toft, circa 1995.

Chapter 3

Anatomy and Neurobiology of Chemical Dependence

HAVING LEARNED HOW THE NERVOUS SYSTEM OPERATES at the cellular level, it is now important to understand that every disease has a disruption of normal cell activity as its basic cause. In the case of diabetes, the cell problem is a lack of sufficient production of insulin by the pancreatic islet cells. With Parkinsonism, the basic cause appears to be a lack of dopamine (DA) function in the basal ganglia of the brain. Of course a lack of chemical production or release is not always the case; sometimes the receptors for the released chemical (insulin or DA in the previous examples) are down-regulated (or insensitive for some reason). Sometimes there is a genetic basis for the lack of production or down-regulation; sometimes there are environmental factors (obesity or trauma, as protagonists in the previous examples) in the onset of the disease. In the brain, disruption of neuron activity (called neurotransmitter *dysregulation*) is associated with the disease of chemical dependence. *Dysregulation* means that the cause could be a disruption of chemical production or release, or it could be that the receptors for the chemicals are not working correctly. The dysregulation may be present before the person takes a drug, or it may be caused by constant (chronic) drug-taking or induced by a psychosocial stressor, such as trauma. Or it could be all three. In any case, the bottom line is that the dependent patient has a disease—neurotransmitter dysregulation—that will not be easy to treat.

Diseases by nature are difficult unless a panacea or magic bullet has been developed to overcome the symptoms or the cause. It is rare to find ways to block a cause of disease in medicine (one of the few examples is the vaccine to prevent smallpox); most of the time, symptoms are overcome so that the quality of life is increased (insulin for diabetes, medicines for Parkinsonism, antidepressant medications).

In this chapter I will discuss the systems involved in the causes of chemical dependence, including neurotransmitter dysregulation, and theories about how dysregulation occurs. I will begin by describing the part of the brain where chemical dependence is known to occur.

The Brain's Reward Pathway

The likely brain site where drugs produce dependence in susceptible individuals is the so-called "reward pathway" in the middle of the brain (Koob, 1992). This is known anatomically as the *mesolimbic dopamine system* (MDS). Another, somewhat older, name for the MDS is the *medial forebrain bundle.* This DA reward pathway contains several major bundles of nerve cell endings where neurotransmitters are concentrated. Neuroscientists believe that the function of these MDS neurotransmitter systems is disrupted, due to genetic "miswiring," long-term exposure to a drug, or (more likely) a combination of genetic heritability, drug exposure, and environmental influences.

Based upon current literature and speculation, two general theories regarding the development of chemical dependence as a brain disease have been developed. The first theory concerns changes in brain sensitivity to drugs over time, called *neuroadaptation.* Most people appear to develop impaired control over drug use (dependence) through prolonged exposure to a drug. Such people have months or even years of drug use before they become dependent. This drug exposure apparently leads to a gradual dysregulation of the MDS neurotransmitter systems. Pathways in the MDS become active (or less active) in the drug's presence and still more active (or less active) with repeated drug exposure. This process—and others like it—involves a neurobiological concept known as *synaptic plasticity*, as the changes in question occur at the synapses between neurons. A major weakness of the neuroadaptation theory is that it does not adequately explain why some people who use drugs heavily over a long period are resistant to neuroadaptation or, if it does occur, do not lose control over their drug-taking behavior. Some scientists assume that genetic susceptibility is the key to the expression of symptoms with long-term drug exposure, but genetics cannot provide the entire answer. There may, for example, be environmental/psychological factors that are necessary for the symptoms of chemical dependency to be expressed. Although such environmental/psychological factors could not alone drive (cause) the disease, for some people, their presence may be crucial for the disease to become fully developed.

A second theory is that susceptibility for the disease is in the MDS at birth, and that long-term neuroadaptation is less important than genetic predisposition in the causation of chemical dependence. It seems reasonable that people who become dependent early in life with relatively little drug exposure have the greatest genetic "tendency" to develop the disease. In this theory, genetic vulnerability and other factors cause the disease during use of a drug, sometimes with first-time use (for which scientific studies are lacking), sometimes within the first year of use (for which there are some studies with cocaine), and sometimes not for many years (for which there are many studies). Accompanying this theory is the dramatic explanation that "the disease is in the brain, and the out-of-control drug use is only a symptom of the disease."

Both of these general theories are reasonable, given the lack of conclusive studies on the causes of chemical dependence. Indeed, a combination of these two theories (i.e., there could be different mechanisms in different individuals) is very likely.

Anatomy of the MDS

The main MDS areas, moving from the center of the brain forward, are the ventral tegmental area (VTA), nucleus accumbens (NAcc), and the frontal and prefrontal cortex (Figure 3.1). Most current work using brain imaging is focused on the frontal lobes, but so far almost no studies have looked at the function of the VTA or NAcc in the brains of alcohol- and other drug-dependent patients.

The first important brain area in this system is the VTA, located in the center of the brain. Neural terminations of the VTA projections (where nerves make final connections) to the forward part of the brain are widespread, consisting of subcortical (NAcc), archicortical (amyg-

Figure 3.1
The Reward Pathway

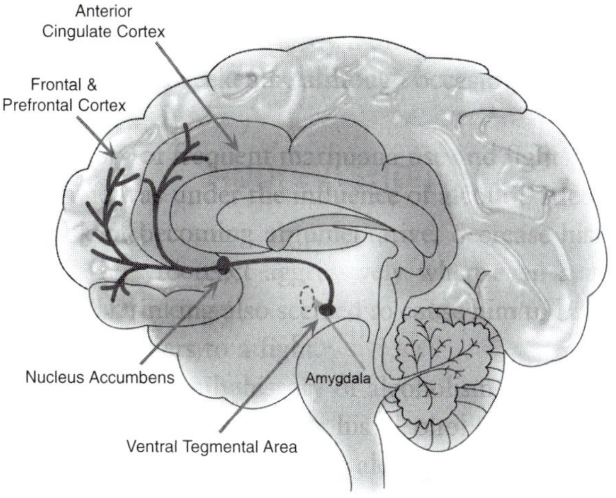

dala), paleocortical (anterior cingulate cortex), and neocortical (frontal and prefrontal cortex) areas. Because essential portions of the circuit are below the area of the neocortex and consciousness (subcortical), drug dependence develops without conscious recognition. The effects of drugs on projections to the frontal lobes are what eventually lead to the impaired control over drug use, through a reduction of cortical decision-making functions. Thus, such characteristics as "lack of willpower" and "personal weakness" do not play a significant role in the development of drug dependence. Some scientists prefer to discuss issues of conscious control, choice, decision, motivation, or drive. It is important to recognize that such psychological characteristics *are* involved in the major drug-use disorder of chemical *abuse*, but not in chemical dependence.

The extensive research on the neuroanatomy and neurophysiology of the MDS is interpreted somewhat differently among researchers, as we will see later. Figure 3.2 illustrates the extensive interactions among the major subareas of the MDS in the rat brain, as proposed by Cami and Farre (2003). Notice that mesocorticolimbic DA systems originating in the VTA include: neural projections from the cell bodies of the VTA to the NAcc, amygdala, and prefrontal cortex; glutamate (GLU) projections from the prefrontal cortex to the NAcc and the VTA; and projections from the GABA nerve cells of the NAcc to the prefrontal cortex

(Hjelmstad, 2004). Opioid interneurons (short nerve cells) regulate GABA-inhibitory action on the VTA and influence the firing of norepinephrine (NE) neurons in the locus ceruleus. Serotonin (5-HT) projections from the raphe nucleus extend to the VTA and the NAcc. The figure also shows the proposed sites of action of the various drugs of abuse in these circuits. Medications to reduce drug craving and to overcome neurochemical dysregulation are beginning to target these circuits (Johnson, Ait-Daoud, Akhtar, & Ma, 2004).

Figure 3.2
Interactions Among Subareas of the MDS in the Rat Brain

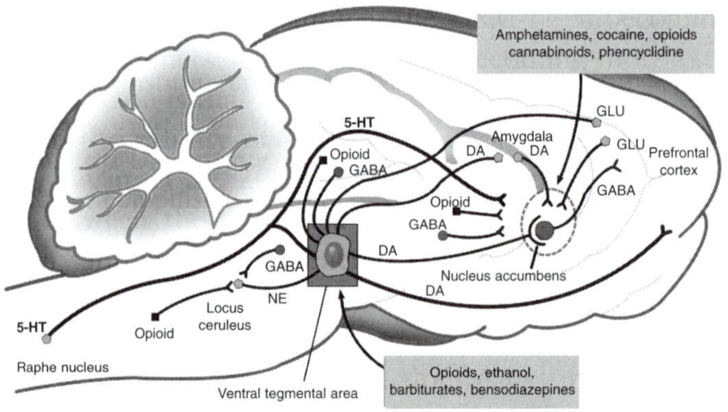

Adapted with permission from Cami, J. & Farre, M. (2003). *New England Journal of Medicine, 349*, 975–986. Copyright 2003. Massachusetts Medical Society. All rights reserved.

Knowing the Disease Before Studying It

In my experience, most drug abuse or "addiction" researchers have never knowingly talked with an "addict" or problem drug abuser, attended a treatment session or 12-step meeting, or attempted to learn firsthand what the problem/disease they're studying is all about. Treatment professionals, on the other hand, are aware of the symptoms of the problem/disease and what it does to the person physically, emotionally, socially, and spiritually. It makes sense that in order to be able to set up meaningful testable hypotheses, scientists also must be aware of the signs and symptoms of the disease and the impact of the disease on the individual.

In Chapter 1 I identified the key characteristic of chemical dependence as "impaired control over the use of drugs." Other descriptors that have been used in scientific studies are "recurring desire to take drugs even after many years of abstinence," "continued vulnerability to relapse after years of drug abstinence" (Kalivas & Volkow, 2005), and "compulsive drug-seeking and drug-taking behavior persisting despite serious negative consequences" (Cami & Farre, 2003). Such descriptions provide the framework for experiments that can discover the mechanisms behind such pathological drug-taking behavior. Consistent with this idea, chemically dependent people often report that they "need" a drug—which is beyond "liking" or "wanting" a drug. Often, chemically dependent individuals report that they no longer feel euphoria—a sense of well-being—when taking the drug, but they must continue using it anyway to remain functional, to feel normal, or to satisfy a subconscious instinctive urge.

What is this "need" that chemically dependent people feel? Neurobiologists now believe that the need relates to "dysregulations" of the MDS (meaning the system is not working normally) that cause the person to feel that the drug is "correcting" the brain's problem. The problem, as will be seen in the theories presented below, is caused by a sensitivity to drugs because of genetic vulnerability or neuroadaptation caused by continued exposure to drugs over a period of time. Most likely, either one of these causes, alone or in combination, is the problem. Drug-taking, combined with pre-existent or developing dysregulations of the major MDS neurotransmitter systems (DA, SER, GABA, GLU, endorphin, acetylcholine, or endocannabinoid), leads to an instant or later-developing dysregulation of the MDS that causes the person to "connect" to certain drugs to "balance" or "correct" the brain dysregulations. Whichever drug produces the best "connection" turns out to be the "drug of choice" (better: drug of ***no*** choice) for that person. Of course, dysregulations of several neurotransmitter systems would produce multiple dependencies or "co-addiction" to more than one drug.

According to some theories (see Incentive Sensitization, later in this chapter), "liking" is associated with the pleasurable effects of a drug, whereas "wanting" is related to the urge or craving to take the drug. On the other hand, "needing" suggests that the body (more specifically, the hypothalamus of the brain) demands or requires the drug to function normally, in a manner similar to the body's instinctual need for sex, water, and air. This makes sense when we understand that one of the anatomical relationships of the MDS involves the hypothalamus—a structure that regulates such essential processes as eating, drinking, sexual drive, and breathing.

The "need" for drugs is crucial in understanding why people can't stop using chemicals that are toxic and able to produce death. Some people have even related chemical dependence to obsessive compulsive disorder (OCD), a psychiatric illness where people cannot stop repetitive behavior or control having specific repetitive thoughts, images, or feelings. Obsession means "thinking about it all the time," and compulsion is "doing it all the time." Certainly chemical dependence meets these descriptions. Thus, a provocative question in research on dependence asks why some drug-exposed persons lose control over their drug-taking or drug-seeking behavior and other persons similarly exposed to drugs do not. A directly related question asks, What is the best way to begin to normalize dysregulated brain function to allow these people to regain some behavioral control over use of the drug?

Diagnostic publications tell us that the amount of alcohol or drug used is not a primary indicator of impaired control, nor is the presence of "hangovers," "blackouts," or physical withdrawal syndrome (*DSM-IV-TR*, 2000). The best current models suggest that the drug-dependence process involves brain chemistry changes (neuroadaptation) that are similar to those involved in synaptic plasticity, and that restoration of behavioral control must involve opposite changes at the neurochemical level (Kalivas & Volkow, 2005). Again, the phrase *synaptic plasticity* refers to a type of neurodaptation in which the functioning of a synapse is changed as a result of previous neural activity. All forms of synaptic plasticity are complex and probably involve multiple neurotransmitter systems within the brain.

Neurobiological Theories of Dependence

Drugs that directly affect the MDS of the brain have the potential to produce chemical dependence. Drugs that have little or no effect on the brain's MDS are incapable of producing chemical dependence. Based upon the preceding understanding of MDS function, the current view is that chemical dependence is a type of synaptic plasticity (neuroadaptation) that occurs within the limbic portion of the brain and especially within the MDS. Thus stimuli within the environment (cues, which include drugs and other strong stimuli) play a role in the brain's neural adaptation process. Chemical dependence differs from other types of synaptic plasticity described in neuroscience in that a drug is a very powerful stimulus for inducing changes in brain chemistry. Drugs offer special "advantages" as stimuli for affecting synaptic plasticity because their effects on brain chemistry are probably more powerful than all other types of stimuli, even physiological stimuli (Wilcox & Erickson, 2004). For example, running (or other vigorous exercise) enhances the release of several neurotransmitters within the MDS, including endorphins as well as DA and serotonin. Although an increase in brain endorphins can be substantial following exercise ("runner's high"), this increase is still much smaller than the changes in brain morphine levels produced by a dose of heroin. Such dramatic differences in the magnitude of effect can lead to qualitative differences in the types of adaptation that occur.

In an attempt to describe the mechanisms behind the neuroadaptation and neurochemical dysregulation that underlie the dependence process, several theories have been proposed. They basically fall into four categories, which tend to support each other. In the final analysis, some components of these theories will probably be combined to explain the cause of chemical dependence. It is also likely that several mechanisms will be used to explain the dependencies on different drugs. The four theories all relate to mechanisms of neuroadaptation and are described as:

- Allostasis
- Pathology of motivation and choice
- Incentive sensitization
- Learning and memory mechanisms

What we notice about these theories is that they are well-developed and not mutually exclusive.

The Allostasis Theory

This theory, originally proposed by Koob and Le Moal (1997) and more recently expanded by Koob (2003), points out that "drug addiction" (authors' terminology) has characteristics of both impulse-control disorders and compulsive disorders (Figure 3.3). Impulse-control disorders involve a sense of tension or arousal preceding an impulsive act, whereas compulsive disorders involve anxiety and stress preceding a compulsive repetitive behavior and a release of stress by performing the compulsive behavior (*DSM-IV*, 2000).

Koob (2003) suggested that progression from an impulsive disorder to a compulsive disorder involves a shift from positive reinforcement (something that has pleasant or satisfaction-producing effects) to negative reinforcement (something that stops painful or unsatisfying effects) to drive the behavior. As shown in Figure 3.4, Koob posits three stages of addiction—preoccupation/anticipation, binge/intoxication, and withdrawal/negative affect—as a drug user progresses from impulsivity to compulsivity in a "spiralling distress/addiction cycle." It is impressive that the *DSM-IV* criteria for dependence are represented in this scheme. (Unlike the *DSM-IV* criteria, however, this model requires withdrawal as a condition for "addiction.") Koob claims that many interdisciplinary theories can be superimposed on these three stages that feed into each other, become more intense, and ultimately lead to the pathological state known as "addiction."

The concept of allostasis, defined as the process of achieving stability through change, was originally developed to explain the idea that homeostasis (the body's attempt to retain function within a normal range) is insufficient to explain the "physiological basis for changes in patterns of human morbidity and mortality associated with modern life" (Koob, 2003; Sterling & Eyer, 1988). The allostasis concept was proposed to account for mechanisms of stress and anxiety disorders, as well as (more recently) alcoholism and chemical dependence. The term *allostatic state* might help to explain how movement of physiological parameters out of the homeostatic range can lead to a pathology such as alcohol or other drug dependence through the establishment of a new set point (a point of "stability" or "normalcy").

An example of an allostatic driver of the transition from drug use to drug dependence is physiological withdrawal, which produces changes in reward neurotransmitters opposite to those involved in positive reinforcement. Thus, allostasis as it relates to drug dependence describes the ability to maintain reward function via changes in reward and stress system neurocircuitry. Koob (2003) hypothesized that the function of DA, serotonin, and endorphins is decreased during withdrawal, and that these changes contribute to a shift in reward set point as well as greater

Figure 3.3

Relationship Between Impulse-Control and Compulsive Disorders and Sources of Reinforcement*

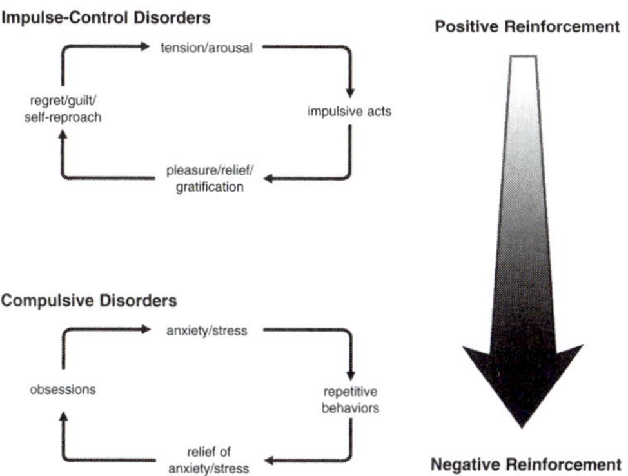

Reprinted with permission from Koob, G. F. (2003). *Alcoholism: Clinical & Experimental Research, 27*, 232–243. Copyright 2003. Lippincott, Williams & Wilkins.

Figure 3.4

The Spiralling Distress/Addiction Cycle From a Psychiatric Addiction Perspective*

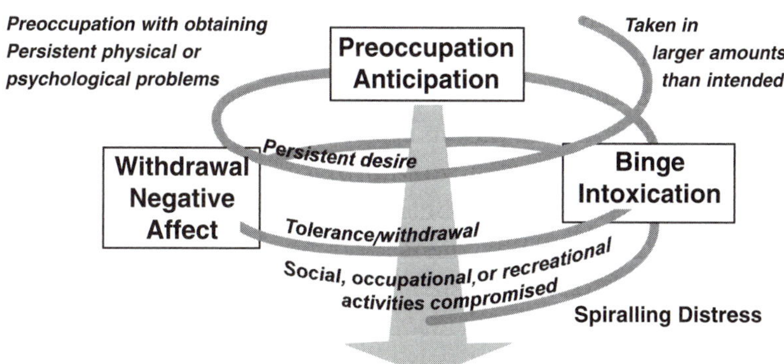

Reprinted with permission from Koob, G.F. & LeMoal, M. (1997). *Science 278*, 52–58. Copyright 1997. American Association for the Advancement of Science.

involvement of the brain stress systems, as measured through hormones such as corticotropin releasing factor (CRF). These changes apparently take place within the neurocircuitry of the basal forebrain macrostructure of the extended amygdala (Koob & Le Moal, 2001). Still in question is the determination of which specific elements in the extended amygdala are critical for the allostatic changes related to neurotransmitter dysregulation.

In summary, this theory is based upon strong experimental evidence, lays a multidisciplinary foundation for the *DSM-IV* diagnostic criteria, and helps to explain the permanent neurobiological changes that occur in portions of the MDS and the extended amygdala that interact closely with each other. A weakness of the theory is that it depends too heavily on an involvement of withdrawal mechanisms as an explanation. In addition, there is no explanation as to why allostasis might occur in some people with drug-use problems and not others who are drinking or drugging to the same extent. Finally, it fails to allow for situations where some "addicts" report "instant dependence."

The Pathology of Motivation and Choice Theory

A report on the neural basis of "addiction" (authors' terminology; Kalivas & Volkow, 2005) provides a detailed overview of cellular adaptations in prefrontal area NAcc circuits and how they may be involved in the production of addiction (chemical dependence). It is assumed in their review that the vulnerability to relapse in dependent individuals is caused by long-lasting changes in brain function as a result of repeated drug use, genetic predisposition, and environmental contributors to learning. These authors reviewed neural circuitry involved in the activation of goal-directed behavior, how these pathways are reorganized to establish behaviors that are characteristic of addiction, and the brain circuits that are critical for craving and drug-seeking. Shown in Figure 3.5, the circuit consists of (1) a final common pathway for initiation of drug-seeking, (2) modality-dependent subcircuits in which different modes of stimuli that induce drug-seeking are related to distinct components of the circuit, and (3) a requirement for DA transmission for relapse to the drug when a cue previously associated with drug delivery, a stressor, or a single dose of the drug occurs.

Kalivas and Volkow (2005) described three temporally sequenced

Figure 3.5
Final Common Pathway Involved in Drug-Seeking*

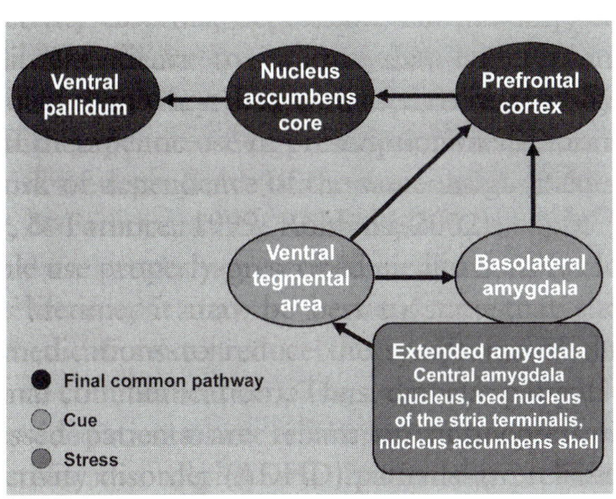

Adapted with permission from Kalivas, P.W. & Volkow, N.D. (2005). *American Journal of Psychiatry, 162*, 1403–1413. Copyright 2005. American Psychiatric Association.

stages of addiction: (1) acute drug effects (mostly involving DA circuits), (2) a transition from recreational use to patterns of use characteristic of addiction (e.g., repetitive use), and (3) end-stage addiction, characterized by an overwhelming desire to use the drug, a diminished ability to control drug-seeking, and reduced pleasure from other, everyday rewards. They stated that repeated use of a drug (during stages 2 and 3) causes a gradual involvement of the prefrontal cortex and its GLU projections to the NAcc. They provided detailed descriptions of the neurochemical and pharmacological studies that relate to this progression of stages to addiction. It also appears that the vulnerability to relapse in end-stage addiction is sustained for years and is accompanied by equally enduring cellular changes.

This theory emphasizes the idea that GLU projections from the prefrontal cortex (the brain area involved with decision-making and judgment) to the NAcc make up the final common pathway for eliciting drug-seeking behavior. Dopamine function is involved only in the early stages of drug use but can progress to addiction through a transference to GLU function.

A strength of this theory is that most of the contemporary research studies are included, except for just a brief mention of other neurotransmitters. So for at least DA and GLU, the neurochemical dysregulations cited earlier have been confirmed in a number of experiments. A weakness of this theory is that it doesn't effectively address the speed of onset of some chemical dependencies, and it also lacks a complete discussion of how genetics might be involved.

The Incentive Sensitization Theory

To date, the most popular concept of neuroadaptation in the development of drug dependence is the incentive sensitization theory. This idea receives the most support from psychostimulant research and is reasonable for central depressant drugs as well. This model suggests that the anatomy of chemical dependence involves the MDS, with an emphasis on "NAcc-related circuitry." This view immediately brings the model into line with ideas on the anatomy of natural reward and emotional processing within the limbic system. The model focuses on how drug cues trigger excessive incentive motivation for drugs, leading to compulsive drug-seeking (Vanderschuren & Everitt, 2004), drug-taking, and relapse (Robinson & Berridge, 1993).

The essential role of the NAcc-related circuitry is to provide salience (meaning) to environmental stimuli associated with reward. The model predicts that repeated exposure to drugs sensitizes, by means of associative learning, the DA and GLU pathways that predominate in the MDS, leading to *increased* pathway activity with continued drug use. This is in opposition to what occurs in pathways associated with tolerance, where there is a *decrease* in a drug's effect with repeated administration. Sensitization of the pathways is, in turn, postulated to lead to enduring plastic ("learned") changes in MDS function that are remarkably persistent.

An important feature of sensitization for "addiction" concerns individual differences in susceptibility to the process. In animal populations, studies have shown that some individuals readily "sensitize" to a drug whereas others are more resistant. (This might relate to the human condition in which not all drug users become dependent.) Susceptibility might be affected in this case by genetics, sex hormones, and stress hormones. The theory also provides evidence that sensitization is environment-dependent (Robinson & Berridge, 2003).

There have been many attempts to find the causes of brain sensitization, and many of these could contribute to the final answer. Neuroadaptation is thought to involve many long-lasting changes in NAcc-related circuitry. For example, sensitization appears to be accompanied by an increase in DA release in the NAcc (Robinson & Berridge, 2000). Also, distinct changes in GLU (an excitatory chemical) neurotransmission have been found in sensitized animals (Vanderschuren & Kalivas, 2000). It is also possible that drugs can affect the anatomy (as seen under a microscope) of neurons in the NAcc and prefrontal cortex during sensitization. Robinson & Kolb (1997) showed persistent changes in the length of dendrites and the extent to which dendrites are branched. This appears to be associated with an increase in density and types of dendritic spines, which contain excitatory GLU synapses.

Thus it is now well accepted that brain sensitization is accompanied by a major reorganization of brain reward systems (Robinson & Berridge, 2003). Some of these changes can occur quickly, mirroring the often-repeated observation that some people develop chemical dependence very early in life or with only a few exposures to the drug.

Strengths of this theory are that it is very comprehensive, has much research to support it, and is congruent with the phenomena of onset and relapse reported by persons with the disease of chemical dependence. Weaknesses relate to the fact that there are still some concerns about cause and effect with some of the observations in animals, and it is not clear whether the explanations of drug effects found in animals can explain mechanisms of human disease. On the other hand, O'Brien and Gardner (2005) have argued that human and nonhuman models have made "enormous" contributions to our understanding of "addictions." Finally, the model does not seem to acknowledge some dependence situations in which patients have become tolerant to the pleasurable effects of a drug, yet continue to seek the drug to avoid withdrawal effects.

The Learning and Memory Mechanisms Theory

Learning and memory have long been associated with "consolidation" of stimuli and information coming into the brain. A form of neuroadaptation, "consolidation" suggests that long-term changes in neuronal circuitry take place. Originally these changes were thought to occur only in the brain area known as the hippocampus, but we now know that the changes probably occur in multiple and more complex brain areas. Because of similar neuroadaptation mechanisms, the concept of consolidation fits nicely in a discussion of synaptic plasticity as it relates to the causes of chemical dependence. In fact, learning and memory mechanisms are a logical extension of the theories described above.

Everitt and Robbins (2005) have reviewed neural systems of reinforcement in drug addiction, which they described as transitions "from actions to habits to compulsion." They pointed out that the reinforcing effects of addictive drugs are associated with many dimensions. Drugs, they said, act as "instrumental reinforcers." That is, they increase the likelihood of responses that produce them, which results in drug self-administration or "drug taking." Stimuli in the environment that are closely associated in time and space with the effects of self-administered drugs gain "incentive salience" (meaning "connected to the incentive to take the drug") through Pavlovian conditioning and later become cues for relapse. For example, needles have incentive salience for intravenous heroin users.

Drugs produce subjective effects, which include "feelings" or distortions in sensory processing. Through a series of transitions from initial drug use through loss of control over the drug-taking behavior, the behavior becomes habitual and eventually compulsive. Everitt and Robbins provided evidence that these transitions depend on interactions between Pavlovian (unconditioned or reflexive) and instrumental (reinforced by repetition) learning processes, and they hypothesized that such changes represent a transition at the neural level from prefrontal cortical to striatal control over drug-seeking and drug-taking behavior, as well as a change in ventral to more dorsal parts of the MDS.

In another view of the same events, Hyman (2005, p. 1414) stated, "evidence at the molecular, cellular, systems, behavioral, and computational levels of analysis is converging to suggest the view that addiction represents a pathological usurpation of the neural mechanisms of learning and memory that under normal circumstances serve to shape survival behaviors related to the pursuit of rewards and the cues that predict them." The survival behaviors referred to by Hyman include food and shelter and opportunities for mating. These natural goals serve as "rewards," and behaviors with rewarding goals tend to persist strongly and increase over time. Associated with these goals are (1) internal motivational states such as hunger, thirst, and sexual arousal, which increase the incentive value (i.e., likelihood of causing a response) of goal-related cues and the pleasure of consumption, and (2) external cues related to rewards such as the sight or odor of food, which increase the likelihood that goal-directed complex behaviors will occur, even in the face of obstacles.

There is experimental evidence that DA release can affect stimulus-reward learning to shape the behavioral response to reward-related stimuli (Schultz, Dayan, & Montague, 1997). In addition, intracellular signaling mechanisms that produce synaptic plasticity are candidate (speculated as likely choices) mechanisms for addiction because they can convert drug-induced signals, such as DA release, into long-term changes in neural function and ultimately into the remodeling of neuronal circuits, especially in the MDS. Presumably synaptic plasticity mechanisms include those that change the strength or "weight" of existing connections and those that could lead to synapse formation or elimination and changes in the structure of dendrites, axons, or other neuronal functional components (Chklovskii, Mel, & Svoboda, 2004; Hyman, 2005).

The merging of learning and memory mechanisms with neuroadaptive mechanisms for chemical dependence is exciting, as there are many similarities that help us conceptualize the cellular components that change over time and how they might ultimately be manipulated to reduce the symptoms of chemical dependence. On the other hand, the same questions exist for learning and memory as for chemical dependence—namely, how do different stimuli/drugs disrupt neurotransmitter signaling in different circuits; what are the functional consequences of the disruption; and how do addictive drugs/stimuli permanently alter synapses and circuits?

Importance of Chemical-Dependence Theories

The theories described above provide likely mechanisms by which dependence-producing drugs lead to dysregulations of the mesolimbic dopamine system and associated brain areas. These dysregulations provide a core belief for a *disease* state. Many health-care professionals now recognize that chemical dependence is a chronic medical illness. The "chronic" nature of chemical dependence involves its tendency to recur—the possibility of relapse rarely goes away for addicts. Other factors make chemical dependence "medical": first, the genetic basis for chemical dependence (discussed in Chapter 4) and second, the permanence of changes in brain chemistry and anatomy that result from long-term drug exposure in at-risk persons. In chemically dependent people, imaging studies have shown that visual cues normally associated with drug-taking (e.g., drug paraphernalia) activate the amygdala (involved in learning of associations between rewarding stimuli and an emotional reward), the prefrontal cortex (involved in executive behavior), and the NAcc (involved in evaluating significance of cues). Thus, cues may induce relapse in dependent patients who are unaware of the reasons for their behavior. These reasons may involve psychological processes of memory, closely associated with emotional recall, along with defense mechanisms used to protect ego stability and the person's self-concept (in other words, how "good" they feel about themselves).

A Critical Transition Point

The above theories basically describe ways by which "neuroadaptation" occurs. But neuroadaptation theories are only important when the process occurs in vulnerable individuals (because of genetics or unidentified environmental triggers)—those who "have what it takes" to become dependent.

People in treatment and recovery often describe a point in their lives when a "switch" was turned on in their brains, at which time they perceived they were no longer able to control their drug-taking behavior. Likewise, at some point during the treatment and recovery process, some people exclaim that "the switch has been turned off" and they are able to once again control their drug use. Could these "switches" be related to brain chemistry changes?

Scientists once held the view that DA is the "pleasure transmitter." This has turned out to be a simplistic explanation in the context of chemical dependence. Chemical dependence is more than the seeking of pleasure (or the avoidance of pain or withdrawal). Newer neurobiological findings and theories now involve brain areas that are modulators or extensions of the MDS, such as the amygdala, prefrontal cortical areas, anterior cingulate, and others (Spanagel & Heilig, 2005). These "extended" brain areas allow the addition of "salience" (meaning) and emotional and cognitive memory to the pleasurable effects. It could be that the environment in which the drug is taken, how great an impact the drug has on the emotions produced by the experience, and the significance of the entire drug-environment-response phenomenon can determine the likelihood that drug use will be repeated. Some drugs appear to be capable of affecting these adjunctive brain areas to "transition" drugs from pure pleasure to chemical dependence, where pleasure is no longer important in maintaining drug-taking behavior. Thus some drugs "have what it takes" to produce chemical dependence, and others (even though they may produce a change in mood or energy) do not.

Note that in Chapter 1 I talked about how drugs in many cases do not produce chemical dependence; rather, chemical dependence driven by genetics is a disease in which compulsive use of the drug is the symptom. In individuals who "have what it takes" to get the disease, the genetic tendency to become dependent is triggered by use of the drug. In other cases, drugs produce neuroadaptive changes in the MDS, which lead to triggering of the disease state. Thus, some drugs "have what it takes" to produce chemical dependence, and this dependence only occurs in individuals who "have what it takes" to develop the disease.

The bulk of the scientific evidence fails to prove that caffeine is "addicting," at least in a way that is characteristic of cocaine and amphetamine (see Chapter 5 for details). This topic will continue to be controversial and perhaps never will be resolved. What is important about the example of caffeine is that it is similar to many drugs (antidepressants, lithium, neuroleptics used to treat schizophrenia, anti epileptics, and antiseizure medications) in that it produces positive pharmacological actions and often alters mood and thinking but does not have the neurobiological qualities that allow individuals to lose control over their use. These drugs are entirely different than those that are clearly dependence-producing, such as cocaine, heroin, alcohol, and nicotine.

Alcohol Dependence

The development of alcohol dependence, as with other chemical dependencies, requires the participation of multiple neurotransmitter systems, described in Chapter 2. These include the DA, serotonin, opioid, GABA, GLU, acetylcholine, and endocannabinoid systems (see the Appendices). Relapse prevention involves therapies directed at these same neurotransmitters (see Chapter 8).

It is difficult to come up with a unified understanding or story that takes into account all the individual research studies on neurotransmitters and how they contribute to alcohol dependence. What follows are two descriptions of neurotransmitter involvement in alcohol dependence to illustrate how the disparate studies can be put together to make sense. The first is paraphrased from a scientific peer-reviewed journal article; the second is paraphrased from a well-conceived article written by a science journalist for a popular magazine. Although the explanations offer different viewpoints on how the data fit together to explain alcohol dependence, both make sense.

Explanation #1

Johnson (2004) described an intricate model involving multiple neurotransmitters:

> Acute alcohol suppresses [diminishes] the firing rate of ventral tegmental area [VTA] GABA neurons, which leads to less suppression of VTA DA neuronal activity. This disinhibition [excitation] leads to VTA DA neuronal firing and DA release in the nucleus accumbens. With chronic drinking, VTA GABA neurons are hyperexcitable, mainly because of increased GLU input, less GABA tone from the NAcc, and rebound firing of GABA neurons because of their long-term suppression from repeated alcohol ingestion. This leads to VTA DA hypofunction and decreased release [compared with the acute condition] of DA in the NAcc.
>
> To explain the acute effects of topiramate, a drug that reduces drinking in alcohol dependent patients: During acute drinking, the GABAergic [GABA] influence of topiramate probably predominates, particularly in the NAcc. This leads to greater inhibition of NAcc DA neurons. Greater GABA tone from the NAcc to the VTA suppresses [reduces] VTA DA cell firing. Topiramate concomitantly [at the same time] inhibits the excitatory effects of glutaminergic neurons on DA neurons in the VTA and NAcc. These combined actions of topiramate should lead to profound suppression of DA neuronal activity and DA release in the NAcc. Hence, topiramate reduces the DA-mediated reinforcing effects of acute alcohol. (p. 1139)

Explanation #2

Arnst (2005) described a portion of the scientific literature on alcohol's effects this way:

> Alcohol releases a neurotransmitter called GABA, instrumental in creating a sense of euphoria. Too much GABA can impair muscle control and slow reaction times, so the brain releases a stimulating chemical called glutamate to keep it in check. When alcohol is cut off, glutamate levels remain high and can cause irritability and discomfort. To relieve those unpleasant feelings, the brain craves another drink. As more GABA and glutamate are released, brain cells change their structure to accommodate the excess chemicals, making them dependent on these levels. When alcohol is withdrawn, painful emotional and physical reactions are set off.
>
> GABA may be the reason people drink, but glutamate is the reason they can't stop. This powerful neurotransmitter is a key player in the brain's learning centers, and excess amounts create deeply embedded pleasurable memories of drinking. Years after a person quits, these memories can be triggered by a place, person, or even smell associated with drinking, setting off intense cravings. Such cue-induced cravings are the main reason for relapse. (p. 97)

Arnst explained the acute effects of Campral and Vivitrex (new name: Vivitrol), drugs that reduce craving in alcohol-dependent patients, as follows:

> Campral helps alcoholics resist these cravings by checking production of glutamate, bringing the brain's chemistry back into balance. Vivitrex dampens cravings by a slightly different mechanism, calming opioid receptors in the neurons that are overstimulated by alcohol. (p. 97)

The preceding descriptions have their own strengths and weaknesses. The first is written by a scientist, using terminology that might not be very clear to other scientists (especially those not in the field) and to nonscientists. However, it is more scientifically accurate than the second description, as each word has a concise meaning. The second description, written by a journalist, is easier to understand but is not totally accurate from a scientist's viewpoint. Both descriptions, however, are based upon excellent science and are interesting depictions of small segments of scientific results. If scientists are happy with the way that journalists describe their research, journalists will provide most of the treatment professionals' information about new addiction science. However, many scientists are not happy with the accuracy or completeness of such reporting. When that happens, it demonstrates that perhaps scientists would be better communicators of such knowledge—if they learn good communication skills and if they take the time and effort to educate nonscientists about new research findings.

Alcohol Dependence Often Does Not Occur Alone

Many clinicians believe that it is difficult to find a "pure alcoholic" these days. What they mean by that statement is that most patients who are alcohol dependent are often using other drugs or suffer from an Axis I (major) or Axis II (personality) mental disorder. Such clinical "co-addictions" or "co-occurring" disorders make sense if there is more than one neurotransmitter dysregulation of the mesolimbic dopamine system, and if the neurotransmitter dysregulations occur in brain areas other than the "dependence" area (mesolimbic dopamine system). Axis I disorders have postulated sites of dysregulation; for example, anxiety and depression are related to limbic system dysregulation, attention deficit hyperactivity disorder to frontal lobe dysregulation, etc. The number of patients who have more than one co-occurring chemical dependency is not known. Through basic animal studies relating specific neurotransmitters to various drugs, multiple neurotransmitter dysregulations have been postulated to be the reason for anecdotally-observed co-dependencies involving the following (Erickson, 2003): alcohol (glutamate); opioids (endorphins); cocaine, amphetamines (dopamine); benzodiazepines (GABA); nicotine (acetylcholine); marijuana (endocannabinoids). Alcohol not only works on the glutamate system, it has some effect on all other neurotransmitter systems (Erickson, 2003).

The following case study illustrates a patient with multiple problems:

Case Study: John

John was a 60-year-old man with no prior history of or treatment for alcohol- or drug-use problems. He sought assistance due to recent heavy drinking. He had been a social drinker most of his life, but over the previous 2 years his alcohol consumption had gradually risen. Neither he nor his wife could explain why his drinking had spiraled upwards. A family history revealed no known history of alcohol problems in immediate or extended family members, even looking back two generations. There was also no family history of mental health disorders.

To reduce anxiety related to a heart condition, John had begun taking Valium at 10–15 mg per day 14 years ago (as directed by a family physician), as well as an antihypertensive and beta-blocker medication prescribed by his cardiologist. His drinking remained normal—about 1 to 2 beers per day—for 12 years after starting the Valium, but then it began to change. His daily consumption first increased to 3 or 4 beers, then several months later to a six-pack, and finally to 2 six-packs per day. He then shifted to concentrated beverages, such as a pint of whiskey per day. If he did not drink alcohol, he needed to take greater doses of Valium to remain calm.

John was given a diagnosis of alcohol dependence with physical withdrawal and benzodiazepine dependence with physical withdrawal. He detoxified from alcohol and Valium and began outpatient treatment sessions, in conjunction with weekly A.A. meetings. Twelve months later he continued abstinence and his overall health improved.

This case illustrates several concepts. First, the probable cause of John's codependence on alcohol and Valium was a GABA dysregulation in the mesolimbic DA system, as described earlier in this chapter. Both alcohol and benzodiazepines are known to have an effect on GABA receptors in the brain, and either drug class can "connect" to the GABA receptors and alter them in a way that causes the person to become chemically dependent. Second, there was clearly a mechanism of cross-tolerance between alcohol and Valium occurring, so that the absence of one caused a need for the other, with the required doses of each drug escalating. Third, there was an element of self-medication for anxiety that probably precipitated the use of the drugs, which in turn led to chemical dependence because of John's escalating long-term drug use (causing neuroadaptation of the mesolimbic DA system to occur). Fourth, there was a possible chronic drug interaction occurring, whereby the long-term use of one drug (Valium) along with regular moderate alcohol use stimulated liver metabolism, resulting in an increased capacity to metabolize alcohol.

Different Views of Chemical Dependence

All the neurobiological theories described in this chapter appear to require chronic drug use for the production of chemical dependence. But two weaknesses of those theories involve the facts that (1) many people drink or drug heavily and never develop chemical dependence, and (2) some people develop dependence very quickly or with rather minor drug exposure. The incentive sensitization theory comes closest to explaining the variability in dependence vulnerability, but the clinical observation that many chemically dependent individuals become dependent with only 1 or 2 binges of drug use minimizes the significance of drug use and enhances the idea that people are born with a vulnerability to chemical dependence. An intriguing way of looking at this entire picture is that (in many cases) the cause of chemical dependence is "not in the bottle, not in the syringe, and not on the glass plate"—the cause is in the brain. Dysregulations in the MDS constitute the disease, just like poor DA function in the basal ganglia is the cause of Parkinson's disease. Drug-seeking and drug-taking are only the symptoms of the disease, just as muscle rigidity and tremors are the symptoms of Parkinson's disease.

Certainly the continued voluntary use of drugs (drug abuse) is an apparent contributor to chemical dependence, but it is not possible to predict who will become dependent on drugs and who will not. We can no longer "blame" someone for becoming dependent on drugs any more than we can "blame" genetically vulnerable people who develop type I diabetes when something goes wrong with their insulin production (and when they eat sugar). The compounding factor regarding chemical dependence is that an addict's behavior and the illegality of drug use affects so many more people (family, friends, and society) than does type I diabetes, even though the medical consequences are substantial with both diseases.

This chapter has provided an overview of the most important neurobiological theories underlying chemical dependence and the neurochemistry involved with drug-use problems. Chapter 8 includes a discussion of mental disorders that co-occur with drug-use disorders. It appears that the neurotransmitter systems involved in chemical dependence are the same as those involved in co-occurring mental disorders. Genetic factors involved in the causation of chemical dependence and mental disorders is discussed in the next chapter.

Chapter 4

The Genetics of Chemical Dependence

AS DISCUSSED IN CHAPTER 3, THE SUSCEPTIBLE BRAIN AREA in chemical dependence is the mesolimbic dopamine system (MDS). It is clear that beyond producing "euphoria" or "pleasure," "addicting" drugs high-jack the MDS to produce chemical dependence, perhaps in a variety of ways. But as I noted earlier, not everyone who consumes pleasure-producing chemicals, or who drinks or drugs too much, develops chemical dependence. There are even clinical cases where individuals are judged to be dependent even though their exposure to drugs has not been overwhelming. Why are there such extreme exceptions to the mistaken idea that "all one has to do to become addicted is use a drug long enough and often enough?"

In the field of alcoholism, where genetics studies have been ongoing since the 1970s, it has long been observed that "alcoholism runs in families." Just as in other medical disciplines, genetics studies on involvement have included family, twin, and adoption studies. These are designed to first identify the percentage of total etiology that genes contribute to the cause of the disease. Second, when there *is* found to be a significant contribution of genetics, the hunt is on for genes that directly cause or are most closely related to vulnerability to the disease in a given individual or set of individuals. Third, identification of the implicated genes provides a strong clue to the actual biological causes of the symptoms.

Finally, therapeutic schemes directed at the implicated genes can be expected to produce vaccines or medications that alter the precise genetic target or gene expression products. These will probably provide therapeutic breakthroughs in reversing the symptoms even more effectively and specifically than early trial-and-error medications that affect only the symptoms of the disease.

The genetics component in the causation of chemical dependence is significant (Mayer & Höllt, 2005), and thus genetic research is receiving great support. Most scientists agree that, unlike with Parkinson's disease, where the heritability contribution is limited, genetic tendency plays a major role in the eventual expression of the disease symptoms of chemical dependence. The genetics story has been developed in much more detail for alcohol dependence than for other chemical dependencies (see the Appendices), and research strategies for gene discovery tend to be somewhat different with alcohol dependence than with other dependencies. This is because the research on drug dependence evolved rather late compared to that of alcohol dependence. In fact, much of the genetics literature on alcohol dependence still uses the nonscientific and broader term *alcoholism* rather than the newer terminology.

Genetics Runs in Families and More

Clinicians have long known that the family background of a person with a drinking problem can tell them more than any other indicator about a diagnosis of "alcoholism," and now, alcohol dependence. When a person with a positive family history of alcoholism has lifestyle problems caused by alcohol, it becomes pretty clear that some form of intensive treatment will be needed.

Case Study: Bill

Bill was a 19-year-old male who was referred to treatment because of uncontrollable alcohol use. He began drinking at age 16 and quickly found he could consume large quantities, which led to various problems. He entered treatment as an outpatient at 17 and had no history of drug use other than some infrequent use of marijuana. He was very bright, articulate, artistically gifted, and was working as a professional model. Neither of Bill's parents drank, and the family history revealed that both parents had a strong family history of alcoholism, including both of their

> fathers, some uncles, and both paternal grandfathers. Both parents chose not to drink because of the impact of their parents' drinking on their own childhood. However, they could not understand why Bill developed a "drinking problem," as he had never been exposed to alcohol use or abuse in the home. Bill did not know what prompted his drinking, but he stated that he often "got this overwhelming desire to drink," and once he began he could not stop until he was "plastered." Bill did acknowledge some problems with anxiety and mild episodes of panic, but he could not pinpoint any cause for these drinking "spells." He met criteria for alcohol dependence with withdrawal but was not diagnosed for panic disorder. Over the next 2 years he had repeated relapses, was arrested for driving while intoxicated, and was detoxified and placed into a rehabilitation program twice for 4 weeks each, once at 18 and again at 19, after which he began regularly attending A.A. At last contact, he had been experiencing continued episodes of relapse drinking.

This case illustrates a patient with a clear genetic vulnerability to alcohol dependence. Genetically driven brain dysregulations often lead to a form of the disease characterized by long-term abstinence probabilities lower than average. The early onset of alcohol dependence in Bill suggests an early-onset form of the disease (for example, Cloninger Type II or Type B; Cloninger, Sigvardsson, Gilligan, von Knorring, Reich, et al., 1988), compared to a late-onset, less severe form (for example, Cloninger Type I, or Type A).

Basic Genetics

Genetics research has its own language. The results, emanating from studies in genetic epidemiology, molecular biology, and molecular genetics, are difficult to understand without some orientation to basic processes. An excellent review of basic genetic processes can be found in an NIAAA periodical ("Alcohol, Research, & Health," 2002) from which the following six sections are excerpted.

DNA: The Molecule of Life

Deoxyribonucleic acid (DNA) is a long, threadlike molecule that contains all the genetic information needed to sustain life. The coded information is transmitted from one generation to the next. A single strand of DNA is composed of a chain of building blocks called nucleotides, each of which consists of two subunits. These are (1) a modified sugar molecule (i.e., deoxyribose phosphate), and (2) one of four molecules (organic bases) called adenine (A), thymine (T), guanine (G), and cytosine (C). Nucleotides are held together in sequence by strong chemical bonds between adjacent sugar phosphate subunits, which leaves the bases exposed.

The DNA molecule is typically a pair of nucleotide strands intertwined to form a double helix—a three-dimensional configuration resembling a spiral staircase (Figure 4.1). The sugar phosphate backbones form the outside of the helix. Relatively weak chemical bonds join the organic bases within the helix together. The bases form the steps of the "staircase." The formation of base pairs between two DNA strands are governed by strict rules based on chemical structure, with adenine always binding to thymine, and guanine always binding to cytosine. When bases bind to each other it is called complementarity; thus, the two strands of a double helix are *complementary*. The principle of complementarity is the basis of the ability of DNA to store biological information and pass it from generation to generation.

Figure 4.1
DNA Molecule*

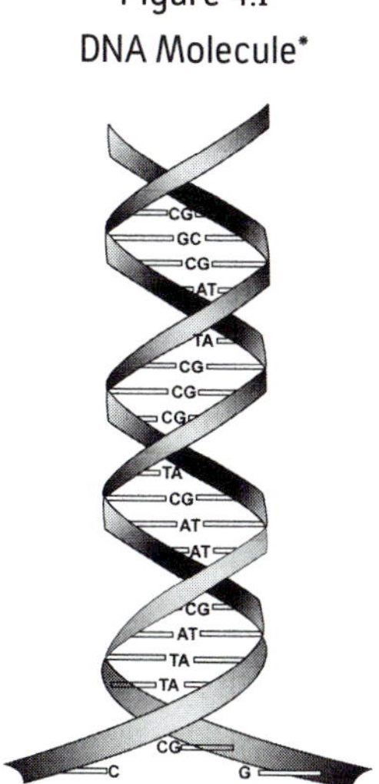

*Adapted from Dick, D.M. & Faroud, T. (2002). *Alcohol Research & Health, 26*, 172–174.

Figure 4.2
Human Chromosome Set*

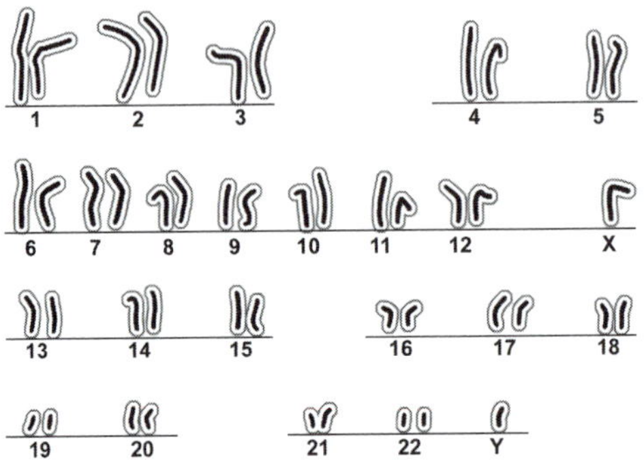

*Adapted from Dick, D.M. & Faroud, T. (2002). *Alcohol Research & Health, 26*, 172–174.

In most organisms, the DNA is "swaddled" by protein molecules and tightly packed into larger structures that are seen as rod-shaped chromosomes during a certain phase of the cell cycle. Chromosomes come in matched pairs that vary in size and shape, and they are found inside the nucleus of almost every cell in the body. The number of chromosomes in each cell depends on the organism. Humans, for example, have 22 pairs, plus two sex chromosomes. Figure 4.2 illustrates the total 23 chromosome pairs, in this case of a male (indicated by the presence of the X and Y sex chromosomes). Whenever cells in the body grow, their chromosomes duplicate before the cell divides. This ensures that each daughter cell (a cell resulting from the replication and division of a single parent cell) will receive a complete set of paired chromosomes. Reproductive cells, on the other hand, are formed during a specialized type of cell division that places only one member of each chromosome pair in each egg or sperm cell. When an egg and a sperm cell come together during fertilization, their chromosomes combine so that the developing offspring contains a full set of chromosomes, inheriting an equal share of genetic material from each parent.

Proteins and the Genetic Code

The basic structural and functional molecules of living things are called *proteins*. As physical components of the cell's structure, they contribute to an organism's basic structure and form, and simultaneously fulfill many functional roles. For example, some proteins play major roles in biochemical and metabolic events within cells. Others carry messages between cells or circulate through the body in the blood, functioning as hormones, immune system components, and transporters of oxygen and other substances critical for life. When discussing the genetics of chemical dependence, the most important proteins are those that serve as *enzymes*. Enzymes can move freely in the cell or are attached to a cell structure, and they can initiate and facilitate almost all of the numerous chemical reactions that sustain life.

Proteins are composed of chains of amino acids. Twenty different amino acids are known to participate in protein formation, and the function of a protein is determined by its sequence of amino acids. Some researchers suggest that the human body can produce up to one million different proteins as needed, but fewer than 100,000 are probably present in a cell at any one time.

The sequence of amino acids in a protein is determined by the sequence of nucleotide bases in a stretch of DNA that encodes a protein. Each amino acid consists of a triplet, a sequence of three DNA bases. Because four different bases can be combined into 64 different triplets, more than one triplet represents most of the 20 amino acids. After more than a decade of research, scientists finally finished breaking the genetic code, which involved matching every triplet to its corresponding amino acid. Amazingly, every organism on the planet shares the same genetic code. Thus, the DNA nucleotide combination A-T-G (adenine-thymine-guanine) always codes for the amino acid methionine, regardless of where it may appear within the overall DNA coding sequences of different proteins.

DNA at Work: Gene Expression and Protein Synthesis

The term *gene expression* has several definitions; in this discussion it is used to refer to all processes involving DNA-directed protein synthesis. Because chromosomes containing DNA are held in the nucleus (whereas protein synthesis occurs in cytoplasmic structures called ribosomes), gene expression involves the use of small helper molecules, composed of ribonucleic acid (RNA). These relay the genetic information from one cell structure to another. RNA differs from DNA in two respects: (1) ribose replaces deoxyribose in the sugar phosphate subunit of each RNA nucleotide; and (2) thymine is replaced by uracil (U), which also binds (i.e., is complementary) to adenine. Three families of RNA molecules play major roles in gene expression—messenger RNA (*mRNA*), transfer RNA (*tRNA*), and ribosomal RNA (*rRNA*).

During the first stage of gene expression ("*transcription*"), an mRNA molecule that is an exact copy of the relevant DNA region is produced. The second stage of protein synthesis ("*translation*") involves all three major forms of RNA. During translation, the ribosomes recruit tRNA molecules, including their attached amino acids. With the help of multiple enzymes and regulatory molecules, the amino acids are then detached from their tRNA carriers and linked to each other to form the desired protein ("*protein synthesis*"). Protein synthesis is the basis for all tissue formation.

Genes

The term *gene* has no single definition. The complexity of this term is due to the ever-increasing, and changing, understanding of how genetic information encoded in the DNA is converted into the different types of proteins found in each cell of the organism. Because there is no single agreed-upon definition, the ambiguity tends to impede understanding and conceptual agreement among researchers in the various subdisciplines. Some scientists have even proposed abandoning the term altogether. Because the term "gene" is so prevalent and has been associated so closely with the genetic knowledge base to date, other authors have suggested that a better goal might be to keep refining its definition and promote its accurate use. For our purpose, a gene can be most easily defined as a combination of DNA segments that together are capable of producing one or more functional proteins. (These are simply proteins that do something: provide structure, action, or play some other role in tissues.)

Genetic Variability and Why There Is No Gene for Chemical Dependence

It is incorrect to say that a person "inherits the gene" for a disease, as all humans generally carry the same number and types of genes. But many genes exist in different variants, called *alleles*, and individuals can inherit different alleles, making each person genetically unique. A *genotype* is the mixture of specific alleles contributing to a particular person's size, shape, or personality. In contrast, the term *genome* refers to the total genetic material of an organism. The observable physical or behavioral characteristics (and internal physiological differences) resulting from a specific genotype make up an individual's *phenotype*.

A DNA region containing several alleles is said to be polymorphic (multistructural). Most polymorphisms help us understand normal variation among individuals. For example, various alleles of a gene that affects eye color cause a person to have brown or blue eyes. Sometimes, however, abnormal alleles produce proteins that are inactive or function abnormally, leading to the development of disease. For example, a defect in a single gene causes cystic fibrosis. Genetic defects arise from mutations, from changes in nucleotide sequence due to exposure to X-rays or toxic substances, or from unknown causes. When polymorphisms occur in less than 1% of the population, they are considered mutations.

Most human traits are too complex to be determined by a single gene with two or more alleles. Many traits, such as height or intelligence, vary continuously across a population and interact with environmental influences. The fact that they can also be affected by emotional/psychological response and factors is less well understood. Such traits, called *quantitative traits*, are influenced by the cumulative effects of multiple genes, each of which may contribute a relatively small effect. Genes influencing a quantitative trait are called *quantitative trait loci* (QTLs). Virtually all behavioral characteristics are quantitative traits, including those influencing (for example) alcohol consumption and its effects on the person. Thus, there is no single "gene," or even "allele," for alcoholism. Instead, a person's risk for the disease is determined by a combination of multiple polymorphic genes interacting with the environment.

Genomics and Proteomics

Each cell must produce a specific set of proteins to fulfill its functions, and protein synthesis usually must be adjusted in response to changing internal and external events. Thus, gene expression is regulated by an assortment of proteins and other substances that tell genes in different cells when to turn on and off. As a result, only a fraction of the estimated 35,000–40,000 genes present in each cell is switched on at any given moment, producing no more than 6,000 primary translation products (proteins). However, the complete set of proteins that can be produced in an organism, called the *proteome*, is considerably larger and more complex than the organism's genome. In fact, whereas genomes are relatively stable, proteomes are constantly changing. Some researchers speculate that the number of different protein molecules expressed by the human genome may be closer to a million than the standard estimate of 100,000.

Genomics is the comprehensive study of structures and functions, whereas *proteomics* studies the interactions among whole sets of genes and proteins. These represent serious attempts to study gene function and protein interactions. Researchers have postulated literally hundreds of mechanisms to explain the discrepancy between the size of the genome and that of the proteome. Thus, several modifications can lead to the generation of more than one protein from one gene.

Conclusions

The preceding discussion shows the complexity of the genetic basis of alcoholism (and other addictions), which probably involves numerous genes, each of which has only a relatively small influence. To identify those genes and their contributions, it is critical that researchers use both "traditional" genetic approaches to study individual genes and their functions plus more recent genomic and proteomic approaches that allow for the examination of the structures and functions of whole gene or protein systems. Combining these approaches should help researchers gain a better understanding of the genetic underpinnings of chemical dependence and other related and complex disorders.

Overview of Genetics Studies

The technologies being used to find the genetic contributions to alcohol and other drug dependence are extremely varied and complex. From epidemiologic studies to sophisticated gene arrays, scientists have been exploring this area for over 25 years. It is one thing to notice that "alcoholism runs in families" and quite another to predict the risk of a given individual to alcoholism by looking at DNA in tissue samples. The research now available looks at everything from twin studies to the chromosomes that are likely to have "addictive disease genes." Reviewing all the literature on this subject is beyond the scope of this book, but it is possible to introduce the various models and methods and to look at what scientists have found regarding the heritability of alcohol and other drug dependence.

Alcohol Dependence: A Complex Genetic Disease

There is a great deal of evidence from family, twin, and adoption studies showing that genetic factors contribute to the risk of "alcoholism." These factors explain 40–60% of the variance (i.e., of all the possible causes of "alcoholism," 40–60% relate to genetic vulnerability). Adoption studies show that children adopted at early ages tend to exhibit the same vulnerability to alcohol dependence as their biological parents, rather than their adoptive parents, do (Cloninger, Bohman, & Sigvardsson, 1981). These studies do not show a 100% risk of developing the disease, even with exposure to the drug. Having the "genes for alcoholism" does not mean that the person will develop the disease. Implicit in these statistics is the fact that there are unknown nongenetic contributing factors that account for the remaining 40-plus percent causes of chemical dependence.

As is typical of many medical and psychiatric disorders, "alcoholism" is genetically heterogeneous (multiple genes and alleles are involved), with a variety of factors increasing or decreasing the risk. For example, antisocial personality disorder and attention deficit hyperactivity disorder (ADHD) increase the risk for alcoholism, whereas gene variants for the enzymes that break down alcohol and acetaldehyde (ADH and ALDH, respectively) decrease the risk (Schuckit, 2000). ADH breaks down alcohol to acetaldehyde, and ALDH breaks down acetaldehyde to harmless products. There is normally a large variation in the activity of these enzymes among people.

There are numerous genetic studies that fall into one of two general categories: human studies, including the Collaborative Study on the Genetics of Alcoholism (COGA), and animal studies.

Human Studies

Researchers are currently trying to identify the specific genes involved in patterns of drug abuse and chemical dependence. Although studies have convincingly demonstrated that genes play a role in the development of chemical dependence, the same studies have also provided strong evidence for environmental factors. Genetic and environmental factors probably interact to result in disease development (Dick & Foroud, 2002). Gene expression (how the genetic code is passed on to critical proteins) can be affected by drugs (Rhodes & Crabbe, 2005), but whether this is related to the cause of chemical dependence is still not understood. New developments in genetic technologies are increasing our understanding of chemical dependence. Following are some of the studies.

The COGA Study

COGA is a large-scale, federally funded effort to identify and characterize the genetic risk factors for alcoholism (Bierut, Saccone, Rice, Goate, Foroud, et al., 2002). The study involves more than 1,000 alcohol-dependent subjects and their families. Researchers are conducting comprehensive psychological, physiological, electrophysiological, and genetic analyses of the participants. These studies have identified several traits (not psychological traits), or phenotypes, that seem to be genetically determined. These phenotypes include the presence of alcohol dependence, the level of response to alcohol, the presence of coexisting depression, and the maximum number of drinks a person consumes per occasion. Scientists have found regions on several chromosomes that are associated with these phenotypes and need to be studied further.

First, COGA investigators recruited alcohol-dependent people from chemical-dependence treatment centers. The patients (also called *probands*) and their family members were invited to participate in the study. All participants were interviewed to assess various characteristics: the presence of alcohol abuse and dependence, the presence of other psychiatric disorders (such as depression) and other medical illnesses, and the participant's family history of "alcoholism" (the term used in early studies when interviewing people about their families; more recent studies use the term *alcohol dependence*). Alcohol dependence was diagnosed using *DSM* criteria (previous editions of the *DSM* were used, mostly *DSM-IIIR*) and criteria for "definite alcoholism" as specified by Feighner, Robins, Guze, Woodruff, & Winokur (1972). The investigators also collected blood samples for later analysis, and the participants underwent additional biological measurements including measures of brain activity (electroencephalograms and event-related potentials, ERPs). ERPs are measures of changes in ongoing electrical brain activity that occur as a person responds to a stimulus. They can be measured reliably and provide strong evidence that the patterns of these brain waves are genetically determined (Porjesz, Almasy, Edenberg, Wang, Chorlian, et al., 2002). The participants also completed several questionnaires, such as the "self-rating of the effects of alcohol" scale (Schuckit, Edenberg, Kalmijn, Flury, Smith, et al., 2001), to determine their response to alcohol.

COGA was the first comprehensive human study to look for specific genes in diseased versus control populations. Researchers did not know in advance which chromosomes would carry genetic factors influencing the development of alcoholism and related phenotypes, so the analyses began with a survey of all chromosomes—the entire human genome.

So far, the analyses have identified several chromosomal regions, particularly on chromosomes 1, 2, 3, 4, and 7, that appear to be linked to several alcohol-related phenotypes and are now the targets of more detailed analyses. The observation that some of these areas appear to be linked with more than one phenotype strengthens the evidence that genetic factors in those chromosomal regions contribute to the development of alcohol dependence. A "protective region" on chromosome 4 appears to be in the general vicinity of the alcohol dehydrogenase (ADH) genes. Researchers believe the allele in this region may reduce the risk for alcohol dependence in an individual.

A great deal of interesting data has come out of the COGA studies. Future work will revolve around the identification of genes that are located within the chromosomal regions that have shown linkage with alcohol dependence and other phenotypes, and it will aim to identify polymorphisms within those genes. The large number of children and adolescents in the original population sample will prove invaluable as these young people pass through the age of greatest risk for developing alcohol dependence. These efforts will eventually lead to the identification of genes that affect the risk for alcohol dependence and related phenotypes.

Candidate Genes

COGA and other studies have looked at genes that are expected to play a role in the development of alcoholism, based upon animal studies indicating that certain neurotransmitter dysregulations are at the heart of the disease. Somewhat controversial is the idea that the dopamine D2 receptor gene (DRD2) or the serotonin transporter gene affects the risk for alcoholism. Because DRD2 may be associated with reward or pleasure, some authors have proposed that the gene that produces this receptor is involved in alcoholism. Results on this receptor are mixed (Blomqvist, Gelernter, & Kranzler, 2000; Bowirrat & Oscar-Berman, 2005). Other studies have shown a weak association between the serotonin transporter gene and alcohol dependence (Feinn, Nellissery, & Kranzler, 2005). Still other studies have found alcoholism susceptibility areas on several chromosomes (1, 2, 6, 7, 10, 12, 14, 16, and 17) using different methodologies (Hill, Shen, Zezza, Hoffman, Perline, et al., 2004). Genomic screens for loci associated with alcohol dependence in Mission Indians have identified several previously recognized chromosomal loci and some new regions of the genome that may be unique to that population (Ehlers et al., 2004). Some data suggest that GABA receptor genes may be involved in alcohol dependence (Edenberg, Dick, Xuei, Tian, Almasy, et al., 2004), but these results have not yet been confirmed (Dick, Edenberg, Xuei, Goate, Hesselbrock, et al., 2005).

The "Low Level of Response" Phenotype

Schuckit and colleagues (2001) have spent a lifetime documenting the "low level of response to alcohol" and the significance of this risk indicator in the population. People who are at high risk of developing alcoholism (for example, many children of alcoholics) consistently report that they need more alcohol than other people to become intoxicated. These people are described as having a low level of response to alcohol, and this trait is a powerful predictor of subsequent alcohol dependence. Twin studies have indicated that this trait is genetically influenced. Qualitative measurements using the "affected sibling design" found evidence for genetic linkage of the "low level of response" phenotype with the same region on chromosome 1 that was linked with the "alcohol dependence" phenotype (Bierut et al., 2002). Further studies are needed to examine more in-depth linkages on other chromosomes.

Other Types of Human Genetic Approaches

Dick and Foroud (2002) have described four general types of genetic approaches: the linkage approach, association studies, population-based assoctiation studies, and family-based association studies.

The *linkage approach* is a classical genetic approach that is a powerful tool for discovering the disease gene in single-gene disorders, such as classical inherited diseases. The rationale goes like this: There are many polymorphic sites in the genome of normal individuals in whom there is no corresponding phenotype. If scientists can locate a disease-related gene close to a position than can be marked, the marker will be inherited in close correlation to the disease phenotype. (A marker position is a place on a chromosome where a DNA sequence is known to occur. It is used to track a particular gene that has not yet been identified.) The size of the correlation is expressed by the so-called *lod score* (algorithm of odds). A lod score of zero indicates no correlation.

Several problems arise when this approach is used to study a disease involving more than one gene. First, the impact of each individual gene is low, requiring large numbers of individuals and marker loci (positions) to be studied. It is difficult to exactly identify the site of the gene on the chromosome. Second, a given phenotype (chemical dependence in this case) may be related to different genes in different individuals, requiring the study of a highly heterogeneous population. However, the approach is more promising if the individuals under study belong to the same pedigree (for example, families of heavy drinkers). One study using this approach elicited significant lod scores on chromosomes 1, 2, and 7 (Reich, Edenberg, Goate, Williams, Rice, et al., 1998).

Association analyses are more likely than linkage analyses to pinpoint the gene or genes that influence a disorder or behavior. In this approach, scientists search *candidate genes* for polymorphisms in humans. Choosing candidate genes (e.g., the DRD2 gene for dopamine-induced reward) is actually a guess, made on the basis of available scientific studies. Table 4.1 shows the selection of candidate genes, indicating that selection is usually based upon the pharmacodynamic action of the drug under study.

Population-based association studies are methods that compare the genes of groups of people. For example, some analyses involve two samples: people with a disease and people without the disease, hopefully matched for age, ethnicity, and other factors, so that they differ only in their disease status. Investigators would then compare the frequencies of

Table 4.1
Products of the Most Important Candidate Genes Studied for Association with Addictive Disease*

System	Connection with addiction	Gene product	Function
Opioid	Target for opiates	MOP	Receptor
		DOP	Receptor
		KOP	Receptor
		Proenkephalin	Endogenous ligand
		Prodynorphin	Endogenous ligand
Dopamine	Part of the common reward system, target for cocaine	D2	Receptor
		D4	Receptor
		DAT1	Transporter
		DBH	Metabolism
		MAO-A	Metabolism
		COMT	Metabolism
Serotonin	Involved in aggressive behavior, as observed in alcoholics	HT1B	Receptor
		5-HTT	Transporter
		TPH	Synthesis
GABA	Possible target for alcohol	GABR-A1	Receptor subunit
		GABR-A6	Receptor subunit
		GABR-B1	Receptor subunit
Alcohol metabolism	Essential for alcohol detoxification	ADH1B	First metabolic step
		ADH1C	First metabolic step
		ADH2	First metabolic step
		ALDH2	Removes a toxic metabolite
Cannabinoid	Target for cannabis products	FAAH	Synthesis of endogenous ligand

5-HTT, serotonin transporter; ADH, alcohol dehydrogenase; ADLH, aldehyde dehydrogenase; COMT, catechol-O-methyltransferase; DAT, dopamine transporter; DBH, dopamine-beta-hdroxylase; DOP, δ opioid receptor; FAAH, fatty acid amide hydrolase; GABA, γ-aminobutyric acid; KOP, κ opioid receptor; MAO, monoamine oxidase; MOP, μ opioid receptor; TPH, tryptophan hydroxylase.

*Table 4.1 – Adapted with permission from Mayer, P. and Höllt, V. (2005). *Current Opinion in Pharmacology*, 5, 4–8. Copyright 2005. Elsevier.

various alleles of a marker within or near the candidate gene. These are rather simple studies that still require an evidence-based candidate gene, and when the number of candidate genes is large it is likely that the effects of each gene are small, making them more difficult to measure. It is also difficult to measure which combination of genes along with other factors may influence the development of the disease.

Family-based association studies attempt to overcome the pitfalls of the population-based association scheme by avoiding the necessity of including a matched control sample and instead analyzing, for example, a nuclear trio consisting of an affected person and his or her parents. For these 3 people, the genotype of a marker in or near the candidate gene is determined. Because a person's genetic makeup includes 50% genetic input from each parent, if each parent carries two different alleles of the marker gene, one allele from each parent will be transmitted to the affected offspring and one allele will not be transmitted. With proper statistical analyses, researchers can determine that a particular allele of the marker being tested is associated with development of the disease.

Animal Studies

Animal models are being used to study genes related to drug (e.g., alcohol) use and its consequences. Such models can improve the efficiency of identifying genes underlying human alcoholism. For example, scientists can use well-characterized animal lines to address genetic issues regarding alcohol-related behaviors that are genetically more complex. In animals it is assumed that fewer genes affect the behavior of interest. This of course would make the isolation of candidate regions on chromosomes and genes faster and more efficient. Animal models also allow breeding strategies that cannot be performed in humans. Now that most animal genomes have been fully characterized, scientists are able to recognize that there is a high degree of similarity of linked regions of genetic material across many species. As a result, researchers who identify a certain DNA region in mice as important in alcohol-related behaviors can infer the approximate location of the corresponding DNA region on a human chromosome.

Early animal studies that spawned current research focused on the development of models of alcohol preference. The 1960s saw the first studies on genetic selection for voluntary alcohol consumption in the rat (Eriksson, 1968), giving the field the AA (Alko alcohol) and ANA (Alko nonalcohol) rat lines that ultimately were used to study differential brain function under the influence of alcohol (see Kiianmaa, Nurmi, & Sinclair, 1994). Beginning in the 1970s, naturalistic alcohol-preferring and nonpreferring mouse models were used to study voluntary alcohol preference and behavior (see Randall & Lester, 1975). Later, other rodent models were developed (P, alcohol-preferring; NP, alcohol nonpreferring) and have been used extensively to study mechanisms of brain differences in response to alcohol (Smith, Learn, McBride, Lumeng, Li, et al., 2001). They have also provided the theoretical foundation for understanding neurochemical mechanisms of alcohol preference as it might relate to alcohol dependence (Melendez, Rodd-Henricks, Engleman, Li, McBride, et al., 2002). More recent refinements of the early rat strains (HAD, high-alcohol-drinking; LAD, low-alcohol-drinking; HAP, high-alcohol-preferring; LAP, low-alcohol-preferring) are elegant models for providing evidence that the preference for alcohol is genetically driven, and they have helped us to understand the gene alleles that are responsible for this behavior (see Bice, Foroud, Carr, Zhang, Liu, et al., 2006).

The research on animal models for studying human alcohol phenotypes is rich and extensive (Phillips, 2002). It includes many sophisticated genetic approaches: the use of knockout and transgenic mice, quantitative trait locus (QTL) mapping, virus-mediated gene transfer, random mutagenesis, and gene expression profiling (Phillips, 2002). The research on animals for genetic modeling of other drug responses is more recent and less extensive, and it focuses on studies of intravenous and oral self-selection models and some selectively bred strains (e.g., methamphetamine, see Kamens, Burkhart-Kasch, McKinnon, Li, Reed, et al., 2005; opioids, Carlson, Saulnier-Dyer, & Moolten,1996). In some cases, animal strains differing in response to alcohol have been tested for their response to other drugs (e.g., amphetamine in P and NP rats, D'Aguila, Peana, Tanda, & Serra, 2002).

These studies generally focus on finding a gene position for a specific drug trait. For example, a QTL for morphine preference was detected on chromosome 10 in a region containing the mu-opioid receptor gene (OPMR1; Berrettini, Ferraro, Alexander, Buchberg, & Vogel, 1994). A weakness of such a finding is that only a coarse localization (or "hot spot") of the underlying gene on the chromosomes can be found with this method, as the regions of interest still contain several hundred genes, although some studies have characterized smaller areas of 121 genes on chromosome 1, and 78 genes on chromosome 13 (Mayer & Hollt, 2005). Additionally, so far no reports show relevance of rodent QTL results to humans.

Although a great deal of information has come from animal studies, the techniques that have been developed have not yet reached their full potential (Dick & Foroud, 2002). It is turning out to be extremely challenging to identify the genes involved in chemical dependence. Yet people have already become concerned about application of that knowledge. If genes are ever identified, will they be detectable in fetuses and newborns, and if so, how will that information be used? Can such information be used for genetic counseling? What about gene therapy? Will replacing diseased genes with normal ones prevent or reverse the disease—or have unintended consequences such as new illnesses or syndromes? Will germline gene therapy, where the malfunctioning gene is replaced by a properly functioning gene in the germ cells (egg and sperm) be the answer? What about pharmacogenetics—the application of knowledge about a person's genetic makeup to predict his or her response to a particular drug? All of these are exciting questions that hopefully will be answerable through animal research as it becomes applied at the human level.

Progress in the Genetics of Chemical Dependence

As discussed in Chapter 1, the liability to chemical dependence is widespread throughout the population, but from genetic studies we know that individuals with chemical dependence in first-degree relatives are at greater risk. We now know that a larger component of what is inherited is the variation among individuals in the fundamental neurobiology of chemical dependence (Chapter 3). Scientists have now identified some possible causative genes and certain risk genes (Goldman, Oroszi, & Ducci, 2005). For the future, large datasets and new tools in genetics and molecular neurobiology offer a promise of even more progress.

Chapter 5

Stimulants and Depressants

BECAUSE GENETIC VULNERABILITY IS NOT the only cause of chemical dependence, other factors must be examined, and the pharmacological characteristics of drugs are therefore of great importance. Because drugs affect the brain in so many different ways, pharmacologists have grouped drugs into categories according to their commonality of effects. For example, drugs that increase activity in people are called *stimulants*, whereas drugs that slow down people are called *depressants*. These are the categories we will discuss first, in this chapter, since they are "traditional" in the sense that their effects have been known for centuries. Because alcohol, a depressant, is such a major factor in drug-use problems in society, it has its own chapter (Chapter 6). In Chapter 7, I discuss drugs that do not fit nicely into the CNS stimulant-depressant categories, have scientifically been forgotten, or are very controversial scientifically. All the drugs to be discussed in these three chapters have a high potential for misuse and some degree of dependence production.

Before discussing stimulants and depressants, I'd like to offer an overview of several basic concepts that relate to the action of any drug. These concepts should help the reader overcome myths about drug action. I want to discuss what a drug is and whether alcohol is a drug, talk generally about how drugs alter consciousness and emotion, and how drugs are categorized by the U.S. government based upon their abuse potential.

Fighting Myths

There are many outmoded statements regarding the ability of drugs to produce chemical dependence—for example, "Any drug that affects the brain can produce addiction." (New research illustrates that many centrally active drugs, even some that affect mood, do not produce "addiction" or chemical dependence. Most notably, antidepressants, lithium used for treating mania, and neuroleptics to treat schizophrenia do not produce chemical dependence, or "addiction.") Another is "The greater 'high' one gets with a drug, the more addicting that drug will be." (Nicotine has the highest "addiction" liability but has low euphoric quality compared to cocaine or heroin, which produce enormous euphoria and chemical dependence.) This chapter is intended to provide a basis for understanding that many of the "street facts" about drugs and "addiction" are actually myths.

What is a drug?

A drug is any chemical other than food or water that produces a therapeutic or nontherapeutic pharmacological action (effect) in the body. ("Pharmacology" is the study of how drugs change the function of the body.) Chemicals, on the other hand, are a broad class of substances (including drugs) that may or may not produce noticeable effects in the body. Many chemicals (such as tin, lead, and gold) have mainly toxicological (harmful in high doses) effects on the body. Most foods are not drugs. Is sugar a "drug"? This somewhat humorous question is actually a serious one when asked by people in recovery from alcohol and other drug dependence. The reason is that sugar is related to a very strong "craving" in some individuals, leading some to believe that sugar must affect the same brain pathways as "addicting" drugs. So far, however, the research on sugar and where it acts on specific brain pathways is nonexistent.

Alcohol is a drug, not a food (in spite of the calories it provides). Drugs are generally categorized as medicinal (pharmaceutical, therapeutic), legal (licit), or illegal (illicit). Respective examples of each of these categories are aspirin, nicotine, and heroin. Nicotine is a chemical that is also a drug. Sometimes a drug can fall into more than one category, depending upon how it is used. For example, cocaine is therapeutic and licit when used as an anesthetic for eye surgery, but it is illicit when used to get "high." The group of "legal" drugs includes dangerous chemicals that have only toxic actions (e.g., inhalants, legal but often restricted for sale). When drugs are taken in high doses, more often than recommended, or in ways that harm an individual or those around the user, the drug is abused. (A better term is *misused*, as people don't hurt or mistreat drugs, but *misuse* in the United States generally refers to the overuse of prescription drugs.)

A Range of Drug Actions

Many chemicals can be ingested to cause an altered consciousness in people seeking euphoria, insight, or relief from suffering. These chemicals are called *centrally active drugs* because they act on the CNS—the brain and spinal cord. They include very simple molecules (such as ethanol or beverage alcohol), compounds that are found in nature (such as nicotine, marijuana, and cocaine), and products (synthetic) manufactured for recreational or curative purposes (such as LSD and amphetamines).

All of the drugs discussed in this chapter and the next two chapters have a direct effect on stimulating dopamine (DA) release in the brain's mesolimbic reward pathway. As indicated in Chapter 3, release of DA in the nucleus accumbens produces a sensation of pleasure, and the anticipation of obtaining these drugs activates the limbic pathways in a manner that (in susceptible individuals) leads to chemical dependence.

Although drugs acting on the CNS produce some pleasurable effects in certain people, most are toxic to some degree, usually in a dose-related manner. Greater toxicity (side effects, organ damage) is seen with increasing doses of drugs over longer periods of time in people who have a "toxicological" sensitivity to these drugs. Side effects occur when a drug's actions "spill over" into unintended sites in the brain or body. For example, low doses of morphine given for pain may have a side effect of drowsiness as the drug spills over to the sleep centers in the brainstem. With higher doses, side effects of nausea and constipation may occur as the drug affects other brain and body sites of action.

D.E.A. Schedules of Drugs

Drugs that can be abused are controlled by the Drug Enforcement Administration (D.E.A.) through categories listed in the Controlled Substances Act of 1970. Schedule I drugs include those that have no accepted therapeutic use (examples: marijuana, heroin, ecstasy). Schedule II includes drugs that are used therapeutically but have high potential for abuse, such as cocaine, amphetamines, and potent opioids such as morphine. Schedule III drugs have "some" potential for abuse (less than those in Schedule II), such as certain drugs used to treat obesity. Schedule IV drugs have "low" potential for abuse and include antianxiety medications such as Valium and Xanax. Schedule V drugs are subject to state and local regulation and include low-potency opioid compounds used to treat diarrhea, among others. (Note: The Controlled Substances Act uses the term *abuse potential* of drugs when determining the schedules. This is not the same concept as *dependence liability*, discussed in Chapter 1.)

Central Nervous System Stimulants

Stimulants significantly increase CNS activity in a number of brain areas, particularly parts of the cerebral cortex ("grey matter," the site of intelligence in humans), as well as other brain areas susceptible to their actions. Such stimulation is manifested as an energetic euphoria, increased motor activity, increased talkativeness, inability to sleep or (in milder doses) an antifatigue effect, reduced appetite, and stereotypic (repetitive) behavior. Some of these drugs have a very high chemical dependence potential, whereas others have none or very little.

Cocaine

Cocaine is a powerful, short-acting CNS stimulant. It goes by many names, including C, coke, nose candy, and snow. There are three forms of the drug: hydrochloride salt (injected intravenously or snorted as "lines"), free-base (smokable, made by cooking cocaine hydrochloride with baking soda and ether, thereby removing the hydrochloride), and crack (made from free-base into a waxy product that crackles or "cracks" when smoked). The three usual routes of administration (intravenous, snorting, and smoking) produce different euphoric onsets in the brain, with smoking being the fastest and intravenous being the slowest. Fewer studies have been done on the onset time of other less popular routes such as intramuscular, subcutaneous, vaginal, or anal.

Cocaine is not a new drug; South American Indians have chewed coca leaves for their antifatigue effects for thousands of years. Cocaine has a legal use as a local anesthetic for eye procedures. However, we usually hear about cocaine use, abuse, and dependence, and how its use waxes and wanes in different parts of society. It is generally considered today to be one of the drugs with the highest abuse potential and dependence liability.

Cocaine has been widely studied by neuroscientists because of its now well-known action at the "cocaine receptor site" in the brain. This site, a dopamine transporter (DAT), is blocked by cocaine, causing an increase in DA in the synapse. This increase in usable DA is mainly the reason for the CNS stimulatory effects that are so characteristic of cocaine's pharmacology.

Drugs like fluoxetine (Prozac) work in the synapse similarly to cocaine, but with several differences. Fluoxetine is a selective serotonin reuptake inhibitor (SSRI), meaning that it blocks mainly the uptake of serotonin at the serotonin transporter (SERT). This leads to an increase in serotonin in the synapse to overcome clinical depression. It also appears that people with a major depressive episode have lower SERT binding (suggesting lower SERT activity) in the amygdala and midbrain, two areas involved in emotion (Parsey, Hastings, Oquendo, Huang, Simpson, et al., 2006). So it works on a different neurotransmitter than cocaine. Also, fluoxetine (and other drugs like it) acts throughout the limbic system of the brain, which is where we feel our emotions. It does not have a specific and powerful action on the reward pathway (mesolimbic DA system), which is why it does not produce chemical dependence. We assume, then, that for something to be able to produce chemical dependence ("addiction"), it must have a major action on the pleasure pathway.

Following prolonged use of cocaine (especially with high doses), nerve cells (neurons) become fatigued, their DA is depleted, and the user experiences a "crash." The crash consists of prolonged sleep, followed by periods of clinical depression (drug-induced mood disorder, depressive type), drug craving, and anhedonia (inability to experience pleasure). This is the withdrawal syndrome that is so characteristic of cocaine, and it differs markedly in intensity from withdrawal from depressants such as opioids. In fact, withdrawal from cocaine and other stimulants has been characterized as "nonphysiological," as most of it goes unnoticed unless the withdrawing person is verbal or complaining.

Acutely, deaths have been caused by dangerous doses of cocaine (either high doses or lesser doses in a sensitive person). These can produce increased blood pressure leading to hemorrhagic strokes in the brain, or cardiac arrhythmias leading to a heart attack. Sometimes convulsions cause death through acute respiratory failure (the breathing stops) or hyperthermic crises, in which the body temperature rises dramatically. Clearly, we must not take this drug lightly or presume that it has a low level of risk.

There is some "street lore" indicating that crack cocaine is more "addicting" than cocaine powder. This belief is based on the observation that users prefer crack to powder cocaine because of its faster onset ("the better the high, the more addicting"). Second, there appear to be more crack users than cocaine powder users in society (however, this may be due to the fact that crack is less expensive). Third, people in low socioeconomic groups tend to use crack, whereas more affluent individuals are known to use cocaine powder, and the idea that the "street-using" population contains more addicts persists. There is some scientific evidence (mainly from animal studies) that rapid delivery of drugs to the brain facilitates "addiction" (Samaha & Robinson, 2005). But from a pharmacological point of view, crack and cocaine powder are the same. And if the drug "connects" to brain transmitter systems in a specific way, it does not make sense that one form of the drug should produce a higher level of chemical dependence than another form.

Another popular myth is that babies can be born "addicted" to crack. Researchers and clinicians are requesting that terms such as *crack baby*, *crack-addicted baby*, *meth baby*, and *ice baby* not be used, as they have no scientific basis (Lewis, 2005). These pejorative terms inaccurately describe babies whose mothers have probably used not just one drug, but several. In addition, the use of such terms often prevents babies from getting proper help because of stigma and prejudice against the mother. Also, many of these children catch up developmentally by age 2 or 3 with proper postnatal care, adequate parenting, and social interaction with other children. Some of their so-called problem behavior has been attributed to chaotic or violent family environments and poor parental attachment.

Not everyone who uses cocaine becomes dependent. The incidence of dependence to cocaine has been estimated at 17–18% of all users (Anthony et al., 1994). There are anecdotal reports of some people becoming dependent on cocaine with the first use of the drug. In a recent scientific study, 5–6% of cocaine users became dependent ("addicted") within the first year of use (O'Brien & Anthony, 2005). Of course, some people who use cocaine never become dependent.

Case Study: Marcos

Marcos was a 37-year-old attorney who drank alcohol moderately several times a week for years, and had no history of drug-use problems. However, he did have a positive paternal family history of alcohol dependence. He tried cocaine for the first time at age 36. He described the feeling as "exhilarating" and snorted it twice more that evening. He decided to use again the following week, with similar positive experiences, and then began seeking sources for cocaine. He rapidly moved from using once or twice a month to weekly, and then to daily, use. He was obsessed with obtaining and using this drug, and stated that he was "constantly chasing the high." When he felt too high he used alcohol to "slow down the feeling of racing." He was soon going on "coke binges," after which he experienced significant mental and physical exhaustion for 48 hours or more.

Having and using cocaine seemed to preoccupy Marcos's thinking 24 hours a day, 7 days a week. He had deliberately tried to cut down on both the amount he used and how often he used it, but then he would suddenly find himself using again as if "he was on autopilot." His job performance suffered and he was consequently referred for an evaluation. Given the risk of losing his license to practice, he agreed to treatment and entered a short-term residential program.

> Marcos did not know if he could quit the drug completely. While in treatment, he stated that he was "not like everyone else"—"not an alcoholic, a drug addict, or a pot head." He saw himself as unique and special, claiming that only cocaine users knew what he had experienced. Upon discharge, he began mandated weekly group therapy and Cocaine Anonymous meetings and underwent random urine testing for a year. During the first 3 months Marcos had several brief relapses, but he regained abstinence and continued to make gradual progress.

Marcos's case suggests a moderate level of severity of cocaine dependence that seemed to respond to treatment. Maintenance of long-term sobriety and abstinence with cocaine dependence is difficult without intensive detoxification, long-term monitoring, and a commitment to getting well and staying drug-free. Marcos's prognosis, however, appears to be good in overcoming the dysregulation of his brain's mesolimbic DA system.

Amphetamines

There are several drugs in the amphetamine class, including dextroamphetamine (Dexedrine), methamphetamine (Desoxyn), methylphenidate (Ritalin), and mixtures (Adderall). The number of users who become dependent on amphetamines has been estimated at 11% (Anthony et al., 1994). Amphetamines have biobehavioral actions similar to cocaine, but with a longer duration of action after a single dose. Their cellular mechanism of action differs a bit from that of cocaine: Instead of blocking DAT, they cause a release of DA from the nerve cell, with additional but lesser effects on norepinephrine and serotonin release. This different mechanism is the reason for the unique therapeutic actions of amphetamines, including uses in the treatment of narcolepsy, ADHD, and as an adjunct in weight control.

Every so often, we experience a methamphetamine ("meth") epidemic in the U.S., with escalating emergency room and treatment admissions for methamphetamine users. Pharmaceutical companies have had to reformulate over-the-counter cold remedies to remove pseudoephedrine, a key chemical in the manufacture of meth. Pharmacies have had to take the remedies off the shelf and place them under controlled access. There are several reasons for these epidemics. Methamphetamine is easy to make, yields a large profit in its manufacture and sale, and is highly euphoric. Additionally, the penalties for its use and sale are not as great as for heroin and other drugs. The downside? It is almost as dependence-producing as cocaine, more dependence-producing than alcohol, can fairly easily lead to overdose, and may have long-lasting effects on brain function.

"Traveling laboratories" in the backs of pickup trucks are able to supply methamphetamine to users throughout the country. As with any street drug, purity and potency are problems when drugs are bought from illegal sources. Sometimes the residues of manufacturing chemicals and added adulterant substances are more toxic than the pure products themselves.

Many people want to learn how to stop people from manufacturing, selling, and using meth, and they are eager to know whether the drug produces long-term brain damage. Prevention measures (education and family support, along with criminal prosecution) might reduce some abuse of this drug, but there are growing indications that meth might cause long-term psychological distress, if not long-term damage to brain cells. The pharmacological mechanism is the same as other amphetamines, producing an increased release of DA and norepinephrine into the cell synapse, thereby increasing downstream excitation. The end behavioral result is (in low doses) to increase attention and alertness and to reduce fatigue. In higher doses, amphetamines increase movements, ranging from purposeful behavior to fidgeting and eventually to stereotyped (repetitive) movements that cannot be stopped until the drug wears off. Many long-term users report they cannot feel "normal" (like they felt before drug use) after stopping the drug, but any chronic toxicity caused by methamphetamine may be the result of major psychological changes while taking or after taking the drug rather than direct brain cell toxicity. Future studies on these victim reports might help to clarify the actual causes of such dysphoria (lack of well-being) as well as ways to overcome it.

How does methamphetamine compare with cocaine? They are two different drugs, but both cause an end result of CNS stimulation. Cocaine is mainly a naturally occurring ingredient in a certain plant, whereas methamphetamine is synthetic (made from other chemicals). The reason they are often confused is because they both are a white powder and can be taken by injection, smoked, or by "snorting." Like cocaine, methamphetamine also comes in free-base and smokable forms, known as "ice." One of the street names for meth is "crank," and one of the street names for coke is "crack," which also adds to the confusion.

How does methamphetamine work? Methamphetamine is a "psychostimulant" that causes a euphoric response almost as intense as cocaine. It acts longer than cocaine (in single doses), but has a slower onset of action. Methamphetamine has therapeutic uses in the treatment of narcolepsy (a sleep disorder) and as an adjunct to obesity control, when prescribed. It appears to increase the release of DA from brain cells, which leads to an overall generalized stimulation of the brain.

Can a single dose of methamphetamine harm the fetus? Some animal studies suggest this is the case, especially when focusing on long-term neurodevelopment. Some scientists suggest that methamphetamine can harm DNA. The general consensus is that multiple doses of methamphetamine in the mother may harm the fetus. But more research is needed to determine whether the single-dose studies in animals are replicable in humans, what percentage of babies are affected (if at all), and who might be at highest risk. In the meantime, pregnant women are best advised not to use methamphetamine.

Several studies indicate that students who appropriately take prescription stimulant medications (such as Ritalin and Adderall) to treat ADHD have relatively low rates of tobacco, alcohol, marijuana, and ecstasy use compared to students who illegally use prescription stimulants. Because stimulants taken therapeutically in this way also produce lower incidences of chemical dependence than stimulants used illegally, parents need not be concerned about the clear benefits of stimulants in treating a child who has ADHD.

What is "ephedra"? This is an herbal supplement that produces a euphoria ("high") like an amphetamine but is less potent in doing so. Manipulation of its chemical structure led, in the past, to the discovery of amphetamines, so it has an interesting history. Recently, the Food and Drug Administration's attempt to regulate supplements led to the banning of products containing ephedra. The FDA claims that ephedra has been linked to numerous deaths. Is it "addicting"? Probably not, although there are no studies to answer this question.

EL CAMINO COLLEGE LIBRARY

Caffeine

Caffeine is the least potent of the CNS stimulants. It is mainly found in coffee, cola drinks, specialized products (such as Red Bull), and other beverages. Mostly used in moderate doses (e.g., 200–300 mg, roughly 2–3 cups of coffee, with variation among individuals) for its energizing and antifatigue effects, caffeine can increase alertness, alter sleep patterns, reduce fatigue, and cause headaches, gastritis, nervousness, dizziness, and heart palpitations. Caffeine also produces a mild and incomplete level of tolerance and a mild to significant (depending on the person's sensitivity) withdrawal syndrome: headache, feeling of weariness, weakness and drowsiness, impaired concentration, fatigue and work difficulty, depression, and nausea and vomiting, as well as withdrawal feelings. Most physicians are aware of the acute and withdrawal effects and will recommend that caffeine consumption be reduced or eliminated in patients with cardiac abnormalities, insomnia, anxiety, fibrocystic disease, and gastrointestinal disease. In addition, most obstetricians recommend caffeine cessation during pregnancy, based upon some degree of distress to the fetus produced by caffeine. Unlike alcohol and nicotine, caffeine produces its effects without life-threatening medical consequences.

Compared to cocaine and amphetamines, caffeine is a mild stimulant of the CNS. The neurochemical mechanism of caffeine on the brain is incompletely understood, but it might involve an action at the adenosine receptors in the brain. Such an action is not the same as seen with cocaine and amphetamines, which have a more direct effect of increasing DA in the synapse. Whereas many caffeine users (and some scientists) lightly state that "caffeine is addicting," most of this understanding is based upon the erroneous idea that withdrawal (which caffeine produces) is the same as "addiction." Also, because caffeine produces stimulation, some falsely believe that the effect leads to "addiction."

Caffeine is controversial scientifically with regard to whether it causes "addiction." Juliano and Griffiths (2004) have provided data on the reinforcing effects of caffeine, as well as tolerance and withdrawal produced by caffeine in animals. They have also provided evidence for such phenomena in humans, and the data are numerous. Griffiths and Mumford (1995) indicated that caffeine is less potent than amphetamine and cocaine in its reinforcing qualities in both animals and humans. Similarly, Nehlig (1999) and Smith (1996) agreed that caffeine has reinforcing effects and produces tolerance and withdrawal. However, they say, these effects are incomplete and do not favorably compare with powerful stimulants such as amphetamines and cocaine. Garrett and Griffiths (1997) suggested that caffeine's effect on DA activity is similar to that of amphetamines and cocaine. These data, however, have not been significantly replicated by other laboratories. Furthermore, whereas caffeine appears to have a "downstream" enhancement of DA activity, amphetamines and cocaine have direct effects on DA transporters on presynaptic cells. So far, then, available research indicates that caffeine is not able to switch the brain from "pleasure" to "chemical dependence" because it does not powerfully and selectively affect DA function in the shell of the NAcc, the main "addictive" center of the brain that is affected by the more powerful CNS stimulants.

Thus, the literature on caffeine-producing chemical dependence is underwhelming, as caffeine does not have a major effect on the portion of the mesolimbic DA system involved in the development of chemical dependence. The public and news media are much more likely to state that caffeine is "addicting" than are scientists. Further, the National Institute on Drug Abuse does not recognize caffeine as a harmful or "addicting" drug.

Overview

When CNS stimulants act on the pleasure pathway of the brain (the mesolimbic DA system), the result is a range of pleasurable or euphoric feelings, depending on the drug ingested, the dose, the drug purity, the frequency, and the route of administration. When these drugs act on other parts of the brain, other things happen, such as increased muscle movement, jitteriness, increased talkativeness, and even (with cocaine or amphetamines) hallucinations. Although hallucinations can sometimes occur with these drugs, more common symptoms are grandiosity, delusions of superiority or power, and ideas of reference, especially those of a paranoid type. Delusions can lead to hallucinations, usually of tactile form (formication) but sometimes visual and auditory as well. The olfactory type of hallucinations is rare. The part of the brain that is most affected by the drug determines the pharmacological actions and side effects, in spite of the fact that the drugs work on the same place on the cell in every part of the brain.

Central Nervous System Depressants

These drugs cause a slowing of nerve cell activity in all or a portion of the CNS. However, a slowing down of one portion of the brain might produce a "speeding up" (release of inhibitions) in another area, leading to behavioral excitation. A practical example of this is the stimulation that is seen with 1–2 drinks of a depressant like alcohol. Even though alcohol is a CNS depressant, it produces this paradoxical behavioral stimulation, which is the first phase of the biphasic response to alcohol—a social euphoria followed by drowsiness, slowing of reaction time, and reduced judgment (depression).

This chapter looks at three CNS depressant categories: benzodiazepines, barbiturates, and opioids. Alcohol is covered separately (Chapter 6) because of its unique societal impact.

Benzodiazepines

Benzodiazepines (once erroneously called "minor tranquilizers") are effective in reducing anxiety (*anxiolytics*, popularly called *sedatives*) and in promoting sleep (*hypnotics*). Anxiolytic benzodiazepines include alprazolam (Xanax), chlordiazepoxide (Librium), and diazepam (Valium). Hypnotic benzodiazepines include flurazepam (Dalmane), triazolam (Halcion), and temazepam (Restoril). (Rohypnol, not legally available in the United States, is a benzodiazepine with amnesia as a major effect.) These drugs are thought to increase the function of gamma aminobutyric acid (GABA) in the brain. Because the GABA system is an inhibitory system, increasing its function tends to suppress overactive symptoms, two of which are anxiety and insomnia. (The recent use of antidepressant medications for treating anxiety suggests that other neurotransmitters besides GABA—e.g., serotonin or DA—may be involved in the neurobiological mechanism of anxiety.)

Individual benzodiazepines differ in their rate of absorption and metabolism. In general, the ones that act quickly also tend to lose their effects quickly. Thus, some drugs are more effective for major acute anxiety attacks or for difficulty in falling asleep. Other drugs have greater utility in addressing free-floating chronic anxiety or early-morning awakening.

People can abuse benzodiazepines by using them longer than prescribed by a physician, especially when they persistently use them to address a problem that requires making behavioral or psychological changes, such as adjusting to a high level of stress or mental discomfort. In general, benzodiazepines should be given in a fixed number of doses (30 to 60-day supply), with reevaluation of the problem by a physician before a prescription refill. Hypnotic benzodiazepines should not be prescribed for longer than 2 weeks, as these drugs suppress rapid eye movement (REM) sleep, the most restful stage of sleep. If such drugs are prescribed for longer than 2 weeks, there is a significant chance of "rebound insomnia" in which it is difficult to differentiate continuing sleep problems from the excitatory withdrawal effects of the drugs.

Chemical dependence on benzodiazepines does occur (estimated at about 9% of users; Anthony et al., 1994), often in combination with alcohol. Detoxification practitioners often use benzodiazepines to reduce withdrawal hyperexcitability from alcohol. In either case, with or without alcohol, dependence on these drugs is problematic, as detoxification can take months. This is because some of these drugs and their active metabolites have a relatively long half-life (the time it takes for one half of the drug to disappear from the body), due to high lipid solubility. Thus benzodiazepines stay in the body much longer than most other drugs. Counseling or 12-step programs are needed to maintain abstinence, both during and after detoxification. Some people have acute withdrawal problems for up to 15 days after cessation, plus long-term symptoms for weeks or months, including body aches and anxiety. Some of these drugs (including Ativan, Valium, and Dalmane) have a tendency to cause paradoxical excitement in some people, especially those with aggressive or impulsive traits.

Alprazolam (Xanax) is a popular antianxiety benzodiazepine that can lead to chemical dependence in individuals with a susceptibility to this disease. Anecdotally, it appears to have a greater ability to produce chemical dependence than other benzodiazepines. Although it can produce a long-lasting withdrawal that is uncomfortable (just as with other benzodiazepines), the simple phenomenon of withdrawal does not mean it has produced chemical dependence in that person. The exact dependence liability of Xanax in comparison with other benzodiazepines has not been established.

Barbiturates

Barbiturates are old CNS depressant drugs that fall into the sedative-hypnotic category. Although they have been mostly replaced by benzodiazepines and are not used to any great extent because of their very high dependence liability, there are a few indications for the therapeutic use of barbiturates. For example, they are used to reduce epilepsy and in the emergency treatment of convulsions (phenobarbital), as well as for general anesthetic purposes (thiopental). Thus they are worthy of mention because of drug diversion and their continued availability on the street. These drugs are very dangerous, especially when mixed with alcohol. Such drug combinations have led to the deaths of movie stars and other famous people in the past. The withdrawal can be even more severe than alcohol and even lethal if not medically managed, producing classic delirium tremens, hallucinations, and seizures.

Barbiturates can produce all degrees of depression of the CNS, ranging from mild sedation to general anesthesia. Barbiturate-induced inhibition of targeted tissues occurs mostly at synapses where neurotransmission involves the inhibitory neurotransmitter GABA, acting at one type of GABA receptors called GABA-A. Certain barbiturates, particularly those such as phenobarbital and mephobarbital, have good anticonvulsant activity. The antianxiety properties of the barbiturates are not as useful as those produced by benzodiazepines. Except for the anticonvulsant activities of phenobarbital, the barbiturates possess a low degree of specificity for certain uses (i.e., a few barbiturates can induce sleep) and margin of safety. There is always some evidence of general depression of the CNS when these drugs are used therapeutically. Pain perception and reaction are relatively unaffected until unconsciousness occurs, and in small doses, the barbiturates increase the reaction to painful stimuli. Thus, they cannot be relied upon to produce sedation or sleep when the person has even moderate pain. Finally, when barbiturates are given in anesthetic doses, they have effects on excitable tissues such as the heart and parts of the peripheral nervous system. Thus, there can be serious effects on cardiovascular and other peripheral functions during acute barbiturate intoxication, leading to overdose and death.

The National Institute on Drug Abuse chart on Selected Prescription Drugs of Abuse (NIDA, 2006) lists several barbiturates that are available and abused: pentobarbital sodium (Nembutal), secobarbital (Seconal), amobarbital (Amytal), and phenobarbital (the longest-acting, and least likely to produce chemical dependence). The only legal possession of these drugs is through a doctor's prescription.

Opioids

Some people erroneously believe that opioids are "narcotics." Actually, the term *narcotic* is outmoded. Formerly used to describe analgesic opiates, marijuana, and cocaine, the word now appears to be misunderstood by people who use it. *Narcotic* literally means "drugs that produce sleep or grogginess." The new, more accurate terms for sleep-inducers are "sleep aids" and "hypnotics."

Natural opiates are derived from the opium poppy and include morphine, codeine, and semisynthetic compounds derived from them, such as heroin. The term *opioid* is broader, including all agonists (drugs that activate opioid receptors in the brain, such as morphine) and involving drugs that block opioid receptors (*opioid antagonists*, such as naltrexone, ReVia). Methadone (Dolophine) is a synthetic opioid with a long half-life. Buprenorphine (Buprenex, Subutex, Suboxone) is a synthetic opioid that has "partial agonist" properties (i.e., it does not fully activate opioid receptors, which limits its euphoric potential). These proprietary products are used in the treatment of chemical dependence (see Chapter 8).

The primary use of opioid analgesics such as morphine is analgesia (treatment of pain). They are very effective in reducing the affective ("suffering") component of pain, producing a dreamy euphoria in which worldly cares disappear. A secondary use is in treating coughs ("antitussive effect"). A third use is in treating diarrhea, because of the constipatory side effect of less powerful opioids.

Opioids work by mimicking the activities of naturally occurring (endogenous) peptides known as endorphins, enkephalins, and dynorphins. Four opioid receptors in the CNS are the binding sites of action: mu, sigma, kappa, and N/OFQ. Opioid *agonists* activate a receptor directly to produce analgesia or euphoria; opioid *antagonists* block one or more of the receptors to prevent the action of an agonist. Endorphins (and brain chemicals like them) are naturally occurring "morphinelike" chemicals in the brain and spinal cord that affect pain sensitivity in individuals. They are also released in the brain during exercise, childbirth, certain types of stress, relaxation, and perhaps when people take drugs such as heroin and alcohol. Endorphins work by activating opioid receptors—the same receptors that are affected by opiate painkillers (strong analgesics). There is a rich and detailed history on the discovery of opioid receptors, endogenous peptides, and mechanisms of action (Gutstein & Akil, 2001).

There are several ways in which opioids (and other psychoactive drugs) may be administered. These are: (1) orally (morphine is relatively ineffective when taken orally, whereas methadone is very effective), (2) pulmonary (opium-smoking began in China), (3) insufflation ("snorting"—opium itself is not well absorbed by this route, but heroin can be taken this way), and (4) injection-intravenously, intramuscularly, or subcutaneously (probably the most effective). (*Intravenous* means into a vein, *intramuscular* means into a muscle, and *subcutaneous* means between the layers of the skin.) Injection methods are the most dangerous if the needles are not sterile or have been shared with others, leading to transmission of hepatitis and other viruses such as HIV from user to user.

In comparison to other drugs, opioids have relatively few serious side effects, which means that chronic use of these drugs does not produce organ pathology as occurs with alcohol or smoking. The acute dangers of opioids, however, are significant (Dasgupta, Kramer, Zalman, Carino, Smith, et al., 2006): They have a high potential for chemical dependence production (approximately 23% of people who use heroin become dependent; Anthony et al., 1994) and accidental overdose. Pure or pharmaceutical-quality opioids are obviously safer than street drugs, in which adulterants can cause harm. Opioid overdoses cause respiratory depression, a state that can be rapidly reversed (through timely emergency intervention) with a specific opioid antagonist such as naloxone (Narcan).

Two characteristics of opioid use are (1) large amounts of rapid tolerance buildup, and (2) severe uncomfortable withdrawal with chronic use (which is not usually fatal unless the person is medically compromised by a serious condition like hypertension or heart disease). Tolerance develops to the euphoric and analgesic effects as well as to some other side effects, such as nausea. Tolerance does not develop to all side effects (such as constipation, small pupil size). Clinicians are now capable of withdrawing patients from opioids such as heroin in a comfortable manner, through the use of drugs such as clonidine (Catapres), which reduce the discomfort of the side effects, and through the less dangerous method of acupuncture. But a drug-free heroin addict is not cured! Addicts can be detoxified, but they are still chemically dependent. It takes more than removal of the drug from the body to overcome drug dependence. Patients require counseling or N.A. to have any chance at lifetime abstinence. For some, methadone or buprenorphine treatment is a better method for maintaining abstinence from heroin, for reducing the craving for heroin, and for getting away from the heroin environment. However, these medications are most effective when used in conjunction with behavioral therapy, vocational or employment counseling, and support groups. This is similar to the best results being achieved when using antidepressants along with cognitive or interpersonal psychotherapy. For those who cannot or do not wish to become totally abstinent from opioids, methadone or buprenorphine maintenance is another option (see Chapter 8).

Opioids have a long history of being used legally as painkiller. Morphine, for example, has several characteristics: It is an old, powerful analgesic (the "prototype" painkiller) and is as useful today as it has been for over a century for the treatment of pain. It has powerful cousins such as Dilaudid, Demerol, and oxycodone. Finally, it is the product of the breakdown of heroin.

Everyone has heard of the abuse of Oxycontin, Vicodin, and other pain relievers. Another opioid, fentanyl, is a painkiller used for relief of chronic and postoperative pain, and there are reports that the sustained-release patches containing fentanyl are being abused. Is this a problem with the drugs, or a problem with being able to control the behavior of recreational drug users? Obviously, whenever a new medication becomes available, especially one that is in a new form that provides more drug when abused, people are going to try to use it. This is more of a social and cultural problem than a pharmacology problem.

OxyContin (oxycodone) is a popular analgesic drug. This is an orally active sustained-release opioid drug used for pain control. Its effects are designed to last about 12 hours. Like other opioids, this drug can be abused and is capable of producing chemical dependence in susceptible individuals. OxyContin is a highly abused drug, mainly because many drug abusers like it. There is no evidence, however, that it produces a greater incidence of chemical dependence ("addiction") than other powerful painkillers such as morphine. When abused, OxyContin tablets are often crushed and ingested, taken intravenously, or snorted, giving a "high" that the manufacturer did not intend. Deaths from OxyContin have received much publicity, making some people believe it should be banned nationwide. But anyone who believes this is grossly overreacting. First, does OxyContin cause more overdose deaths than other opioids? The answer is no, as all opioids can be taken in overdose, especially in combination with other drugs. Second, does OxyContin cause more dependence than other opioids? There is no evidence for this, even though it is *abused* just as much (if not more) than other opioids (recall that "abuse" and "dependence" are two different overuse conditions). Third, this medication is much better than most other opioids for reducing pain. Therefore, the benefit of the drug greatly outweighs its risks.

Speedballs

A "speedball" is a street name for a combination of a CNS stimulant and a CNS depressant. One of the most popular speedballs is a combination of cocaine and heroin. Another (although not usually called a speedball) is amphetamine and alcohol (taken orally). People take these for one of the following reasons: (1) to increase the euphoric effect (sense of well-being) over that achieved with either drug alone (both depressants and stimulants produce a type of euphoria), (2) to slow down or offset the first drug's actions (for example, an amphetamine can "perk up" a person who is drowsy from alcohol), or (3) to produce a unique euphoric effect that cannot be achieved with either drug alone. In general, mixing such drugs is dangerous, for the effects are not always predictable and the side effects (such as respiratory depression, even due to different mechanisms in the brain) can be additive.

How Stimulants and Depressants Hijack the Brain

Most of the drugs discussed in this chapter (and many of those discussed in Chapter 7) have a specific action on identified receptors in targeted brain areas, although much of the research on the cellular level is not yet complete. When drugs target specific areas, they have unique pharmacological and behavioral effects. Thus, most drugs are known to affect specific neurotransmitter systems, and if those neurotransmitter systems are available and vulnerable to the drug, specific effects occur. For example, when a prescription opioid is given for pain, the opioid will attach to opioid receptors throughout the brain. But receptors tend to be more plentiful in brain areas where people perceive pain and pleasure, such as spinal pain paths, the relay area called the thalamus (where diffuse pain is perceived), and the mesolimbic reward pathway. Certain pain medications have an attraction for affecting one, two, or all three of these brain areas, depending upon the molecular structure of the medication, its diffusion capability in reaching specific brain sites, its rate of metabolism, and other factors. Thus in a given individual, pain perception may be decreased, pain pathways may become blocked, and the person's pain is relieved. This individual may or may not experience "pleasure" from the therapeutic use of the medication. Another person who uses the opioid to get "high" may experience the pleasure he or she seeks and continue to take the drug. Another person using the drug to get "high" may not feel much effect or may have unpleasant effects and thus move on to another drug of abuse. A fourth person might take the drug to relieve pain, experience pleasure or relief, and continue to take the medication long after the organic pain has resolved.

The site of drug use (the environment surrounding drug use, called the *setting*) can have a major impact on what the user experiences. For example, drinking two beers in a closet is usually not as exhilarating as drinking two beers with friends while watching a football game. The expectation of the drug's effect (known as the *set*) also determines what kind of pharmacological outcome a drug user will have. For example, self-injecting an opioid into a vein will be more pleasurable to a person seeking a drug high than in a new tentative drug user who has a fear of needles. So when we speak of the "set and setting" of drug use, and how it produces different responses to the drug, we can understand one more cause of "drugs of choice" and the great variability in drug response from person to person. This variability is based upon factors including the drug itself, but the drug purity, potency, route of administration, dose, individual susceptibility, health, age, gender, environment, and many other factors influence the outcome.

Although set and setting play a major role in people's acute responses to drugs, these factors have not been shown to be of direct importance in the production of chemical dependence. Vulnerability to chemical dependence is probably more related to genetic factors than to environment and expectation. We know that even though each abused drug has its own unique effects (which is why nicotine feels different than marijuana or methamphetamine), stimulation of the DA component of the reward system is a common denominator. When any of the drugs mentioned in this chapter enter the brain, they artificially simulate a highly rewarding environment. The DA released into the MDS affects memory and executive function circuitry to drive the person to repeat the experience. With each successive use, the circuitry becomes stronger and more compelling, creating dependence on the drugs.

Thus it is important for treatment professionals to recognize that the drugs described in this chapter have their own unique pharmacology, but that they all have a common effect on enhancing the activity of the brain's reward pathway. Knowing this is the beginning of understanding that different drug problems require different approaches to help abusers and dependent patients get better and overcome their hijacked brain function. This is why there are so many options for treatment, as discussed in Chapter 8. The next step is to recognize that science is getting close to "seeing" the effects of these drugs on the brain, using methods outlined in Chapter 9.

Chapter 6

Alcohol

PHARMACOLOGISTS BELIEVE THAT ALCOHOL IS A DRUG. A drug is any chemical that changes normal physiology and function in the body and in high doses produces a toxicological or harmful effect. People who argue that alcohol is not a drug (e.g., it is a food, it is not like "heroin," it is a caloric nutrient) have a reason for their beliefs, but the scientific consensus is clearly that alcohol is a drug. The reason it is separated from other drugs is that it has a unique place in society, it has a tradition of beneficial use that transcends its overwhelmingly negative effects, and it is legal to buy and sell (for anyone who is "mature enough" by law).

Beverage alcohol (scientifically known as ethanol, ethyl alcohol, or grain alcohol) has many uses: as a solvent in liquid pharmaceutical preparations, as a blocking agent when injected around a nerve, and as a skin disinfectant (along with isopropyl alcohol), to name a few. Most people know it as drinking alcohol, which, despite its beneficial social and medical effects when used in moderation, is responsible for many of society's problems, including drunk driving, family discord, violence, and aggression. These problems can plague both people who use it recreationally and those who use it to self-medicate for anxiety, depression, grief, or just everyday troubles.

People often wonder how alcohol can be a legal, socially accepted drug when most other mood-altering drugs are illegal to possess, sell, or use. Alcohol's use is historical, and to prohibit its sale and use would break established cultural, religious, and social traditions, as well as cause significant federal and state tax-revenue losses. Prohibition, which occurred in the U.S. from 1920 to 1933, was generally considered a failure, for it spawned bootleg manufacturing operations and increased trafficking in illegal alcohol sales. Interestingly, the rate of alcohol use, abuse, and liver cirrhosis in the U.S. declined greatly during this period, but the number of "alcoholics" remained about the same.

Terminology

As discussed in Chapter 1, there are two major alcohol problems: abuse and chemical dependence.

Abuse is intentional alcohol overuse or misuse (e.g., as seen on and around college campuses). The main characteristic of alcohol abuse is that people will moderate or stop their abusive drinking when they decide that the adverse consequences are worse than the desirable effects of drinking. The second major problem with alcohol is pathological *dependence*, popularly known as "alcoholism." The number of drinkers who become dependent has been estimated at 10–15% (Anthony et al., 1994). Chemical dependence is a brain-chemistry-driven, loss-of-control-over-drinking disease characterized by the inability to continually moderate use or remain abstinent, even under adverse consequences. Alcohol dependence requires formal treatment or specialized programs to help individuals maintain abstinence. (Note: The term *alcoholism* is widely misunderstood and stigmatizing. To recovering people, *alcoholism* means problem drinking that destroys lives—a less restrictive use of the term than in scientific studies.)

Binge Drinking

Binge drinking is episodic drinking, during which a large number of drinks is consumed in a short period of time. The term conjures up the picture of out-of-control consumption of alcohol in a 2- or 3-day period, as "on a weekend binge." Some researchers have defined a "large number" as at least five drinks (for males) and four drinks (for females) in a sitting (in describing drinking by college students, Nelson, Naimi, Brewer, & Wechsler, 2005). Such drinkers may or may not be intoxicated, depending on the duration of drinking in one sitting. Is it binge drinking if a person drinks 40 bottles of beer in a 12-hour period? What about the person who drinks at a constant rate for 3 days during an outdoor festival, and then never drinks again for 2 weeks? Is this binge drinking or social drinking? What about the lady who has four drinks a day for a week while on a Caribbean vacation? One recommendation is to describe binge drinking as "a prolonged (usually 2 days or more) period of intoxication." Others have suggested the terms "high-risk periodic drinking" or "heavy episodic drinking." Obviously, the term *binge* is imprecise.

Social Use

"Social use" of alcohol, in my view, consists of an occasional drink or two in the company of friends: a glass of champagne at a wedding, a cold beer after a softball game, or a glass of wine with a meal. Contrary to popular belief, social drinking does not kill brain cells, nor does it adversely affect any major body organ. Two-thirds of the U.S. population drinks alcohol, but the number of social drinkers has not accurately been measured, mainly because of conflicting definitions of "social" drinking.

Moderate Use

"Moderate use" of alcohol has been defined by the Department of Agriculture and the U.S. Department of Health and Human Services (1990) as 1–2 drinks per day—one drink for women, two drinks for men. These guidelines exclude women who are pregnant or trying to conceive, people who plan to drive, people taking medications, recovering alcoholics, and people under the age of 21. The interest in "moderate" drinking is underscored by research showing beneficial effects of moderate drinking on cardiovascular function, and perhaps on the prevention of type II diabetes and occlusive (clot-related) strokes. Moderate drinkers are allegedly at reduced risk for atherosclerotic heart disease, compared to alcohol abstainers and heavy drinkers. The mechanism of this protective effect is incompletely known (see the last section in this chapter). Finally, drinking "moderately" is a goal of some people with alcohol problems, as is discussed in Chapter 8.

Heavy Drinking

"Heavy drinking" is not only associated with number of drinks per episode but also involves duration of drinking. The scientific definitions of "heavy drinking" range from five glasses of wine a day (i.e., in a 24-hour period) to unlimited drinks, including the amounts drunk by highly tolerant "alcoholics." Still, the term is slippery: We can be sure that a quart of rum over a 4-hour period is "heavy drinking," but what about five beers in an hour? As a pharmacologist, I have problems with the subjective labels of "social," "moderate," and "heavy" drinking because they are not clearly quantitative, but rather in the eyes of the beholder. Thus any numbers of drinks associated with these terms are merely guidelines.

Problem Drinking

"Problem drinking" is defined as any consumption of alcohol that results in significant risk of physical damage, psychological problems, accidents, legal problems, or other social problems. "Problem drinking" includes the two *DSM-IV* related diagnoses described earlier: intentional alcohol abuse and pathological alcohol dependence.

Unhealthy Use

This is a broader classification including many of the preceding terms. It involves a spectrum of drinking associated with varying degrees of risk to health in medical patients (Saitz, 2005). The prevalence of this type of drinking is estimated as "high"(7–20%) in outpatients, higher (30–40%) among patients treated in emergency departments, and highest (50%) in trauma patients.

Case Study: Mary

Mary was a 30-year-old divorcée who lived at home with her parents and recently had been convicted of drunk driving. She reported a number of episodes of drinking in excess and appeared to have tolerance but no evidence of withdrawal or other drug use. Her drinking occurred most often while socializing with friends, but initially she had no legal incidents while under the influence. Her parents often raised concerns about her alcohol use, but she discounted their concerns.

> Mary had been steadily employed as a waitress and as a dining room manager for several large restaurant chains. However, when she held positions of significant responsibility, she often ended up "feeling under pressure." She then became stressed and resigned or ended up in a disagreement with top management, leading to her being asked to resign or being terminated. In addition to her excessive alcohol use, she had a pattern of impulsive behavior, especially when stressed, and it appeared that there was a long history of conflict between her and her parents. At one point, she found a bottle of her father's heart medication and took a number of pills. She was sent to the ER due to a risk of cardiotoxicity and subsequently was sent to a psychiatric unit and diagnosed with borderline personality disorder, depression, and suicidal risk. Her drug-use pattern was not addressed during treatment.
>
> When Mary was charged with a second DWI, she was forced into drug-abuse treatment. She attended treatment sessions and sometimes attended A.A., but she claimed she did not belong there because she was not "alcoholic."

Mary's sad story illustrates a drinking problem that was not diagnosed, plus other behavioral problems that may or may not have been diagnosed accurately. Mary was a victim of poor diagnosis, little or inappropriate treatment, and therefore her prognosis was poor. This case clearly illustrates that our society needs more resources to help such people, which we might be able to obtain if problem drinking is ever addressed at a level commensurate with the social and public health problems produced by it.

Alcohol Absorption and Metabolism

Ethanol, a simple molecule consisting of two carbon atoms, six hydrogen atoms, and one oxygen atom, is the most abused psychoactive drug. Because the alcohol molecule is so small, it penetrates readily into every tissue of the body. In spite of its easy penetration, it does have specific effects on certain organs and parts of organs. For example, it has a more destructive action on the liver than on the kidney. It also acts more on some nerve cell components than others. This may be due to the higher sensitivity of these components to ethanol, for unknown reasons.

Several factors influence the absorption of alcohol from the stomach into the blood: (1) the amount of food in the stomach, (2) the rate of drinking, (3) the amount of alcohol dehydrogenase (alcohol-metabolizing enzyme) in the stomach lining, and (4) the form of alcohol ("straight" or diluted, and type of diluting beverage). Some studies indicate that carbonated alcohol-containing beverages are absorbed faster than noncarbonated ones.

Alcohol is metabolized (broken down) by the liver into acetate and water. The main metabolizing enzyme for alcohol is known as *alcohol dehydrogenase*. Alcohol dehydrogenase is primarily found in the liver but also occurs in the stomach and (at low concentrations) in other organs of the body. Metabolism produces a compound called acetaldehyde, which is in turn broken down by the enzyme aldehyde dehydrogenase to acetate and water. Acetate from the metabolism of alcohol has no known pharmacological effects.

Blood Alcohol Concentration

What does "blood alcohol concentration" (BAC) mean? This is the amount of alcohol in a person's blood, measured in "grams percent." A BAC of 0.08% means eight-hundredths of a gram of alcohol per 100 milliliters of blood. Sometimes it will be stated as 80 milligrams percent (mg%) or 80 milligrams per 100 milliliters of blood. Finally, the same amount can be designated as 80 milligrams per deciliter (mg/dl). A deciliter is 100 milliliters of blood.

One standard "beverage unit" (BU) of alcohol consists of one 5-ounce glass of wine (12% by volume), one 12-ounce beer (4.9% by volume), or one cocktail containing 1.5 ounces of 80 proof (40% by volume) spirits. All of these contain roughly 14 grams (about one-half ounce) of absolute alcohol. Beverage serving sizes vary, and beers and wines vary by alcohol content. For example, the average alcohol content for most beers (12 ounces) is 4.75–4.9%; for light beers, it is about 3.8% by volume. If a 150-pound man drinks one BU in an hour, this will produce a BAC of about 0.025%, excluding any calculation for liver metabolism. This is approximately one-third of the drink-driving limit of 0.08% in the United States. So if this person drinks four BUs in an hour, he will be at the legal limit after that hour, including a calculation for a 0.02% BAC per hour decline that occurs due to liver metabolism.

It is important to understand that rough calculations of this type utilize "average" values that make determinations of probable BACs easy, without the use of complex calculations. More accurate values can be determined using algorithms that take into account a person's body size, gender, age, and height, which affect the amount of total body water (TBW) in which alcohol can be distributed (Brick & Erickson, 1999). TBW in which alcohol is distributed is called the *volume of distribution*. Also, alcohol is removed by the liver at essentially a constant rate of 0.25 to 0.3 ounces of beverage alcohol per hour, so the BAC (as mentioned earlier) declines by about 0.02% every hour in most people. This is the value for relatively alcohol-naïve drinkers; however, people with significant alcohol drinking experience will have liver enzyme induction and will process alcohol at higher rates, leading to significantly lower BACs. Conversely, liver disease, some medications, and other factors can *decrease* the metabolism of alcohol, leading to higher-than-expected BACs. Finally, after many years of drinking significant amounts of alcohol daily, some people will experience a "reverse tolerance," where they become very sensitive to alcohol again as the liver loses function.

The previous example is for a 150-pound male. Here are two other useful examples: A 200-pound man drinking one BU in an hour will experience a BAC of about 0.019% (Ray & Ksir, 2004). This is approximately one-fourth of the drink-driving limit in the United States. Again, about 0.02% BAC will be lost per hour. So if this man has one drink per hour his BAC will remain stable. Of course, drinking faster than the rate of metabolism will produce higher BACs, and a given BAC at the end of a period of drinking will be the rather straightforward result of number of drinks consumed multiplied by hours of drinking divided by drinks metabolized.

The second example is for a 100-pound female who drinks one BU in about an hour. This would produce a BAC of 0.045% and would take over 2 hours to be metabolized. If two BUs were drunk within an hour by this woman, it would produce close to an illegal BAC for driving. As is true in all the examples given here, other factors would affect the final BAC and the observed level of "intoxication." Among the factors that influence BACs and level of "intoxication" are body weight, gender, genetics, drinking history, amount of food in the stomach, rate of drinking, presence of other drugs that affect alcohol metabolism, and overall health of the individual.

What happens at certain BACs? At 0.08% (the legal drink-driving limit in the United States) a person's ability to drive a car is significantly impaired; that is, there is a loss of judgment, problems with divided attention tasks, and some perception and muscle movement problems. At 0.15–0.2%, most people are "grossly intoxicated"; that is, they slur their speech and have difficulty walking. At 0.3%, most people will be on the verge of unconsciousness or be comatose. At 0.35–0.4%, death is possible. Of course, there is such variability among people that these are only "textbook" guidelines. Some people are very resistant (tolerant) to alcohol's effects, whereas others are more sensitive. Despite myths to the contrary, BAC levels cannot be lowered by coffee, cold showers, or other methods. Time is needed for the metabolism of alcohol to occur and for alcohol to be removed from the body. This is why alcohol overdoses are so problematic—there is no antagonist or "magic bullet" to overcome the effects of alcohol. Proper treatment of overdose involves hospitalization with respiratory support.

In low doses (1–2 drinks, but it varies among individuals), alcohol produces some of these effects: relaxation, reduced inhibitions, impaired concentration, slowed reflexes, reduced reaction time, and reduced coordination. These effects are magnified as the number of drinks increases, until there is serious impairment that can affect driving skills.

Two of the most important reasons for variability in a person's response to a "drink" are the size of the drink and the type of beverage (as there is great variation in alcohol percentage). Bottled beer or small bottles of wine contain fixed volumes of liquid, but when a person goes to a bar or makes drinks at home, the volume of beer, wine, or whiskey can vary tremendously. For example, tap beer comes in glasses that vary in size from around 8–22 ounces, yet each size is called a "drink." Wine is poured into small or large glasses that are not always "full." Finally, although a "jigger" of whiskey is usually about 1–1.5 ounces, many bartenders "free pour" whiskey, using their experience to approach the amount of a jigger. So beware when someone says, "But I only had two drinks!"

Can alcohol kill people? Alcohol is a very dangerous drug for two reasons. First, people can overdose on alcohol and die either because they suffocate on their vomit or because alcohol can shut down the brain areas that control breathing. Anyone who has a blood alcohol level of 0.35% (about 14–18 drinks in a rather brief period of time) or above is in danger of an overdose. Second, chronic heavy drinkers can die during withdrawal from high BACs. (Death is usually due to seizures when the body experiences hyperexcitability during declining BACs.)

Effects on the Brain and Nervous System

Research shows that alcohol can cause permanent problems with nervous system function. We know that people who drink heavily have memory loss, some confusion, and often problems with feelings and sensations in their hands and feet. ("Heavily" does not mean two drinks per day; rather, several pints of spirits per day would be considered "heavy" drinking.) Although there is great variation from person to person, over the long term almost everyone will have some negative nervous system function with heavy daily drinking.

"Disinhibition" is a phenomenon produced by alcohol. It causes nervous system depression. Everyone's behavior and personality is under some degree of restraint because of prior experiences, laws, customs, personal beliefs, and values. The cortex ("thinking" portion of the brain) is depressed by low doses of alcohol. One function of the frontal cortex (forward lobes of the brain) is to maintain control over the rest of the brain. When alcohol depresses the frontal cortex, the rest of the brain speeds up. Thus, a person feels more likely to take chances, there is poor judgment, and the pleasure pathway is engaged, leading to a euphoric "high." This loss of inhibitions is an early part of the condition known as "intoxication." The way that alcohol produces its intoxicating effects on the brain is not entirely known. Scientists around the world are studying four specific brain neurotransmitter receptors as sites of action for alcohol. These receptors are (1) the n-methyl-d-aspartate (NMDA) receptor, (2) the gamma aminobutyric acid (GABA) receptor, (3) the glutamate receptor, and (4) the nicotine (nicotinic) receptor. Blockade or enhancement of these neurotransmitter receptor systems may hold the answer to how alcohol produces the pharmacological action of intoxication. Generally, most evidence indicates that ethanol (beverage alcohol) binds to hydrophobic (lacking affinity for water) pockets of proteins, altering their function by changing their three-dimensional structure. Proteins that are particularly sensitive to this effect include ion-channels, neurotransmitter receptors, and enzymes (Chapter 2) involved in changing the receptor signal to a nerve impulse. This leads to much of the intoxicating effects of ethanol.

Unlike other drugs, alcohol has no specific receptor to activate in the brain. For example, cocaine's receptor is the dopamine transporter. Heroin's receptor is the opioid receptor, and the receptor for marijuana is the cannabinoid receptor. Scientists used to think that alcohol "melted" (not a scientific term) the nerve membrane in a reversible way, but today scientists are inclined to believe that alcohol has affinity for certain receptors for other chemicals in the brain. For example, alcohol is known to affect the GABA receptor, the NMDA receptor, and probably others to produce its myriad of behavioral and toxicological effects.

Why does alcohol stimulate some people and make other people sleepy? Observation tells us that women generally become sedated with a few drinks, whereas men become "happy," sullen, or angry (although obviously this isn't always the case). This is probably due to differences in metabolism (breakdown of the drug), rate of drinking, brain-cell sensitivity, and other unknown factors.

Does alcohol kill brain cells? Yes, but only when large quantities are drunk over a period of many years. Thus, alcohol abusers and alcohol-dependent individuals (collectively called "problem drinkers") often suffer from Wernicke-Korsakoff Syndrome, amnesia, confusion, and dementia. This effect is due to alcohol toxicity on the hippocampus, or "memory" portion of the brain. Social drinking, however, does not kill brain cells; the effects are totally reversible.

Alcohol and Driving

Impairment of driving is due to many effects of alcohol: reduced judgment, increased reaction time, a euphoric "high" that makes people feel they can drive safely when in fact their ability is reduced, increased risk-taking, reduced ability to focus on roadway markers and other traffic, and (when the effects are wearing off) marked drowsiness that can lead to decreased attention and perhaps periods of nodding off.

The Driving While Intoxicated (DWI) or Driving Under the Influence (DUI) BAC of 0.08% (in all of the United States) gives us a good place to start in understanding how alcohol disrupts motor coordination. Scientific studies have shown that the ability to drive begins to be affected at 0.05% (which is the maximum legal BAC in most European countries). Most people understand that the ability to drive depends upon good judgment, ability to steer, ability to use the brakes, and lack of risk-taking. At 0.08% (DWI limit), there is significant reduction in judgment, increased risk-taking, and some disruption of muscle control.

Somewhere between 0.08% and 0.10% (the former U.S. DWI limit), people begin to have trouble walking (inability to walk a straight line) or standing on one foot. They also often show nystagmus (eyeball drifting and inability to focus on a moving target) and have trouble counting backwards or reciting the alphabet. Thus, "field-testing" for DWI consists of observation of several or all of these last five alcohol-related problems.

About 80–90% of ingested alcohol is metabolized (broken down) by the liver. The rest is excreted in the breath, urine, or sweat. Although alcohol can be measured in any of these for indirect determination of blood alcohol, the best method is via a blood sample. Breath measures of alcohol are somewhat inaccurate depending on how the sample is taken and the type of analytical instrument. Urine alcohol levels are quite variable and are therefore of no value for measuring precise blood alcohol, and sweat samples generally only indicate the presence or absence of alcohol in the body.

Why can some people drink a lot of alcohol and never seem intoxicated? "Seeming" to be intoxicated is a very subjective thing. People might seem pretty normal (especially to those drinking with them!), but inside their heads they are euphoric, dissociated from the real world, dizzy, nauseated, exhilarated, or all of the above. Most people, when they reach a BAC above 0.15% (5–6 drinks in a short period of time) will show signs of intoxication: slurring words, loss of balance, uninhibited behavior, repetitive eye movements (nystagmus), and impaired judgment when placed in a situation where they have to make important decisions (Brick & Erickson, 1999). A few people, however, have a great deal of natural tolerance and rarely appear intoxicated.

Are designated driver programs effective? Designating one person in a group of drinkers to be the sober driver for the evening sounds like a good idea. However, according to a report from the U.S. Task Force on Community Preventive Services, there is little evidence that such programs reduce drunk driving and alcohol-related crashes. Apparently few designated drivers actually abstain from drinking. In some cases, the least-intoxicated person is chosen to be the driver, which defeats the purpose of the program.

Effects on Other Body Organs

In small doses, alcohol is not toxic, which means there are few pathological effects of alcohol on body organs. In general, the more of a drug that body organs are exposed to, the greater the toxicity. Although alcohol is one of the least potent (requires large quantities) of all drugs, it is usually consumed in large doses ("grams per dose"). Thus, over time large doses of alcohol (especially on a daily basis) can cause great toxicity to organs such as the liver, heart, brain, esophagus, and stomach.

If alcohol is metabolized to acetate and carbon dioxide, why is it so toxic? Alcohol is toxic because of its own molecular effects on tissues. In addition, its first breakdown product (acetaldehyde) is even more toxic. However, the liver metabolizes acetaldehyde very quickly through enzymatic action to acetate and water. Because this breakdown occurs at a steady rate, the more alcohol that is consumed, the longer ethanol and acetaldehyde are in contact with tissues and the more damage will be done.

The major negative effects of long-term alcohol consumption are fatty liver, alcoholic hepatitis, cirrhosis (in susceptible persons), gastritis, short-term memory loss, Wernicke-Korsakoff syndrome (in susceptible persons), clinical depression, mild hypertension, pancreatitis (in susceptible persons), and cardiomyopathy (heart muscle degeneration). Very heavy drinkers will often have esophageal varices (dilated veins in the esophagus), brain disease (loss of cognitive function, confusion, amnesia), and (in susceptible people) signs of liver disease.

Organs vary in their response to alcohol. The kidney is probably the organ that is least damaged by alcohol. People tend to think the kidney is affected because urination increases when people drink. But increased urination is due to alcohol's effect on blocking the pituitary's antidiuretic hormone. If problems with the kidneys develop in heavily drinking individuals, they may be due to other alcohol-induced illnesses, such as hypertension.

The pancreas is the main producer of insulin in the body. Problems with the pancreas lead to type I diabetes. Although large doses of alcohol do not cause diabetes, some problem drinkers do develop chronic pancreatitis, a very painful condition that is difficult to treat. Alcohol is alleged to lead to secondary diabetes in susceptible individuals due to impact on the pancreas.

The esophagus, the tube running from the mouth to the stomach, is sometimes heavily affected by chronic drinking, leading to "esophageal varices." These are inflamed veins bulging into the esophagus that bleed with the continued passage of alcohol and food. To be properly treated for this condition, it is critical that the person stop drinking. Varices can be related to the deterioration of the liver and an inability of blood to pass through the liver readily, leading to portal hypertension, causing excess pressure on the esophageal veins.

Unlike the highly "addictive" drug nicotine and its delivery device (cigarette), alcohol apparently has no major effect on the lungs. Nicotine itself probably does not have a major effect on the lungs; rather, the cigarette, with its tars, carbon monoxide, and other ingredients play the largest role in increasing the risk of lung cancer in smokers. Interestingly, about 70–90% of heavy drinkers also smoke, so the combined effects of alcohol and smoking lead to a wider array of probable cancers, including lung, mouth, throat, esophagus, and stomach.

Alcohol has two effects that can make people feel like vomiting. One is the direct effect of alcohol on sensitive stomach linings: It acts as a poison, causing a complex series of events that causes the body to try to get rid of the toxin. The second it is that it has a direct effect on the emetic (vomiting) center of the brain stem to stimulate vomiting. Everyone has a different sensitivity to each of these effects; some people never become nauseated during or after drinking, whereas other people become nauseous with only moderate drinking. It is also possible that acetaldehyde, the main metabolite of alcohol, could cause nausea in some people.

What causes people to die from drinking large amounts of alcohol during their lifetime? The main cause of death is liver cirrhosis. Interestingly, cirrhosis occurs in only about 20% of heavy drinkers (including alcohol-dependent persons). Other causes of death that might be attributable to alcohol include pancreatitis, cancers of certain types, nutritional problems, and weakening of the immune system. Alcohol probably causes more deaths through overdose, car crashes, homicides, drowning, accidents (such as falls), and suicides than through its direct effects on the body.

With respect to cancer, alcohol does seem to increase the risk of breast cancer somewhat, and oral, gastric, and intestinal cancers might also be facilitated by the drug. It makes intuitive sense that because alcohol causes gastrointestinal irritation, particularly of the stomach and esophagus, that it might increase cancer risk. One study has suggested that acetaldehyde, the primary breakdown product of ethanol and a known carcinogen, does increase the incidence of upper gastrointestinal cancer. It is also known that alcohol combined with tobacco use greatly increases the risk of mouth, tongue, throat, and lung cancer. How the complex effects of alcohol, including types of beverages, concentration, and amount of alcohol consumed, interact with genetic factors to cause cancer still requires much more research.

Hangovers and Shakes

Binge or continual long-term drinking often causes withdrawal when a person abruptly stops drinking alcohol. Because alcohol is a depressant in the body, prolonged high doses reduce cell activity. When alcohol is removed from the cells, they recover and return to normalcy in a way that first produces a change in sensitivity toward stimulation. However, this attempt by the body to produce normalcy often leads to over-stimulation ("hyperactivity"), which is known as *withdrawal*. Thus, binge drinking leads to a mini-withdrawal called a "hangover," the symptoms of which include increased gastric acid (stomach upset), early-morning awakening (a type of insomnia), and other symptoms such as pounding heart, headache, dehydration, and electrolyte imbalance. Cessation of long-term heavy drinking can lead to the "shakes" (tremors), delirium (an acute confusional state), and sometimes seizures. Thus alcohol abusers or alcohol dependent individuals must be detoxified ("detoxed") using a longer-acting sedative in decreasing doses to reduce the discomfort and possible death produced by withdrawal seizures. Interestingly, some people are immune to hangovers or severe withdrawal because of "biological variability" (which means "we don't know why all people don't respond the same way").

People with little tolerance to alcohol tend to be more sensitive (less tolerant) to the acute and rebound effects of drinking. There are several types of tolerance, with behavioral, metabolic (liver), and functional (cellular, tissue, brain) being the major ones. (Note that functional tolerance has several synonyms, which can be confusing for some people.) Not everyone becomes tolerant to alcohol, but when it occurs it can be significant. For example, some heavy drinkers consume over a quart of spirits per day.

Hangovers are very uncomfortable for most people. Once begun, they cannot be significantly overcome with any known remedies. The new hangover products available in pharmacies are probably a waste of money; convincing controlled studies on whether they are more effective than placebos (sugar pills) have not been done. Everyone has a favorite hangover remedy, and each one works based upon individual superstition. But there is nothing on the market that will overcome a hangover. The best measure is prevention, which means drinking in a manner that does not allow the BAC to rise above about 0.05% (varies from person to person) throughout an evening of drinking.

Some people drink to relax. But can alcohol *increase* anxiety? Apparently it can, as in small doses alcohol produces "disinhibition," leading to heightened arousal in brain areas involved in mood. Thus, in some already-anxious people, small nonsedating doses can increase anxiety. In higher doses, the well-known antianxiety effects of alcohol kick in. After several drinks or more wear off, alcohol rebound can cause agitation and anxiety after the antianxiety effects wear off. This too can add to an already-existing state of anxiety.

Interactions With Other Drugs

Alcohol unfavorably interacts with many other drugs: benzodiazepines (such as Xanax, Valium, Librium), antidepressants (such as Prozac, Zoloft), insulin, anticoagulants, antihistamines, some antibiotics, and many others. In fact, many prescription drugs carry the label "Do not drink alcohol while taking this medication." In general, alcohol can increase the effects of medications that make people drowsy, alter the metabolism of medications, or reduce the effectiveness of medications. People using alcohol and one of these prescription medications should be aware of such drug interactions and avoid driving.

One major drug interaction concerns oral contraceptives (birth control pills) that slow down the rate at which alcohol is removed from the body. A woman who is on the pill can expect to feel intoxicated or sedated for a longer time than a woman who is not taking the pill. However, although some women may strongly feel this effect, others may not feel any difference at all.

How does alcohol interact with "club drugs"? This is a difficult question, and the only answer is "very unpredictably." As discussed in Chapter 7, there are six main club drugs: methamphetamine, rohypnol, ketamine, GHB, ecstasy, and LSD. There are no established rules or observations for the interaction of alcohol with GHB, ecstasy, or LSD. Alcohol and methamphetamine will either increase or decrease each other's actions, depending upon the dose of each and the timing of taking one with the other. The actions of alcohol and rohypnol and alcohol and ketamine are additive, given that they are all depressant drugs. Beyond this, little is known about their interactions. The best advice is that they are dangerous when mixed, especially with higher doses of either one with the other.

Finally, there is a major interaction when alcohol and antihistamines are mixed. The same holds true with the benzodiazepine antianxiety/hypnotic class of drugs, the pain-killing opioid drugs, and marijuana. This interaction is essentially an additive one, so that the depressant effects of the drugs are greater than either one alone. Although some have called these interactions "synergistic effects" (the effect is more than a simple summation of effects), this is extremely difficulty to measure. "Additive effects" are more likely.

Alcohol Effects in Women and the Fetus

Women metabolize alcohol more slowly than men because there is a smaller amount of alcohol-metabolizing enzyme (alcohol dehydrogenase) in the stomachs of women. Because less enzyme is present, more alcohol passes through the stomach to the duodenum, the main alcohol-absorbing portion of the gut. This effect, combined with a different fat/lean body makeup between men and women, leads to higher BACs in women than men after identical alcoholic drinks.

Women are more likely to have health problems compared to men who drink the same amount of alcohol per day, and they may develop such problems faster than men. These include liver damage, pancreatic dysfunction, and high blood pressure. On the other hand, women are less likely than men to become alcohol dependent. The reason for this is unknown.

Most women reduce or stop their consumption of alcohol during pregnancy, but some don't. Although a little research has suggested that hormone and psychological changes are the reason why many women stop drinking during pregnancy, the exact percentage of those who do stop drinking and why they do so is unknown. Some women drink less during pregnancy, and a small percentage don't reduce their drinking at all, suggesting that they may be dependent on alcohol and require intense intervention and treatment to reduce the harm to their babies.

Fetal alcohol syndrome (FAS) is a major cause of birth defects around the world. In the U.S., conservative estimates are that each day about three to four children are born with FAS. FAS is the only permanent fetal syndrome caused by drugs that produce chemical dependence. This means that women who drink heavily during pregnancy have a great chance of permanently damaging their baby. The signs of FAS are complex, but they include severe birth abnormalities, including characteristic facial defects, sometimes missing fingers, toes, or kidneys, a small brain, low IQ, and probably a shortened life span. These permanent defects place the child at a severe disadvantage in growth and life adjustment. The new term *fetal alcohol spectrum disorder* (FASD) includes FAS and fetal alcohol effects (FAE). FAE following a mother's drinking during pregnancy involves fewer physical and developmental problems (compared to FAS). These could range from learning disabilities to some of the facial defects that are usually seen with FAS. FAE are thought to occur with less drinking during pregnancy, compared to women who drink enough to produce FAS. The teratologic causes of FASD (alcohol-induced malformations) include reduced blood flow to the fetus, a toxic effect of acetaldehyde (the major breakdown product of alcohol); and alcohol-induced increases in prostaglandins (chemicals released during tissue damage).

Some say that FASD is a 100% preventable birth defect. It depends upon your point of view. FASD can occur in any woman who drinks heavily during pregnancy, but it does not appear in *every* woman who drinks heavily (it is not possible to predict which women are likely to have a FASD baby). And although some women who drink heavily are alcohol dependent, most are not. Thus it is certainly preventable in heavily drinking women who abuse alcohol (they will often stop drinking during pregnancy), but an alcohol-dependent woman will need treatment in order to stop drinking. Treatment is not effective overnight; thus the baby will probably have a high risk for FASD. Alcohol use during pregnancy is considered the number one preventable cause of mental retardation and mental deficiency, however. Thus, the most conservative recommendation by some researchers is that pregnant women, or those who think they might be pregnant, should not drink at all. Although there is little scientific evidence on the benefits of alcohol abstinence during pregnancy, this is the safest message. On the other hand, if a woman has a glass of wine now and then while pregnant, the likelihood of hurting her baby is extremely low. If a woman has one glass of wine before she knows she's pregnant, she should not be consumed with guilt if the child grows up with a perceived cognitive deficit (even ADHD). There are more likely causes for such deficits than one alcoholic drink.

Does drinking alcohol increase the quantity of breast milk? This is another of the many myths that seem to be part of our folklore. Recent interesting studies indicate that drinking alcohol can actually reduce the quantity of breast milk, because alcohol affects the release of oxytocin and prolactin, two hormones involved in the production of milk. This doesn't mean that nursing mothers shouldn't drink at all, but they should be careful, as some women are more affected by alcohol than others.

Health Benefits of Alcohol

Health benefits produced by alcohol are always of concern to those who see only the dangerous side of the beverages. A recent review of existing studies (Meyerhoff, Bode, Nixon, deBruin, Bode, et al., 2005) has determined that the health benefits of alcohol depend on a person's age, gender, and overall medical history. The review found that for the general population, two drinks a day for men and one drink a day for women relate to lower mortality and are unlikely to cause harm. (Remember that a standard drink is defined as 5 ounces of wine, 12 ounces of beer, or 1.5 ounces of distilled spirits.)

Alcohol has a mild antioxidant activity in "moderate doses" (1–2 drinks a day). This antioxidant activity tends to overcome the detrimental effects of free oxygen radicals in body tissues. These radicals might increase the risks for cancer, heart disease, and other age-related diseases, so drinking a couple of drinks a day has been said to reduce the risk of these diseases, particularly atherosclerotic heart disease. The other mechanism of this protection might involve alcohol-induced changes in so-called good/bad cholesterol ratios in the blood. Is this best seen with red wine? Some recent studies have indicated that any type of alcohol (in moderation only) can reduce the risk of myocardial infarction (Agarwal, 2003; Mukamal, Conigrave, Mittleman, Camargo, Stampfer, et al., 2003). As always, the harmful or dangerous effects of alcohol on physical and behavioral health should be taken into consideration when making a decision to drink alcohol for healthy reasons.

Chapter 7

Other Drugs

THE CHEMICALS IN THIS CHAPTER ARE NOT traditional CNS stimulants or depressants. They have multiple pharmacologic effects, and in most cases they elicit different behavioral effects in different people. For example, as noted earlier, some cigarette smokers report an "antifatigue" effect of smoking whereas others smoke to "calm down." Such anecdotal reports coincide with the biphasic effects of nicotine on basic cell function (stimulation followed by depression of peripheral nerve ganglia), which are well-known to pharmacologists who have studied autonomic pharmacology (the pharmacology of drugs that affect the sympathetic and parasympathetic nervous systems).

Other drugs in this chapter are unique in their pharmacology and behavioral effects (e.g., marijuana can be classed as a depressant, an analgesic, or a psychotropic drug based upon the multiple effects seen in marijuana smokers). "Club drugs" are a heterogeneous group of chemicals about which relatively little is known regarding their pharmacological mechanisms. Inhalants are nasty tissue-corroding chemicals that have benign uses (paint solvents, airplane glue, refrigerator coolants) but have been found and abused by adolescents seeking a "high." Steroids are dangerous hormones and hormone supplements that are highly abused (but not yet known to be "addicting") by athletes and nonathletes who use them to enhance body structure and self-esteem. Prescription and nonprescription drugs, due to their healing nature, are abused when patients find them very effective (i.e., "magic") or when the drugs promise to overcome uncomfortable symptoms.

Although there is insufficient research on the dependence liability of many of the drugs in this chapter, those that have been researched have been found in many cases to have significant dependence liability. Extensive descriptions of the behavioral effects of these drugs can be found in Brick and Erickson (1999) and Kuhn, Swartzwelder, and Wilson (2003).

Nicotine

Nicotine is known as the most toxic drug that acts at specific receptors in the body. It is packaged in the most lethal drug-delivery system available. It is readily absorbed through skin and mucous membranes. Nicotine, a chemical that has a little-known use as an animal tranquilizer, is the primary psychoactive compound in cigarettes. It is also one of the ingredients in insecticides. Much of the nicotine in cigars and cigarettes is vaporized during burning, but enough remains to cause significant toxicity of the heart and circulatory system and in other organs affected by nicotine in the blood. This should tell us something about the value of this drug. Although the tar, tobacco smoke, and other ingredients volatilized during smoking are probably the cause of heart disease and lung cancer in chronic smokers, nicotine is the ingredient that induces chemical dependence (Dani & Harris, 2005). Thus, nicotine is the reason why many people have difficulty "kicking the habit," and smoking cessation measures are designed to reduce nicotine consumption. The "habit" part of smoking may be related to holding the cigarette, flicking the ashes, or having a cigarette after a meal, with alcohol, or with other drugs. Although the "habit" is not the chemical dependence, the two combined can make smoking cessation extremely difficult. New antismoking laws in states and countries will cause smokers either to stop entirely or to seek effective smoking cessation strategies. Because of the severe dependence involved with nicotine in some individuals, many current smokers will unfortunately die with smoke in their lungs.

Approximately 25% of the U.S. population smokes on a regular basis, and the number of new smokers in the U.S. appears to be declining.

The number of people who quit or die is therefore not quite counterbalanced by the number of new smokers, although the "declining new smokers" trend may reverse itself due to several factors such as increased advertising, reduced education about the negative effects of smoking, changes in adolescent beliefs or values, and other reasons. Since nicotine does not produce a "blockbuster" euphoria, peer acceptance and advertising of cigarettes are the primary causes of smoking in the U.S.

The number of smokers (especially those who smoke over a period of time) who become dependent on nicotine has been estimated to be around 32% (Anthony et al., 1994), the highest known incidence of any drug. Other smokers *abuse* nicotine, which can also be dangerous because the delivery vehicle (cigarette) is so toxic. Nicotine itself affects nicotinic receptors throughout the brain, leading to stimulation (an antifatigue effect) or depression (relaxation), depending upon the user's need for the drug. It also affects peripheral body receptor sites, leading to sweating, nausea, and other autonomic responses, especially before a smoker becomes tolerant to these actions. Finally, the vast majority of cases of lung cancer can be directly attributed to smoking.

Smoking cessation can be difficult (see Chapter 8). Some smokers, mainly those who are not dependent, can stop cold turkey when they commit to doing so. Others, however, require smoking cessation aids, including hypnosis, group therapy, or individual counseling. Smoking cessation medications, including the nicotine patch, gum, and low-nicotine devices such as inhalers, are designed to wean a person off nicotine with few uncomfortable side effects. Even bupropion (Zyban), an antidepressant drug, can be helpful. However, the truly dependent nicotine user will require long-term commitment along with counseling, other support, and hard work to remain smoke-free. Unfortunately, some severely dependent people will never be able to stop smoking despite numerous attempts. A myth about smoking cessation is that everyone who stops smoking gains weight. However, there is great variation in this response. Some people do gain significant amounts of weight, whereas others gain no weight at all. Excessive smoking (three or more packs a day) is very common among patients with severe psychiatric illness, because smoking helps relieve some of their depressive symptoms due to the primary psychiatric disorder. It also helps overcome some of the unpleasant side effects of antipsychotic drugs.

Basic research in mice suggests that nicotine can increase the motivation to seek food (Wellman, Bellinger, Cepeda-Benito, Susabda, Ho, et al., 2005). This goes against the commonly held belief that smoking reduces appetite, which is the reason given by smokers for not wanting to stop. Also, some young women take up smoking to hold down their weight. If the mouse results are confirmed, it suggests that smoking and nicotine might have opposite effects, or that the weight gain seen when some smokers quit may be due to a factor that is not directly related to nicotine's effects on the brain's appetite center.

Nicotine works by activating a specific subtype of receptor for acetylcholine—the nicotinic acetylcholine receptor. In general, nicotine excites nerve cells and increases cell-to-cell transmission. There is evidence that these effects occur in brain regions that are associated with memory and other mental functions, as well as with physical movement. This helps us understand why nicotine has been tested in the treatment of Alzheimer's patients. The opposite effects of nicotine on cell transmission in the muscles directly relate to the use of nicotine in pesticides and animal tranquilizers (i.e., it is toxic to physical movement).

According to some research, regular exposure to secondhand smoke can double a person's risk of heart disease. Anyone who has been in the house of a smoker can recall the lingering smoke odor that permeates fabrics and hangs on walls, floors, and other surfaces. This residue contains tars and remnants of smoked tobacco that can be dangerous. When this material floats in higher concentrations in the air during active smoking, it can be inhaled by others and cause many of the same detrimental effects experienced by the active smoker.

There are reasons that babies born of mothers who smoke during pregnancy are smaller and lighter than other infants. The main reason is that these babies are deprived of oxygen during their fetal growth period. When a person smokes, she inhales tars and carbon monoxide. Both of these reduce oxygen in the blood, leading to long-term effects on the person. Imagine how sensitive a developing fetus can be to such an effect! Babies born of mothers who smoke during pregnancy are also more prone to sudden infant death syndrome (SIDS), perhaps because they have smaller than normal lung capacity at birth. At least one study puts this risk as second only to SIDS caused by placing a sleeping baby on its stomach in a crib.

A recent Canadian study (Gendreau & Vitaro, 2005) has suggested that so-called "light" or "mild" cigarettes have all of the nicotine and most of the toxins found in regular cigarettes. Six types of "light" cigarettes were compared to regular brands and were found to have 5% more nicotine. Out of 44 toxins measured, the lights contained all but four. One Canadian executive has stated that the terms "mild" and "light" should be banned altogether, as there is no benefit whatsoever of these brands to public health (No Health Gain from Mild, Light Cigarettes, 2005).

If it becomes more difficult to smoke and you provide free nicotine patches to smokers in a given city, will overall smoking rates decrease? The answer is "yes" in New York City, where they have done just that. Almost 200,000 fewer people are puffing almost four years after the city banned indoor smoking and raised cigarette taxes. Remember, however, that not all smokers will respond to such measures, especially those who are pathologically dependent on nicotine.

Marijuana

This interesting drug is highly controversial in social discussions regarding the risks and benefits of using drugs. It has no known lethal dose in humans, making it one of the safest drugs from a pharmacological standpoint. The active ingredient, tetra-hydrocannabinol (THC) is used (legally, in tablet form as dronabinol, or Marinol) in the treatment of AIDS and cancer patients. Anecdotal evidence suggests that it is truly recreational when used in low to moderate amounts, yet in higher amounts it probably causes lack of motivation, short-term memory loss, and impairment of driving skills when a person is intoxicated. The main reason marijuana is illegal is that it was included in the Harrison Narcotic Act of 1914, and so far there has been insufficient scientific evidence for—and government interest in—making it legal.

Marijuana is the general term used to describe several varieties of the plant (or any part of it) known as *Cannabis* (*indicia*, *sativa*, etc.). "Street" jargon includes: *blunts* (hollowed-out cigars packed with marijuana), *colas* (buds of the cannabis plant, which are preferred by marijuana users because of their higher content of delta-9-THC, the active ingredient in marijuana), and *hashish* or *hash* (the most potent form, which comes from the resin of the cannabis plant when it is separated from the plant material).

The major or most potent psychoactive ingredient in marijuana is THC. THC is present in marijuana in concentrations from 2–15%. The source of marijuana determines its THC concentration, depending upon the species, growth environment, part of the plant that is harvested, and where it comes from. Is higher-potency pot more "addictive"? The answer is probably not, as potency of a drug does not determine its dependence liability. However, the greater euphoria of higher-potency marijuana can lead to more marijuana use and abuse, as well as more side effects.

The most common route of administration of marijuana is smoking, although some is ingested orally in homemade foods (e.g., brownies) or in a pharmaceutical product known as dronabinol (Marinol). This drug contains synthetic delta-9-THC, and is used for the treatment of nausea and vomiting caused by cancer chemotherapy, as well as to increase appetite in the wasting syndrome of AIDS and anorexic patients. The smoking route is generally more effective therapeutically than the oral route. When smoked, THC enters the circulation almost immediately, reaching high blood levels in 5–10 minutes.

Marijuana produces a dreamy euphoria, which has qualities similar to that of alcohol or opioid intoxication. THC distributes throughout the body, with THC metabolites depositing in the fat stores of the body. The metabolites leave the stores slowly over a period of weeks, and they can be detected in urine samples to indicate that a person smoked marijuana many days ago. Heavy and long-term users can test positive for 30 days, without having used the drug during that period.

Although there is a severe shortage of good information about the sociological and long-term effects of marijuana, there is no shortage of information on where THC acts in the brain. A number of studies have isolated the "cannabinoid receptor" (CB), which appears to be distributed widely throughout the CNS (Pertwee, 2006). In general CB1 receptors are in the brain and CB2 receptors are outside the CNS. Thus marijuana has many pharmacological actions throughout the body, helping us to understand why marijuana seems to have multiple effects on the brain (euphoria, dependence, nausea/vomiting, pain relief), on the eyes (glaucoma), lungs and trachea (asthma), and even on the peripheral nervous system and spinal cord (multiple sclerosis; Pryce & Baker, 2005). The exact mechanisms by which marijuana produces these effects are still under investigation, but we know that activation of CB receptors is involved, and many CB receptor antagonists have been synthesized (Le Foll & Goldberg, 2005). Naturally occurring brain compounds, such as anandamide ("the brain's marijuana"), appear to stimulate the CB receptors. These compounds have been cloned in the laboratory and have become excellent pharmacological tools for studying the nature of the receptor and how it might eventually be blocked. "Endocannabinoid" research is giving the field newer medications (e.g., rimonabant) that block cannabinoid receptors. These may become helpful in treating dependencies on food and chemicals such as nicotine, alcohol, and cocaine.

What are the effects of marijuana on driving behavior? Although some studies (see Asbridge, Paulin, & Donato, 2005) have shown, as we might expect, that the intoxicating effects of marijuana negatively affect driving behavior (altered perception, altered judgment), this subject has been incompletely studied. One study (Wright, 2005) even suggested that marijuana can cause more careful driving. This is very characteristic of marijuana research. Opposing studies often cancel one another out, or there is a perception of research bias. Only an extraordinary emphasis on a large number of excellent studies on marijuana pharmacology and toxicology will help us out of this "marijuana facts vacuum."

Recent research on marijuana indicates an association between marijuana use and psychosis (Verdoux & Tournier, 2004). However, an unanswered question is whether the overuse of marijuana causes psychosis or whether the use of marijuana triggers psychosis in people who would have developed the disease later in life. A third possibility is that some people may have emerging or early symptoms of psychosis that are enhanced by marijuana use. A final possibility is that undiagnosed psychotic individuals might use marijuana to feel better, in much the same way that they use cigarettes.

There are reasons why until recently, relatively little research on marijuana (compared to the amount on cocaine, alcohol, and heroin) has been carried out. Marijuana is difficult to study, for several reasons. Marijuana joints on the street cannot easily be duplicated in the laboratory, because the content of the active ingredient (delta-9-tetrahydrocannabinol, THC) varies greatly in street products. Animals cannot easily be exposed to the smoke, and the native form of THC is not water-soluble; therefore, it is difficult to administer the compound to animals.

Finally, the effects of smoked marijuana on humans varies greatly from one person to another because of expectations of the user ("set") and the type of environment in which it is used ("setting").

Despite these difficulties, research is now underway to measure the true therapeutic potential of smoked marijuana for the relief of nausea and vomiting in cancer patients and the enhancement of appetite in people with severe weight loss. Other alleged medical uses are in the treatment of pain, asthma, glaucoma, multiple sclerosis, Alzheimer's, and parkinsonism, for which there is incomplete scientific evidence.

Whether marijuana smoke is as carcinogenic as tobacco smoke is also being further investigated (Melamede, 2005). Answers to all of these inquiries will help determine whether marijuana can be a medically useful drug in the future. Such studies might also affect how the public views marijuana with regard to the decriminalization and legalization debates.

At this time, however, marijuana remains the most contentious drug in society. Those who wish to legalize it point to its minor toxicity compared to the legal drugs alcohol and nicotine; those who want to ban it from all societal use highlight the criminal consequences of making it legal (such as its likely contribution to more deaths caused by driving under the influence). Probably there will be no solution that satisfies everyone. At some point, however, our society must resolve the enormous negative impact of legal drugs, whether they are prescribed and used for medical benefit or whether they are used primarily to enhance well-being. In either case, they have the potential to produce chemical dependence, and their users must someday be treated if they develop the disease.

Still, some people continue to believe that marijuana is "nonaddicting." The following case study suggests otherwise.

Case Study: Ted

Ted was a 23-year-old Caucasian male who had smoked marijuana for the past 8 years. At age 14, he began using tobacco and then was introduced to marijuana. He occasionally drank alcohol and used other sedative drugs, but his preference was "feeling mellow" from marijuana. He described that state as one of relaxation, calm, and "where nothing can bother me." He most enjoyed the drug when smoking with close friends, all of whom smoked marijuana regularly. He was aware that he became

> "a little anxious" when he did not smoke on a given day, and he kept a supply of the drug on hand.
>
> At age 23 Ted was arrested for driving under the influence after drinking 2 or 3 bottles of beer. He had a blood alcohol concentration of .04%. According to the arrest report he was weaving into the next lane, was visibly intoxicated, and smelled of marijuana. His urine test was positive for marijuana.
>
> Ted's history revealed a progression from periodic to weekly use over 5 years, with subsequent daily use. He believed that smoking helped him focus and do his job. He did not view his use as a problem despite his arrest, yet he acknowledged that he could not stop using and was concerned about how he would "cope" if forced to quit. He entered outpatient treatment per court order and was required to remain drug-free, with weekly random drug-testing. He remained in outpatient treatment for 3 months, had two episodes of positive marijuana test results, and twice tested positive for other drugs when marijuana was not in his system. The court ordered him into a more structured residential treatment program for 6 weeks. Upon discharge, he was seen in aftercare and referred to a 12-step support group. He relapsed a month later, using marijuana and alcohol, and was incarcerated and again referred for treatment.

This case illustrates the severity of marijuana dependence that can occur in some individuals. These people probably have a dysregulation of endocannabinoids or cannabis receptors in their mesolimbic DA system (Maldonado, Valverde & Berrenderro, 2006). Ted's prognosis may not be good, based upon the severity of his chemical dependence and lack of response to several types of treatment. Research on this subject indicates that marijuana is definitely dependence-producing (estimated at 8–9% of users; Anthony et al., 1994), and marijuana withdrawal does seem to occur (Vandrey, Budney, Kamon, & Stanger, 2005). The treatment options for cannabis are still under investigation (Hart, 2005).

Club Drugs

This group of six drugs—MDMA (ecstasy), LSD (acid), methamphetamine (meth), ketamine (special k, vitamin k), and GHB (gamma-hydroxybutyrate; liquid ecstacy), plus the newer drug rohypnol (roofies)— is collectively called "club drugs" because they are used in "rave" parties and clubs where loud music, synchronized lighting, and super-sensory environment is abundant. (This is the list given by the National Institute on Drug Abuse, 2006. Other lists may contain other drugs.) A rave (almost the same as a dance party) is a large get-together, mostly of young people. At raves, disc jockeys and synchronized light shows are featured, and drug use is condoned. The club drugs are used either alone or in combination with alcohol. Most raves are well-attended (generally 100–500 people), and are advertised on the Internet, in music stores (posters), and by word of mouth. Although illegal drugs are bought and used at raves, authorities are usually outnumbered at such places, so the number of arrests is relatively small.

Users of club drugs have said that the drugs enhance people's experiences when used in environments with a lot of people and sensory stimulation. In spite of common belief, all these drugs are dangerous and may trigger dependence (although research is lacking on the dependence potential of ecstasy, GHB, and ketamine). These drugs have effects on neurotransmitters in the brain, and most are dangerous when mixed with alcohol, which is also commonly seen at rave parties and other recreational use environments.

Street drugs are rarely solely what they are alleged to be. For example, what is sold as "acid" (LSD) is often phencyclidine (PCP) or ketamine. Also, MDMA is mixed with methamphetamine, dextromethorphan, and other drugs that may be the precipitant of many unexpected problems that are then alleged to be caused by MDMA. Remember that the source of many street drugs is not a controlled laboratory environment!

MDMA

MDMA (methylenedioxy-methamphetamine), also called *ecstasy* or just *e*, is chemically related to amphetamines but has different effects on brain chemistry. The main pharmacological action of amphetamines is to increase the release of DA (and some norepinephrine and serotonin) from brain cells, which produces increased euphoria and alertness. The action of amphetamines is mainly on the cerebral cortex of the brain. MDMA, on the other hand, causes nerve cells to release serotonin (and to a lesser extent, DA) into the synapse, thereby producing continual nerve stimulation. The main site of action of MDMA is probably the limbic system, where mood and emotions are regulated. It produces a dreamy euphoria, with an antifatigue effect, and users take it to enhance the sensation of music and excessive energy. Animal studies indicate that it can destroy serotonergic brain cells in high doses, but this has not been confirmed in humans.

Ecstasy can be very dangerous when used in high doses. The negative effects are typical of an overdose of drugs that increase serotonin in the brain. There is jitteriness and teeth clenching as the dose moves up, as well as reduced hunger, dry mouth, muscle cramping, and nausea. At high doses, ecstasy causes a large increase in body temperature in some people, which requires relocation to a cool environment. Elevated body temperature over a long period can lead to muscle breakdown, kidney failure, and death, which has been seen in cases where subjects use ecstasy in large groups.

Could MDMA reduce immune system function? Animal studies suggest that it might, but any anecdotal increase in infections in human ecstasy users is more likely related to other factors, such as the venues where ecstasy is used, general health and nutritional status of the user, and cleanliness of the manufacturing equipment. The amount of high-quality research on MDMA is low; therefore, scientists do not know much about the effects of this drug. More studies are needed to confirm any direct negative effect of the pure drug itself on immune system and other functions.

LSD (lysergic acid diethylamide)

LSD is one of the most potent drugs in existence. A characteristic of LSD is that it causes ego-fragmentation, which is a blurring of the psychological boundaries within the sense of self (ego) and the sense of what separates us from the external world. The amount required to produce ego-fragmentation and perceptual distortions of external stimuli that can lead to delusions and hallucinations is in the microgram range (compared to alcohol, which requires doses in the gram range to produce euphoria). LSD is nontoxic to organs in the body, and it is generally considered to have low dependence liability. It is used by "acid-heads" (an old term!) who want to have new experiences and insight. It allegedly allows a person to see everything differently while in a state of "high suggestibility."

The term hallucinogen is commonly used to describe drugs such as LSD, dimethyltryptamine (DMT), mescaline, and psilocybin. The name means "a drug that causes hallucinations," but this is not a completely accurate definition, because not all users have true hallucinations (meaning seeing, hearing, feeling, tasting, or touching something that does not actually exist in external form; not a misperception of reality). Clinical experience has shown that what is called a "hallucination" by pharmacologists is often really a misperception or perceptual distortion, such as when people misperceive their dog, for example, and say it is a giant cat or a lion. The users are experiencing an actual event, noticing a real material object, or engaging in a real conversation, but the drug distorts their perception of the event, thing, or conversation. Such distortions have also been called "illusionogenic" or "delusionogenic." Hence, some people prefer the term psychedelics (meaning mind-expanding or mind-manifesting). Psychedelics such as LSD are also effective in causing ego fragmentation, as well as in blurring reality, dreams, senses, and so on. A common effect of these drugs is synesthesias, or merging of senses, such as seeing music or hearing colors, which people often call "hallucinating." People that seem to actually hallucinate tend to be those with psychiatric illness, a fragile sense of self, or low ego strength.

Tolerance to LSD occurs very quickly but can disappear in about 1–2 weeks if no more drug use occurs. LSD's rapid tolerance is a type of tachyphylaxis, which means "quick adaptation," and it can actually occur during a single use of the drug. Each time a person takes a dose of LSD, subsequent doses during the same use period will have diminishing effects, so that the person has a tendency to increase doses to get a similar effect. Although there is no documented human lethal dose of LSD, the drug supposedly can trigger psychotic episodes and people often experience "bad trips" (scary hallucinations, frightening experiences and sensations). Such hallucinations could be caused by people becoming afraid due to the weird somatic sensations. A "bad trip" is not physiologically dangerous, and the person can usually be "talked through" the experience through suggestive statements while the drug is clearing the body. "Flashbacks," where some part of the drug effect is experienced months after the last use of the drug, is not due to the drug hiding in body tissues; rather, it is probably a sensation due to psychological retrieval from memory of a previous "trip." Flashbacks can be positive, neutral, or negative. In fact, people with relatively sound personality or a grounded sense of self usually report pleasant "flashbacks" as sensations, feelings, images, musical recall, and so on.

Because of the similarity in molecular structure between serotonin and LSD, and in light of few studies of LSD and neurochemical function, it has been assumed that LSD produces its hallucinatory effects through the serotonin system of the brain. It also makes sense that LSD can block some of the effects of the brain's alerting system, the reticular activating system (RAS). The RAS filters incoming sensory stimuli, so that the brain sensory processing systems do not become overloaded. Theoretically, LSD can block the serotonin function of the RAS so that the sensory filter breaks down and many more stimuli enter the brain, with the results being interpreted as "hallucinations." However, there is little scientific evidence for this theory. More research on the brain mechanisms of LSD is needed.

Methamphetamine

This drug was discussed in Chapter 5, and is formally listed by the National Institute on Drug Abuse as a club drug. Refer to Chapter 5 for information on this popular but dangerous drug.

Ketamine

This is a street drug derived from a legal anesthetic that has little use in human medicine. It is pharmacologically a "dissociative anesthetic" (causing a state in which the person feels out of touch with the environment, while appearing to be somewhat "awake"). Ketamine was formerly used in producing anesthesia in patients undergoing surgery, but now it is used mostly for animal surgery anesthesia. Side effects such as psychotic episodes and vivid nightmares (as with LSD, erroneously described as "hallucinations") have reduced the use of this drug in humans. Street users are known to steal the drug from veterinarians' offices or wholesale houses. Like its street companion phencyclidine

(PCP, angel dust), ketamine's dissociative medical properties include a feeling of anesthesia but distorted perception of the world around the user. Due to the dissociative effects, the drugs seem to reduce the ability to selectively attend to and "block out" external stimuli. One reason many PCP and ketamine users react in panic when taking high doses of the drug is that excess stimuli overload their psychological ability to process or block out information. Hence a low-light, low-noise, low-stimulation environment with appropriate low doses of medications (such as benzodiazepines) is often the best treatment. Some users will become catatonic or comatose or develop high blood pressure, situations requiring careful monitoring and appropriate treatment (Domino, 2003).

GHB

Ironically, the street name of this drug is "grievous bodily harm," but the chemical name is gamma-hydroxybutyrate. GHB is a metabolite of the inhibitory neurotransmitter GABA, and today there is some evidence that GHB may itself be a functioning neurotransmitter in the brain. GHB was used as a sleep inducer in the 1960s and 1970s in the U.S., but now it is paradoxically available by prescription (Xyrem) for treating the sleep disorder narcolepsy, in which the drug increases alertness. In the 1990s, body-builders used it to change the ratio of muscle to fat, but now this use is outlawed.

It is very potent and very toxic. Overdoses can occur easily, because the drug readily crosses the blood-brain barrier. Kuhn and colleagues (2003) have speculated that alcohol and other sedatives increase the effects of GHB. Side effects include increased dreaming, lack of coordination, nausea, respiratory distress, and sometimes seizures. GHB was formerly available in health food stores, but since it was taken off the shelves the only source appears to be the black market (either diverted prescriptions or unapproved laboratory sources). This chemical is not routinely analyzed in drug screens.

Rohypnol

This is a benzodiazepine that is legal in countries other than the U.S. Much of the North American rohypnol club and personal use arises from Mexican and South American sources, where the drug is legal.

"Roofies" is one of the street names for this drug, which allegedly was used extensively by roofers repairing homes after a hurricane in Florida. It probably has a mechanism of action similar to that of other benzodiazepines, affecting the GABA receptor to reduce anxiety, promote sleep, and cause sedation. It is because of these effects that the drug is so dangerous, especially when mixed with alcohol. Combinations of rohypnol and alcohol produce a comatose state and are the reason for the nickname "date rape drug." Such combinations pose great risk of lethal overdose. Any combination of benzodiazepines with alcohol is always a risky situation, for at least additive and sometimes synergistic effects may occur, depending on the doses of both drugs.

How long does the effect of this date rape drug last? Although the research is incomplete, indications are that the acute effects of rohypnol last about 4–6 hours. This is similar to the duration of action of Xanax, another benzodiazepine that has significant CNS antianxiety action. If used with alcohol, the effect can be prolonged two or more times, and amnesia is a common effect.

Inhalant Chemicals

Abused chemicals called "inhalants" are most often used by young people or desperate individuals who cannot afford or cannot obtain other drugs such as alcohol. "Huffing" (inhalant use) occurs when fumes or vapors are inhaled through the mouth to get a quick "high." Huffing is now being seen in fourth graders, and deaths from this practice occur in children as young as 10 years old. Inhalants head the list of the most commonly abused chemicals in 12- and 13-year-old children. "Huffable" chemicals include nitrites (e.g., amyl nitrite "poppers" that have the same basic effects as nitroglycerin used by angina patients), nitrous oxide and other gas anesthetics ("anesthesia outside of the operating room"), and solvents (a broad category of highly toxic chemicals found in gasoline, glues, paints, and sprays). They also include paint solvents, air fresheners, cooking sprays, freon coolants, and deodorants. These are legal, cheap, easily available, and difficult to detect when used. One method is to paint fingernails with correction fluid instead of nail polish and then "sniff." Other kids pour solvents on their shirtsleeves and discreetly "huff" without anyone knowing it.

One of the drug-use trends that occurred in the past was the use of typewriter correction fluid, which contains trichloroethane and trichloroethylene. Use of this product is known as "whiting out," and it still occurs today, although not as frequently. Inhalation of fumes of this product has been known to produce sudden death.

Serious solvent intoxication with these compounds is like that of alcohol, but with greatly increased risk for short-term organ toxicity. The risk of a lethal overdose with solvents is significant, with death occurring because the heart rhythm is disrupted. Other risks include reduced oxygen exchange, accidents, and suicide. A large number of first-time users die from the use of inhalants.

Steroids

Although steroids ("roids"; testosterone derivatives, precursors such as androstenedione, and others) used by athletes do not technically fulfill the criteria for "drugs of addiction," users of such chemicals develop a compulsive reliance on them. "Anabolic" steroids are the most often used because they build muscle and enhance performance. Even though the body produces its own steroids for other purposes, the use of synthetic steroids can have devastating effects on sex hormones, liver, and heart. The athlete who contemplates using such drugs must consider the side effect possibilities and the illegality of such drugs.

Interestingly, there is little attention paid to the "addictiveness" of steroids, in spite of the fact that recent animal studies indicate that animals will self-administer testosterone (Peters & Wood, 2004). Although steroids produce a sense of well-being, there is little evidence that they produce chemical dependence in a similar way as heroin, cocaine, or amphetamines (although research is lacking on this). But they are powerful agents that can be abused and are toxic in some people.

Prescription and Over-the-Counter Drugs

Prescription drugs are not particularly dangerous when used under the supervision of a physician. These medications are designed to be used without danger (except in the case of powerful anticancer and anti-AIDS medications, as well as a few others) by most people. However, a small number of people do not react "as expected" to some medicines, and these medications may also interact with other drugs (including alcohol). Some recent studies indicate that teenagers are misusing prescription medications such as opioids and stimulants, as well as over-the-counter products containing dextromethorphan, pseudoephedrine, and other ingredients. Prescription and over-the-counter drugs can be dangerous, and some have dependence potential when used illegally.

There is great concern around the country regarding the misuse, overuse, abuse, and chemical dependence produced by prescription drugs. The concern arises due to the fact that we know very little about why and how people with legal prescriptions come to share their prescription drugs with others or continue to coerce pharmacists and physicians into more refills when the apparent medical need is gone. One major problem is how to tell when an opioid is no longer needed by a pain patient. Often patients will continue to use medications for long periods of time, for fear of withdrawal or ongoing discomfort, when they could be undergoing more beneficial drug-free therapy, as with physical therapy, acupuncture, or meditation.

I believe that the concern about dependence potential with prescription medicines can be reduced by realizing that we are already aware of how to treat people with a diagnosis of chemical dependence on prescription drugs that include opioids, amphetamines, benzodiazepines, and barbiturates. These are the main prescription drug categories that are characterized by chemical dependence, and it is clear that people who are sick and taking these medications are not as likely to become dependent as people who are using these drugs recreationally. The issue becomes clearer when we understand that the following medications do not produce chemical dependence, even though they are falsely alleged to be "addicting": neuroleptics (used to treat mental illness such as schizophrenia), antidepressants (even though people do withdraw from such medications), membrane stabilizers and antiepileptics (such as Neurontin and Topamax), and lithium (for the treatment of bipolar illness). What is not so clear is why some people who are not chemically-dependent on prescription medications continue to feel that they need the medications long after the original medical condition has resolved according to available assessments. For example, it appears as if patients given medications for short-term insomnia will continue to use the medications (and even continue to talk their physicians into prescription refills) long after the cause of the insomnia has disappeared. It is almost as if they use the drugs as a "security blanket" because using the medications is easier than confronting the possibility of another bout of insomnia. Clinicians formerly talked about "habituation" to drugs, which is a perceived psychological need for medications that doesn't seem to fall easily into the abuse/dependence assessment criteria. Knowledge about the preceding concepts should be required in all health professions.

Chapter 8

Dependence Disease Treatment

PREVIOUS CHAPTERS HAVE PROVIDED the neurobiological and genetic evidence that chemical dependence is a brain disease. This brain disease is associated with the use of many different drugs, each of which has a unique pharmacology and association with the brain's reward pathway. Because of this evidence, treatment methods in the field are now being increasingly thought of as neurobiologically based. New medications are designed upon the neurobiological evidence. For example, neurochemical dysregulations in the mesolimbic reward pathway are being at least partially normalized by drugs that affect GABA/glutamate function (acamprosate), endorphin function (naltrexone, methadone, buprenorphine), dopamine function (bupropion), and other neurotransmitter system function. Even the effectiveness of 12-step programs such as A.A. can now be envisioned to involve brain chemistry alterations that will someday be measurable by brain scans that show functional changes (meaning that the chemistry is changing, as discussed in Chapter 10). To understand how this mesolimbic brain dysregulation can be overcome, it is important to look at the different types of treatments available for helping chemically dependent patients.

Philosophy of Treatment

In the 1960s and 70s there were relatively few options for treating people with alcoholism and other drug "addiction" (White, 1998). The traditional 12-step programs were firmly established, outpatient programs and quarter-way and halfway houses were up and running, and 28-day inpatient treatment programs were growing (many were expensive but had good reputations). Unfortunately, in those days if a person could not afford the cost of an inpatient program or didn't want to attend anonymous meetings, there was little else available. If a person was found to be in trouble with drugs on the street (intoxicated or behaving badly), there was always the local drunk tank in the police station or a hospital emergency room that could take the person in until he or she sobered up. During these decades, the abstinence movement took firm hold, with many people in recovery holding the steps firmly to their hearts and minds, and the public and policy makers formed the opinion that people with drug problems could "help themselves." This philosophy was so strong that it still exists today in the form of reduced opportunities for formal treatment, poor insurance coverage for treatment, and a public attitude that alcoholics and addicts "did it to themselves, so they can help themselves." Lost in the public consciousness were those people who couldn't make it in 12-step programs, did not respond to inpatient treatment, or who continued to drink or use drugs and usually died early because of drug-induced complications.

Outpatient treatment, where people could work during the day and take advantage of in-house programs at night and on the weekends, was available. Compared to inpatient treatment, outpatient treatment was less intense, of longer duration, and usually involved sliding-scale payment options. Variations of treatment included living in the treatment center and working during the day, halfway houses, and treatment in prison populations. Both inpatient and outpatient programs depend heavily on individual support, group meetings, individual counseling, and 12-step attendance. Inpatient treatment is usually more intensive, with additional attention to relaxation, meditation, proper diet, and group recreational activities. Whether inpatient or outpatient is "better" is not clear, but both have their advantages and disadvantages, and both have been characterized by unclear outcomes, based upon a lack of interest of many treatment centers in long-term evaluation, and inadequate knowledge of proper outcome methodology. In addition, the definition of "recovery," and which outcome to measure (length of abstinence, relapse frequency, quality of life, quality of sobriety, and so on) is still under discussion.

As most pharmacologists will tell you, the more medications that are available for treating a disease, the better. For example, there are many medications available to treat depression (SSRIs, tricyclics, new generation antidepressants, monamine oxidase inhibitors), anxiety and anxiety disorders (antidepressants, benzodiazepines, propranolol), and hypertension (ACE inhibitors, calcium channel blockers, diuretics), to name just a few. The reason "more is better" is because there is no magic bullet medication for any disease, and no single drug is effective for everyone. Thus it is best to have a choice of medications, so that different options can be tried until one is found that works best.

With regard to chemical dependence, we are much better off than we were in the 1970s. Thanks to major advancements in the neurobiology of chemical dependence, many new options have become available over the past 30 years. There is still a need for more options, primarily in the area of reducing drug craving and need. We are at the point in the medical history of chemical-dependence disease treatment that our options today help more people than in the past, but current treatments will be greatly supplemented and enhanced in the future. At the same time, clinicians must guard against the idea that medications will be the total answer and that psychotherapy and counseling will no longer be needed (or that the number of sessions required to treat this serious, complex, chronic illness can be reduced).

The list of treatment options in this chapter begins with traditional 12-step programs and ends with the newest medications to reduce craving. However, before discussing available treatments, it is important to understand how expectancy (anticipation of outcome) affects treatment effectiveness.

Placebo (Expectancy) Effects

What is a "placebo effect"? Almost every drug (especially those that affect brain function) or treatment has a placebo effect. This is an unexplained therapeutic (or countertherapeutic, "nocebo") effect that does not involve the drug's pharmacology or obvious intervention. If each person in large group is given a sugar pill for problems such as anxiety, depression, or pain relief, approximately 30% of those people will have a reduction in anxiety, depression, or pain. A similar expectancy occurs with nonpharmacological therapy. In most cases, the person prescribing the treatment, the person administering the treatment, and the supportive personnel and the environment contribute to the positive or negative outcome of the treatment. The reasons are not entirely clear, but one thought is that when people are given any medical attention, some will get better due to an "expectancy" of improvement and hope. Good research on new treatments, then, should include a "control" (inactive medication or treatment) to determine how many positive placebo responders are in the experiment. Conservative scientists believe that only treatments that are significantly better than placebo should be marketed or used. Such carefully studied treatments would be called "evidence-based." Less-rigorously controlled studies that do not meet such high standards are nevertheless considered "evidence-based" studies by some non-scientists.

One example of how expectancy can alter a person's response concerns cold remedies, which have few mood-altering effects. Ask anyone about whether the remedies work and the usual response will be that they reduce the duration of suffering from the "flu," suggesting some "curative" aspects of the remedies. But the ingredients of cold remedies are designed to reduce nasal secretions and body aches and provide vitamin support. Some people even believe that cold remedies can increase immune system function, but there is no scientific support for that claim. Thus, people buying cold remedies because they are desperate to feel better usually feel better and thus report that their cold disappeared faster. Essentially the remedy simply reduced their discomfort, in large part through a placebo effect.

Twelve-Step Programs

One of the most popular ways of helping people with alcohol and other drug dependencies is to get them involved in 12-step recovery programs (Moos & Moos, 2005). Experience has shown that many people get better (begin "recovery") by frequent meetings and "working the steps." This doesn't seem like a medical treatment unless we understand that medical detoxification is often necessary if a person is to be able to permanently abstain from the use of a favorite drug before working the steps.

Abstinence-based programs help many people, and 12-step programs such as A.A. have long-held traditions that are extremely powerful, not only for their impact on society but also for individuals who have gained sobriety through such programs. People who are "a friend of Bill W. and Dr. Bob" can be found all over the world, especially in the thousands of meetings that occur weekly in church rooms and hotel rooms on a regular basis. The fellowship of A.A. is particularly strong, with traditions that maintain sobriety along with philosophies that have saved lives and been copied in some form or another in anonymous meetings designed to help opioid-dependent people, compulsive gamblers, overeaters, smokers, and others with desperate problems. The Big Book of Alcoholics Anonymous is almost as popular as the Bible. (For detailed information on the history and traditions of 12-step programs, see White, 1998 and Kurtz, 1979.)

Although outcome numbers are sloppy and do not tell the whole story, the estimate of the number of "alcoholics" helped by A.A. programs is about 5% of the estimated number of "alcoholics" in the nation. (Recall that "alcoholics" include alcohol abusers and alcohol-dependent people who choose to attend meetings to become abstinent.) The 5% figure is computed from the estimated number of alcohol abusers and dependent people in the U.S. (18 million, but figures vary) and a snapshot of attendance at A.A. meetings indicating that at any one time, about 1.8 million people are attending meetings. Thus about 10% of the estimated number of total alcoholics attends meetings. Members estimate about 50% effectiveness (sobriety at the end of 3 years), thus giving a 5% overall effectiveness rate. (This is an anecdotal estimate as formal studies on attendance and outcomes have not been completed.) We can assume that the total number of "alcoholics" helped by A.A. would increase dramatically if more people were educated about the program. But about 80% of alcoholics deny the disease or are not aware they have a problem. (Such sloppy estimates indicate the critical need for more epidemiological studies and for much more research on all types of self-help groups and on why they are effective.) Furthermore, many people never seek help in A.A. because of differing beliefs in the value of spirituality, because of disbelief that "alcoholism" is a disease, and because of stigma and discrimination against "alcoholics," which cause people to hide the shame, fear, and guilt about their problems. Some people just don't want to be called an "alcoholic."

Neurobiological studies are critically needed to track the brain changes in individuals in 12-step recovery. Because chemical dependence (but not chemical abuse) is a brain disease and people get better in 12-step programs, neurobiologists speculate that these programs probably promote some biological change in the brain.

The following case study illustrates the importance of long-term 12-step involvement.

Case Study: Thomas

Thomas, 32, had been treated in a therapeutic community (TC) program in his early twenties due to a history of opioid dependence beginning at age 15. He had entered treatment when faced with a 15- to 20-year prison sentence, and he stayed in the TC program for 18 months. He had remained opioid-free since leaving the TC. However, Thomas's parole officer referred him to treatment after his alcohol use led to a DWI offense.

Tom's history revealed that he began using alcohol after release from the TC. He had rarely used alcohol prior to that time. He never attended N.A. as it was not part of the program. For several years, Tom's alcohol use did not cause problems and his priority was maintaining abstinence to opioids. However, over the last 5 years his alcohol use had slowly begun to increase in quantity. His inability to remain abstinent had also increased, leading to his drinking on the job and the DWI arrest. His history also revealed family problems with alcohol abuse by male relatives, as well as some immediate family history of opioid dependence.

After the DWI, Tom entered an abstinence-based residential treatment program, received supportive education about alcohol dependence, began attending A.A., and was encouraged to attend N.A. After a year, followup revealed that he had relapsed back to alcohol a few times and was trying to remain abstinent by attending A.A. He stated that he was not attending N.A., because his drug of choice appeared to be alcohol.

Thomas's case illustrates the problem with ineffective first "treatment" opportunities and subsequent change in drug-of-choice in chemically dependent individuals. Although some may point out that the TC stopped Thomas's opioid use, it is likely that the TC exposure did not sufficiently correct the endorphin dysregulation in his brain. Appropriate treatment should have given him tools to become abstinent from all drugs, including alcohol. The long-term outlook for Thomas is good if he continues to work the steps, as it appears that Thomas's chemical dependence (exemplified by compulsion to use alcohol, along with other indicators) does respond to abstinence-based programs.

Counseling (Interactional and Behavioral Therapy)

These diverse resources include individual counseling procedures such as cognitive behavioral therapy (CBT), motivational enhancement therapy (MET), and 12-step facilitation (TSF), which were compared in the NIAAA-funded Project MATCH (Fuller & Hiller-Sturmhofel, 1999); motivational interviewing (MI, Miller, 2005); and individual and group counseling as seen in treatment centers. Counseling (including psychoeducational and process/interactional groups, marital and family therapy, stress reduction, and nontraditional methods such as acupuncture) generally involves intensive education, reflection, and counselor guidance of people who are searching for answers about the causes and correction of uncomfortable thoughts, actions, and behaviors. (For more discussion, see Fuller and Hiller-Sturmhofel, 1999; McNeece and DiNitto, 2005.) An emerging model is brief solution-oriented therapy (although it need not be brief), which focuses on a specific issue or problem to be resolved and then shifts to addressing other problems one at a time. The resolution of one major problem often has a ripple effect, improving issues related to the person's chemical dependence. All of these different types of counseling play a major role in the hands of counselors who help people with drug problems.

What is not very clear from the literature is whether these therapies are more effective in helping alcohol and other drug abusers, as compared to alcohol- and drug-dependent individuals. There is still a significant lack of research concerning the target populations of alcohol and drug counselors, in relation to *DSM* criteria. There are some significant questions that need answering: Does counseling increase the chances of a dependent individual's becoming abstinent? Does counseling help alcohol and other drug abusers reduce or moderate their drinking in a way that leads to long-term changes? How can the variability among counselors in techniques and effectiveness be reduced? Can the contributions of counselors somehow be related to the medical domain so as to increase funding for treatment sessions? Can counselors utilize evidence-based treatment methods to convince insurance companies that what they do is valuable to patient outcomes?

A major problem is that diagnostic intake assessments are often poor or not used at all, so that many counseling and formal programs are treating a mixture of drug-abusing and dependent patients. Also, when proper assessments are carried out in formal treatment centers with medical staff, such personnel often don't understand counseling procedures and theory. Furthermore, psychotherapists may not always understand neuroscience and medicine. Because the *DSM-IV* is a medical/scientific evidence-based document, the differential diagnoses between willful abuse and "impaired control due to brain disease" dependence are often not understood by psychologically based counselors. Finally, there is almost no effective evaluation of treatment outcome in most counseling environments.

Exciting new brain-scan research suggests that brain function may change during successful counseling, providing a bridge between counseling theory and neuroscience mechanisms. Although not fully understood, it appears that "all behavior is physical." Psychological outcomes can be demystified when they are shown to relate to brain neurochemistry.

Individuals trained in psychological theory believe that psychological outcomes are based upon inner understanding, resolution of conflict, and retraining of thought to overcome negative influences. Generally there is little consideration given to underlying brain mechanisms of these processes. The emphasis of many counselors is on optimizing counseling outcomes, with brain chemistry changes underlying such outcomes being only an afterthought. Neurobiologists, on the other hand, are mainly interested in mechanisms of brain function at the cellular level, particularly with respect to neurotransmitters and how they work or how they are defective in brain disease. To them, psychological thoughts and theories are based on the physical processes that go on in the brain. They therefore see psychology as brain-based. Recent research in the area of "physiological psychology" and behavioral pharmacology is illustrating the neurotransmitter correlates of psychological concepts such as anticipation, reward, and drug-seeking. One example of how this is being done is a method called *microdialysis*, in which small probes are placed painlessly into specific brain areas (for example, the nucleus accumbens, where dopamine is released during pleasure) of rodents. Such studies are examining (for example) whether the nucleus accumbens' dopamine release is related to the consumption of ethanol (Doyon, York, Diaz, Samson, Czachowski, 2003). Other studies have examined the neurotoxic mechanisms of ecstasy (Jones, Duvauchelle, Ikegami, Olsen, Lau, et al., 2005). On a more complex level, the new technology of neuroimaging has allowed studies of the neural mechanisms of social cognition (Amodio & Frith, 2006) and the "theory of mind" (Saxe, 2006).

Some people believe that if we treat "addiction" through talk therapy (12-step meetings, group meetings, psychotherapy), "addiction" must be a behavioral problem. This is erroneous because the known neurobiological dysregulation, plus the availability of new medications, clearly stamp chemical dependence as a medical disease.

Misunderstood and Controversial Treatments

The treatments in this section are often misunderstood and controversial. This misunderstanding may be related to a lack of neurobiological or neuropharmacological explanations for the effectiveness of these treatments.

Methadone

There are many publications in neurobiological, clinical, and pharmacological journals on the value of methadone in getting people to stop using powerful opioids such as heroin. Perhaps even more importantly, there are successful anecdotal outcomes with this treatment.

Methadone programs are designed to primarily help prescription opioid-dependent patients or heroin users. Users attend clinics where they can take an oral opioid medication and begin to have stability in their lives. Studies funded by the National Institute on Drug Abuse indicate that methadone stabilizes the brain's reward pathway and reduces the craving for heroin (along with the beneficial effect of reducing virus transmission among dirty-needle sharers). In spite of the enormous agreement that methadone is useful, it is still a controversial treatment for three reasons:

- It is not usually an abstinence-based program of treatment.
- There is a misunderstanding that methadone "merely replaces one addicting drug with another."
- Some methadone treatment programs have been criticized for not being run strictly enough. Patients put pressure on personnel to be lenient about the rules concerning no use of other drugs (alcohol and cocaine use is a major problem in methadone users), and personnel readily allow increased doses of methadone and fail to require patients to be active in counseling, employment, and clinic attendance.

There are four characteristics of good methadone programs:

- They require patients to take the oral methadone tablet under observation in the clinic, so they don't steal it and try to sell it on the street for heroin.
- They have regular urine drug testing.
- They require patients to have a job in order to maintain stability and provide money to pay for the methadone.
- They require patients to undergo counseling to try to reconstruct their lives and remain free of illicit drug use, with the possibility that some will be able to cease methadone use in the future. (However, some clinic staff, especially those on methadone themselves, do not believe people can or should become methadone abstinent, and they do not encourage the idea that full abstinence can work for some.)

Experience shows that when some methadone patients routinely attend N.A., they find that some members who have come off methadone are abstinent and that living a life without methadone is possible. This relates to a fourth reason for the methadone controversy: A large number of methadone patients refuse to become abstinent or do not believe they can become abstinent, choosing instead to maintain themselves on the drug. For neurochemical reasons discussed in Chapter

3, it is easy to understand why chemically dependent people would not feel "normal" when not using a drug that affects the mesolimbic dopamine system dysregulation. Methadone clinics have very little leverage in requiring methadone patients to stop using drugs, and undue pressure may push the chemically dependent person out onto the street again.

Methadone use while attending N.A. runs contrary to the embedded beliefs of some individual N.A. groups. Probably too many local group members allege that the use of methadone, psychotropic drugs, and other approved psychoactive medications is contrary to 12-step philosophy—which is not true. The following case illustrates the value of methadone.

Case Study: Lewis

Lewis was a 26-year-old professional who had undergone surgery at age 23. He did not have any prior history of illicit drug use or even of taking opioids for therapeutic reasons. His drug was alcohol, which he drank in moderation once or twice a week. Because he was adopted, his family medical history was not well known. He had always had a low threshold for pain. During his postsurgical care in the hospital, he received Percodan, which was not effective for his pain. He then received Demerol for a few days, which was effective. He felt both pain relief and significant euphoria, stating "I found the missing link to myself." Upon discharge, Lewis was placed on a limited supply of hydrocodone and advised to use aspirin or acetaminophen as he tapered off the hydrocodone. The hydrocodone alleviated his pain, yet he craved the "sense of well-being" he felt when taking Demerol. He used all the hydrocodone earlier than prescribed and obtained a refill. He used up the new medications in less than 4 days. When he asked for more his physician denied a prescription. This prompted him to go to other doctors, complaining of "back pain," to obtain new prescriptions, which he used up rapidly. He felt miserable off opioids and began asking friends if they had "pain meds," and he continued to solicit drugs from doctors. Within months he began purchasing opioids in pill form on the street and began snorting heroin. He initially avoided injecting, because "only junkies would resort to that," yet shortly thereafter he was injecting heroin daily. If heroin wasn't available, he used whatever he could find—benzodiazepines, marijuana, or alcohol—to reduce his distress. He eventually ran out of money and friends, felt depressed, and considered suicide. Finally, he was seen at a methadone clinic, deemed opioid-dependent, and started on methadone.

Despite being on methadone for some weeks, Lewis continued having overwhelming urges to use heroin. He felt the methadone dose was not "enough." He was restless, thought constantly about using, and could not focus. His methadone dose was gradually increased over time until he reached 100 mg per day, at which point he felt comfortable all day, could focus on work, and no longer felt the need to use heroin. Over the next several months, he stabilized, regained 10 pounds, and tried to address his financial problems and reorganize his life.

As this case illustrates, Lewis was dependent on opioids, suggesting a dysregulation of endorphins in his mesolimbic dopamine system. Lewis was typical in that he "connected" to opioids very quickly (although not everyone using pain medications becomes dependent on them) and needed an opioid in his body to "feel normal."

Harm Reduction

Harm reduction, also known as *harm minimization*, is a strategy for reducing harm to the drug users and people close to them. Many people who have achieved abstinence from drugs through 12-step programs are against harm reduction, as the strategy is seen to be antithetical (and even a threat) to abstinence-based programs. But people helped by harm-reduction methods are often drug abusers who may not require abstinence for a better quality of life, or they are chemically dependent people for whom 12-step programs are not attractive or effective. Our profession should have long ago given up the ideas of "one treatment for all," and "abstinence or death," for such thinking creates further stigma and misunderstanding in the minds of the public and policy makers. Yet old ideas die hard and what worked for some people is erroneously assumed to work for all.

It is important to understand what harm reduction is and what it is not. Following are four different types of harm-reduction strategies:

- *Education of the public about the dangers of drunk driving.* This is a harm reduction strategy that is acceptable to everyone!

- *Methadone maintenance.* As discussed earlier, methadone maintenance is a harm-reduction strategy and medical treatment. The basic idea of opioid substitution therapy has been enhanced by the use of buprenorphine (discussed later in this chapter). Although some people in recovery agree with this strategy, others don't for philosophical or emotional reasons, or because of a lack of understanding about this treatment method.
- *Needle-exchange programs.* There is abundant scientific evidence that needle-exchange programs reduce viral disease transmission among needle-sharing users—without increasing the number of chemically dependent people. Such programs also increase opportunities to provide treatment to illicit drug users (Strathdee, Ricketts, Huettner, Cornelius, Bishai, et al., 2006). Providing clean needles to IV drug users living on the street is an intervention and educational opportunity in which providers take the time to talk to the users, tell them about the dangers of dirty needles and suggest that they seek treatment when they are ready.
- *Teaching "alcoholics" to drink socially or in moderation.* The scientific rationale and need for such programs is unclear, and studies on whether alcoholics can return to drinking in moderation are often plagued by an unclear differentiation between alcohol abusers (who may be able to drink socially) and alcohol dependent patients who have a pathological loss of control over drinking. Furthermore, it is antithetical that a person who has impaired control over drinking should be able to practice "controlled drinking." A more important question might be: Why would someone whose life has been ravaged by alcohol ever wish to try to drink again after recovery? This leads to a discussion of "moderation management."

Moderation Management

A national movement known as moderation management (M.M.) is intended to help "problem drinkers." Based upon drinking-reduction programs for drinkers who have problems of mild to moderate severity (Walitzer & Connors, 1999), this program presumably targets those who are not alcohol-dependent and still show consistent ability to control use, such as those who meet *DSM* criteria for alcohol abuse. The goal of M.M. meetings is to provide an opportunity for behavioral change among those who wish to reduce, but not quit, their drinking. Many problem drinkers do not want to attend A.A. meetings, perhaps because of the stigma of being labeled an "alcoholic." Thus, the more options that are available for drinkers, the more people can be helped.

Meetings of M.M. are not as numerous around the world as those of A.A. According to the M.M. website, about 30% of those who attend M.M. meetings go on to attend abstinence-based meetings. Thus, M.M. could be seen as a "triaging" situation, as presumably those who can't achieve moderation management are probably in need of an abstinence-only program. There are so far no studies on the long-term effectiveness of moderation management.

Faith-Based Treatment

For centuries churches and other faith communities have been concerned with the problem of drunkenness. For most of that time intoxication was viewed as a sin and "drunks" as morally wrong. However, in recent decades mainstream churches have begun to recognize that some "drunks" are in fact sick people in need of understanding and help. Many of the major faith communities have national recovery ministries providing prevention, intervention, and referral services. (There are more A.A. and related 12-step meetings held in church facilities than at any other location. Although A.A. is not a religious program, it is a spiritual program, and many people find that organized religion can be an aid to their spiritual growth.) Even with this involvement, however, many pious persons both in the pews and the pulpits have yet to understand the difference between willful alcohol and drug abuse, which is a moral problem, and pathological alcohol and drug dependence, which is a disease. Both conditions require intervention but of entirely different kinds (Erickson, 1995).

As a result of new "faith-based initiatives," funding has become available to religious organizations desiring to help those with alcohol and drug problems. This may be a mixed blessing. On one hand it can put in place many very approachable, affordable, client-centered treatment programs that fill the gap that has occurred as insurance coverage and funding for public programs has diminished. In addition, such groups can be very helpful after people are in stable recovery, seek spiritual growth, and want to give back to the community. On the other hand, a number of these programs lack the research-based knowledge, professionally trained staffs, and proven treatment models needed to achieve positive treatment outcomes. It can be hoped that the funding agencies will set standards and monitor the conduct of these faith-based programs. A valuable resource is *Core Competencies for Clergy and Other Pastoral Ministers In Addressing Alcohol and Drug Dependence and the Impact on Family Members*, available from the Substance Abuse and Mental Health Services Administration (www.samsha.gov).

Vouchers

A voucher program in which DSM-diagnosed chemically dependent patients receive coupons worth money for every week they are drug-free shows evidence that such patients will remain drug-free while receiving the coupons. They can then turn in the vouchers when they wish to receive rewards other than drugs (Budney & Higgins, 1998). Studies have found that the vouchers are effective in maintaining abstinence, suggesting that the "obsession" for monetary reward can be as strong as the "obsession" for cocaine, nicotine, and other drugs. Still to be determined is whether the vouchers work as well in chemical-dependence treatment centers or in the community ("the real world") as they do in experimental studies, and whether there will be resources to pay for the vouchers as a treatment option. In the meantime, this option is intriguing, as there are no medications involved and therefore no side effects.

Detoxification

This process is a medical method of helping chemically dependent patients become free of drugs prior to more extensive treatment that will empower them to remain free of compulsive drug-seeking and drug-using behavior.

Although the general public is not always aware that "alcoholics and addicts" are treated medically, such drug-using populations have, in fact been treated medically for many years. Beyond the so-called drunk tanks in jails and "let them sleep it off" wards in not-so-crowded hospitals, there were opportunities over 50 years ago for physicians to medically monitor alcoholics and addicts who were seen to be a danger to themselves and others. Usually these monitorings included medications to overcome hyperexcitable states (caused by amphetamines or cocaine intoxication and alcohol or sedative withdrawal) and maintenance of depressed respiration following large doses of CNS depressants (alcohol, barbiturates, heroin). Common remedies for detoxifying narcotic-dependent people were naltrexone (to overcome heroin-induced cessation of breathing), Valium (to overcome delirium tremens), and phenobarbital (to reduce "the shakes" caused by alcohol, meprobamate, short- and moderate-acting benzodiazepines, and benzodiazepine withdrawal). But as soon as patients were stabilized, they were either referred to a psychiatrist or family doctor or told "not to come back."

Today, the medical management of alcohol- and other drug-dependent patients is somewhat more advanced. Rarely is delirium tremens (DTs) seen in a clinic today. A benzodiazepine is routinely given to prevent the often fatal seizures and terrifying hallucinations of DTs. In addition, medical management includes supportive care (sometimes medications) during withdrawal so that individuals can detoxify safely and relatively comfortably in a hospital setting.

A special detoxification case involves heroin and other opioids (both chronic and illicit prescription medicines), where there are no documented cases of patients dying solely from acute withdrawal (although they often wish they had). Opioid withdrawal is uncomfortable but rarely lethal. The goal of detoxification in this case is not only to clear the drug from the patient's body but also to maintain a safe haven during the few days after withdrawal when craving for the opioid rises to a point where the person actively seeks the drug. It is during the post-withdrawal period that most patients are lost to treatment. Thus, we now have elegant strategies to withdraw people comfortably so that they can begin recovery. There are medications to reduce nausea, cramping, excessive sweating, heartbeat irregularities, and other uncomfortable withdrawal symptoms. Acupuncture is available to alleviate withdrawal not only from opioids but also from alcohol and other drugs. A newer method, ultrarapid detox, involves sedating or anesthetizing opioid-dependent patients so that they do not experience the withdrawal symptoms. This procedure, however, is expensive, unnecessary given the effectiveness of other withdrawal strategies, and in some cases has led to deaths due to unexpected responses to the anesthetics or the procedure itself. Thus, it is generally not recommended (Collins, Kleber, Whittington, & Heitler, 2005). Some companies that promote this procedure even claim a "cure" for opioid-dependent patients (beware of people promoting "cures" for chemical dependence).

Medications to Reduce Craving and Maintain Abstinence in Alcohol-Dependent Patients

What is the market for medications to treat alcoholism? One source (Anton, O'Malley, Ciranlo, Cisler, Couper, et al., 2006) says 8 million alcohol dependent individuals. Another source, the National Institute on Alcohol Abuse and Alcoholism (NIAAA) website, states that alcoholism ("alcohol dependence" is a more specific definition) has an estimated incidence of around 4% in the U.S., which is approximately 11 million people. Since the Food and Drug Administration is approving medications only for the treatment of alcohol-dependent patients (Litten, Fertig, Mattson, & Egli, 2005), the market is only as good as the level of accessibility, which will be low until physicians assess patients for this disease.

Following are several medications that are or will be helpful in treating alcohol dependence. All of them require individual and group counseling for the best outcome (Feeney, Connor, Young, Tucker, & McPherson, 2006).

Antabuse

Disulfiram (Antabuse) was the first medication used to treat "alcoholism," and it is among the most well known. Not so well known, however, is how disulfiram works. This drug, introduced over 50 years ago, does not work on the brain to affect the neurotransmitter dysregulations in alcohol dependence that were described in Chapter 3. Instead, disulfiram blocks the liver enzyme aldehyde dehydrogenase (ALDH). This enzyme metabolizes the major metabolite of ethanol, acetaldehyde. Alcohol is converted into acetaldehyde, a highly toxic chemical, through the enzyme alcohol dehydrogenase (ADH). Acetaldehyde is then quickly oxidized to acetate and water. However, if the enzyme ALDH is blocked, acetaldehyde accumulates in the blood, causing a "sickness"—flushing (vasodilation of the skin), rapid heart rate, nausea and vomiting, and faintness. (Calcium carbimide, a drug used in Europe, has a similar action and effect.) Deaths have been known to occur when a lot of alcohol is drunk or if the person overreacts to the acetaldehyde. This "acetaldehyde sickness" is used as a threat to people who take Antabuse, as they must not drink alcohol. Thus a "conditioning period" may be given (Antabuse plus a small amount of alcohol) to show a person what can happen if alcohol is consumed. It is clear that people who are abusers of alcohol respond better to the therapeutic effects of Antabuse, because the threat of getting sick is sufficient to keep them sober. However, alcohol-dependent people tend to either not take the medication or drink through the acetaldehyde reaction. Thus Antabuse has not been found to be as successful since other medications for treating alcoholics, as compliance is a problem. A recent German study, however, found that disulfiram or calcium carbimide was effective in producing an abstinence rate of greater than 50% in a 9-year study of alcoholics (Krampe, Stawicki, Wagner, Bartels, Aust, et al., 2006). The authors indicated that such results support the concept of comprehensive, long-term outpatient treatment of alcoholics and speculated that alcohol deterrents can be used as a "predominantly psychologically acting ingredient" of successful alcoholism therapy. The option to take Antabuse under supervision (or go to jail) has also been mandated for drunk drivers by some judges who believe that compliance will not be a problem when the medication is court-ordered.

Recently, Antabuse has been considered as a medication to treat cocaine dependence (Vocci & Ling, 2005). There is some evidence that disulfiram has some dopaminelike effects in cells, so the rationale for such clinical use is not totally unknown. The dopamine connection is seen in the recommendation that Antabuse should be contraindicated for anyone with schizophrenia, schizoaffective disorder, or any history of related illness. These illnesses are believed to be related to excess dopamine activity.

Anti-Craving, Anti-Relapse, Abstinence-Enhancing Medications

Table 8.1 lists medications that have been approved or are being studied for their effects in alcohol-dependent patients. These medications presumably affect specific neurotransmitters to block the effects of alcohol or somehow reduce the craving for the drug (Johnson et al., 2004). However, they are not "magic bullets" and will not reduce drinking on their own.

Table 8.1
Medications to Treat Alcohol Dependence

Generic Name	Trade Name	Neurotransmitter Affected
naltrexone	ReVia, Depade	endorphins (antagonist)
naltrexone long-acting	Vivitrol	endorphins (antagonist)
acamprosate	Campral	glutamate (antagonist?)
*topiramate	Topamax	glutamate/GABA
*ondansetron	Zofran	serotonin

*In clinical studies only, not yet approved by the U.S. Food and Drug Administration

Naltrexone

Naltrexone (ReVia, Vivitrol) is a full opioid antagonist (as compared to partial antagonists) and was the first medication approved to treat alcohol dependence after Antabuse. It was previously used to treat opioid dependence by preventing the euphoric or rewarding effects of opioids in patients. As such, it was not very successful because compliance to the medication was poor. However, earlier studies indicated that alcohol could affect endorphin function in the brains of animals, and that endorphin function was abnormal in human alcohol drinkers at risk for alcoholism (Gianolakis, Krishnan, & Thavundayil, 1996). When several studies indicated that naltrexone could reduce risk of relapse in patients undergoing counseling for alcohol dependence, the Food and Drug Administration approved it for use in patients. Since that time it has been used somewhat in such patients, but it has been used more in the criminal justice system to reduce the use of alcohol in multiple-DWI offenders sent to treatment.

Naltrexone presumably reduces the euphoric effects of alcohol in some patients by blocking the "endorphin" rush caused by alcohol. This might explain why it doesn't work in every patient (it appears to be only about 50% effective), since not all patients have an endorphin rush. It also is now well established as a beneficial medication in patients (O'Malley, Rounsaville, Farren, Namkoong, Wu, et al., 2003), with few side effects and the ability to be given with other medications such as acamprosate and antidepressants. Physicians need to know more about this medication, as most do not know when to write prescriptions for it, which is probably the reason it is underutilized (Kranzler, Koob, Gastfriend, Swift, & Willenbring, 2006).

A new sustained-release form of naltrexone (Vivitrol) provides drug action for 30 days. The intent of the product is to overcome the lack of compliance among patients. Early studies have shown efficacy and few side effects (Garbutt, Kranzler, O'Malley, Gastfriend, Pettinati, et al., 2005).

Acamprosate

This drug, calcium acetyl homotaurine, was first shown to be effective in Europe and is now approved by the U.S. Food and Drug Administration for the treatment of alcohol dependence. The mechanism of action is thought to involve the restoration of a normal NMDA receptor tone in glutamate systems (Kiefer & Mann, 2005). It decreases nerve transmission in the neocortex and reduces alcohol intake in alcohol-preferring rats. Several clinical studies have shown consistently that acamprosate treatment is superior to placebo in maintaining abstinence. In all but a few controlled clinical studies, the proportion of treated patients abstaining at the end of the study was twice as high as placebo-receiving patients. Treatment durations of up to a year have been studied. A literature-based meta-analysis (large statistical analysis of many studies), in which the original clinical trial data from 17 trials were reanalyzed, concluded that acamprosate is effective and suggested that the treatment effect could increase with prolonged use of the medication (Mann, Lehert, & Morgan, 2004).

The effects of naltrexone and acamprosate seem to relate to different aspects of recovery from alcohol dependence. Naltrexone is more effective in maintaining abstinence, whereas acamprosate seems better able to decrease alcohol drinking. However, there are only a few direct comparative studies on the two treatments (Kiefer & Wiedemann, 2004). More evidence has recently become known about their effects because of a large multicenter project sponsored by the U.S. NIAAA, called Project COMBINE (Anton, O'Malley, Ciraulo, Cisler, Couper, et al., 2006). This project is continuing to look at combinations of medications as well as combinations of medications with psychotherapy to determine the most effective means to reduce alcohol dependence.

Treatment of Heroin Dependence

There are two medications available to treat opioid dependence: methadone and buprenorphine.

Methadone

Methadone, an agonist (activator) of the opioid receptors in the brain, was discussed earlier. It reduces craving for heroin and other opioids and allows people to be placed in a safer environment for treatment. It appears that providing methadone treatment in a primary-care setting works. Heroin-dependent patients who are stable on methadone have healthy outcomes, according to a recent study (Schwartz, Jaffe, Highfield, Callaman, O'grady, 2006). Clinicians say that primary-care facilities can get successful results in helping patients recover from heroin dependence, while providing treatment for other health problems and improving physician attitudes about "addiction."

Buprenorphine

Buprenorphine has long been available for pain relief under the trade name Buprenex. It is now approved by the U.S. Food and Drug Administration for the treatment of opioid dependence under the trade names Subutex and Suboxone. Subutex is the single-entity medication and Suboxone is buprenorphine mixed with naloxone. Buprenorphine is a partial agonist (activator) of the opioid receptor, which means it does not have total agonist activity like methadone. In other words, its effects plateau as the dose is increased. This is important in opioid treatment, because the craving for an opioid like heroin can become so powerful that dependent patients often "slip" (where the urge to use again becomes so great that they have to take the drug) during treatment and try to increase their dose of an agonist to feel better. The partial agonist characteristics of buprenorphine make this less likely to happen. To prevent street abuse of buprenorphine, Suboxone has been formulated with naloxone to block the effects of buprenorphine when the drug is abused by injection. The naloxone blocks the effects of the drug at the opioid receptor.

Buprenorphine is a schedule 3 medication according to the Drug Enforcement Administration, compared to methadone's schedule 2 classification. This indicates that buprenorphine has less "abuse potential." Buprenorphine has the advantage that dependent patients cannot increase the dose to get high during moments of intense craving for heroin. Some methadone advocates have indicated that this is a weakness of the newly approved drug, as the ability to get reinforcement from methadone is one of the motivators for people to stay on methadone. The answer is simple: One drug is best for some patients and the other is best for other patients, just like there is no one drug that works for all people with depression, anxiety disorder, or schizophrenia. Many U.S. treatment facilities and primary-care physicians are already adopting buprenorphine. In many cases it is used for detoxification of patients during treatment (Koch, Arfken, & Schuster 2006).

Treatment of Nicotine Dependence

There are four general types of treatments available for treating dependence on nicotine (Rigotti, 2002). Novel treatments for the future are also under consideration (Lerman, Patterson, & Berrettini, 2005).

Bupropion (Zyban)

This antidepressant also has a trade name of Wellbutrin for the treatment of clinical depression. Bupropion primarily reduces the severity of nicotine withdrawal and the depression accompanying smoking cessation. Some sources indicate that it may reduce craving for nicotine (Mooney & Sofuoglu, 2006). It is probably less than 50% effective for this indication; nevertheless it is one of the few medications available to aid a person who wants to stop smoking. Combined with a nicotine patch or gum, it can be more effective. Unlike the patch or gum, it should be given about a week before a person's "quit date" so that sufficient blood levels can be reached. Some people, perhaps those who have unsuccessfully tried to stop smoking through other means, find bupropion to be a "miracle drug" in that they totally lose the craving for nicotine. Such reports are anecdotal, however, and it is not possible to predict who will respond positively to the medication.

Nicotine Replacement Therapy: Patches, Gum, and Low-Nicotine Devices

Nicotine replacement therapies (NRTs) are designed to replace nicotine in cigarettes and therefore should be used in a dose-reduction manner when treating someone who wishes to become nicotine-free. Many people are beginning to recognize the harmful effects of smoking and wish to stop. Some people find it easy to stop and do so "cold-turkey." (These are probably nicotine users and abusers.) Other people, however, find the "habit" of smoking more difficult to break and require some help in the form of nicotine replacements and counseling. (These are probably nicotine abusers who have perhaps a more severe form of abuse than those who can stop cold turkey.) Still others have a very difficult time stopping, even with nicotine replacement and will power. (These are probably nicotine-dependent people.) A few have a very, very difficult time stopping, even with nicotine replacement, bupropion, and counseling. (These people are probably "very" nicotine-dependent and require extra conscious effort, counseling, and many attempts to stop.) Finally, there are those whose nicotine use will cause an early death, as there is no existing method to help them. (These are the people who begin smoking soon after coronary bypass surgery, or who continue to smoke in spite of emphysema, lung cancer, and heart disease. They are severely nicotine-dependent.) Some experts believe that the morbidity and mortality from tobacco is as high or higher than with alcohol dependence. Thus smoking during recovery from alcohol and other drugs is a significant problem for abstinence and recovery. ("I'll take care of my smoking problem later." "One addiction at a time!") Many people in recovery from alcohol die of a tobacco-related illness long after stopping the use of all other drugs.

Some people choose to stop smoking but maintain themselves on nicotine patches or gum for years. When asked why they do this, they respond that they are proud to have reduced the chances of lung cancer and heart disease because they are now avoiding the tars and carbon monoxide of cigarettes. But they "need" nicotine to feel better each day. Such people are nicotine-dependent but argue that "one patch a day" is safer than "two packs a day." The long-term effects of this prolonged exposure to nicotine are not known. Given the profound cardiovascular toxicity of nicotine, I believe that many of these "nicotine maintenance" patients will die of stroke or a form of heart disease.

The Newest Anti-Smoking Therapies

NRT and Zyban were the earliest smoking cessation remedies, and it was several years before newer medications became available. Now, two new medications, varenicline and rimonabant are available. Varenicline (Chantix) is pharmacologically known as an alpha4beta2 nicotinic receptor partial agonist, which means that it activates the brain's nicotinic receptors in a manner similar to nicotine, but with less affinity (effect). Its therapeutic usefulness comes from the idea that by activating the same receptor as nicotine, varenicline will reduce nicotine craving and withdrawal. Indeed, one of three randomized studies on varenicline in the July 2006 issue of the *Journal of the American Medical Association* (Jorenby, Hays, Rigotti, Azoulay, Watsky, et al., 2006) reported that varenicline is more effective than bupropion or placebo for smoking cessation. Side effects of this drug are described as being minimal; nausea is most commonly reported. One-year outcome studies indicate smoking cessation in about 50% of patients given the drug. There are still unanswered questions about drug interactions, long-term side effects, and possible dependence production, which may require widespread use in the general population to be answered.

Rimonabant (Acomplia) is the only medication of the new endocannabinoid class of drugs that is in clinical study in the U.S. This drug is a cannabinoid receptor antagonist (receptor blocker), and has been used in the United Kingdom for treating obesity and smoking. As this is written, the U.S. Food and Drug Administration has granted a letter of approval for rimonabant for the treatment of obesity, but has not yet approved it for smoking cessation. Estimates are that it might be approved for this use in 2007. This could turn out to be an extremely beneficial medication, since so many people gain weight when they stop smoking. Rimonabant could actually help people maintain body weight when they stop smoking, but only larger studies and use by the general public will provide the final answers.

Smoking is such a dangerous pastime that more tools for recovery from nicotine dependence are urgently needed. Anyone concerned about side effects of the medications mentioned above should remember the medical rule of risk-to-benefit. In other words, the significant benefit of smoking cessation greatly outweighs the possible side effects of anti-smoking medications, including the four mentioned above. Another treatment rule is that such medications should always be accompanied by supportive counseling to help the person in their search for a healthier lifestyle.

Gaps in Medication Treatment of Drug Dependence

Currently there are no medications available to treat individuals who are dependent on amphetamines including methamphetamine, dextroamphetamine, and methylphenidate (Ritalin); benzodiazepines including alprazolam (Xanax), diazepam (Valium), and chlordiazepoxide (Librium); dissociative anesthetics including phencyclidine (PCP) and ketamine; or marijuana, LSD, cocaine, or ecstasy. Treatment of patients with these drug problems relies on supportive care, counseling, and 12-step programs.

New Developments

New medications in clinical study for the treatment of *alcohol dependence* include:

- Nalmefene, which works on the endorphin system, much like naltrexone
- Baclofen, an antianxiety agent that works on the GABA system
- Rimonabant (Acomplia), which works on the endocannabinoid system
- Ondansetron (Zofran), an antiemetic, antinauseant that has been found to reduce drinking in dependent patients; presumably works on the serotonin system
- Topiramate (Topamax), an antiseizure medication that reduces drinking in dependent patients, possibly by acting on the GABA/glutamate transmitters

New medications in clinical study for the treatment of cocaine dependence include:

- Disulfiram (Antabuse)
- Gabapentin (Neurontin), a mood stabilizer and anticonvulsant that works on the GABA system
- Modafinil (Provigil), an antinarcolepsy medication that works on the glutamate system
- Topiramate (Topamax), a medication to treat seizures and migraine headaches that has also been found to reduce alcohol drinking in dependent patients (Johnson, 2005)

There are also some novel approaches under study for the treatment of cocaine dependence (Sofuoglu & Kosten, 2005), including GABA medications, vasodilators, and immunotherapies. These are necessary because of the tremendous treatment problem presented by cocaine dependence, which has proved resistant to most of the medications that have been tried.

These and other new medications currently in clinical trial offer hope to people who are dependent on drugs. Their anticraving and antirelapse effectiveness as well as side effects and contraindications await further discovery. In addition, new research on combinations of medications and counseling (for example, naltrexone and cognitive behavioral therapy) will provide even better ways to help dependent people than are available today. Future research on genetics should provide genetically derived medications that will be even more specific to brain proteins involved in chemical dependence and have fewer side effects (Edenberg & Kranzler, 2005). Even then, however, it appears that counseling will always be necessary to reduce the cognitive, behavioral, and emotional effects of drug abuse.

Vaccines

Vaccines are being developed for the treatment of nicotine, cocaine, methamphetamine, phencyclidine, and other chemical dependencies (Pentel & Malin, 2002). Vaccination was first mentioned as a strategy for treating chemical dependence more than 25 years ago (Bonese, Wainer, Fitch, Rothberg, & Schuster, 1974). In chemical-dependence research, vaccines are produced with antibodies that bind the drug in question and change its pharmacokinetics to produce a therapeutic tool. The major intent of a drug vaccine is to reduce the extent or rate of drug distribution to the brain (Nutt & Lingford-Hughes, 2004). This mechanism is more similar to a medication than to vaccination against an infectious disease.

Pain and "Addiction"

The unique therapeutic problem of pain and "addiction" to medications used to treat pain has gained much attention in the last decade. Domestic and international surveys have estimated that the prevalence of chronic pain in adults is as high as 40% (Verhaak, Kerssens, Dekker, Sorbi, & Bensing, 1998). This has led to a need for pain therapies, many of which involve powerful opioid analgesics.

This topic actually covers two areas of major clinical importance. First, when people use opioids for chronic pain, the logical questions in the field of drug abuse are: "How many of the people using therapeutic painkillers will become addicted?"; "How can we tell when someone is addicted?"; "How do we prevent it?"; and "How do we help them when they become addicted?" The easy answers, based upon the latest research, are: "Not as many become addicted as most people expect"; "It is not easy to tell who is addicted"; "For those who have what it takes to become addicted, there is not much to be done"; and "We can help them more easily than we thought." The second conceptual area concerns how to treat chemically dependent patients who are in pain. This is a much more problematic area and the interested reader is referred to excellent reviews by Compton and Athanasos (2003), Savage and colleagues (2003), and Portenoy and colleagues (2005).

The best place to start in approaching the second difficult therapeutic situation is by looking again at the differences between conscious abuse of drugs and pathological drug dependence (as described in Chapter 1). Assuming that physicians are giving people opioids for chronic pain of an organic cause (injury, disease, surgery, etc.), most people will respond to the therapy as expected. Some will have a "natural tolerance" and will require doses somewhat higher than normal. As the chronicity of the pain is identified, some increase in dosage will be necessary as the individual uses the medication and tolerance occurs. A major characteristic of opioids is that they produce high levels of tolerance. For example, a usual dose of heroin to produce analgesia and euphoria is in the milligram range. Yet anecdotal reports are that some street users are injecting grams of heroin to produce a "high." Thus chemically dependent patients who are in pain will require pain management that allows dose-to-effect strategies. Concern about return to active drug use in a recovering patient is best handled by a physician who is trained in addiction medicine.

It is important to recognize that methadone patients feel acute pain and may need full narcotic analgesia when undergoing surgery, postsurgical care, or after they have been injured or in a traumatic accident. Too often physicians presume that methadone patients will not feel pain and therefore do not medicate properly, assuming the patient is simply trying to get medicated to feel high. Methadone patients develop tolerance to the respiratory depressant effects of opioids, but that does not correlate with not feeling pain.

People who are in recovery from alcoholism often state that they want no pain medications. On the other hand, when confronted with severe pain, they readily allow pain medications to be used. Most do not return to alcohol use, nor do they become dependent on the pain medications.

Co-occurring Drug Use and Mental Disorders

The neuroscience research described in Chapter 3 has shown that dysregulations of the mesolimbic system (probably at the level of receptor function) involve at least seven neurotransmitters: dopamine, serotonin, acetylcholine, endorphins, glutamate, GABA, and endo-cannabinoids. These same neurotransmitters have been implicated in several neurological and psychiatric illnesses (mostly axis I, major mental disorders), but of course involve brain areas other than the mesolimbic dopamine system:

- Chronic pain: reduced endorphin function (spinal areas, thalamus, sensory cortex)
- Parkinsonism: reduced dopamine function (basal ganglia)
- Schizophrenia: increased dopamine function (several brain areas)
- Clinical depression: reduced serotonin function (limbic system)
- Anxiety and panic disorders: reduced GABA function, reduced serotonin function (limbic system)
- Attention deficit hyperactivity disorder (ADHD): reduced dopamine function (prefrontal cortex)
- Obsessive compulsive disorder: reduced serotonin function (mesolimbic system and related areas)
- Posttraumatic stress disorder (PTSD): reduced serotonin function (several brain areas)

It is clear that an imbalance of neurochemical systems in several brain areas is associated with co-occurring disorders. Co-occurring disorders, also called *dual disorders* or *concomitant disorders*, appear when two or more illnesses occur at the same time, with no solid cause-and-effect relationship. Some of the most common associations are PTSD and drug use (Breslau, David, & Schultz, 2003), alcohol dependence and depression, schizophrenia and nicotine use, cocaine use and anxiety, alcohol use and ADHD, opioid use and chronic pain, and Parkinsonism and depression.

A related subgroup includes individuals with axis II disorders (personality disorders). Although there is little evidence that personality traits and temperament are related to major dysregulation in the brain, many psychological characteristics have both biological and genetic bases (Vanyukov, Moss, Kaplan, Kirillova, & Tarter, 2000), and innate psychological traits are enhanced or diminished by environmental influences. Personality traits are ingrained, largely unconscious, psychological characteristics for viewing the self, viewing others, and understanding or interacting with the world. For some people, personality traits are rigid and extreme to the point of significantly impairing their functioning. Such individuals meet the criteria for an axis II personality disorder. Drug-use disorders (both abuse and chemical dependence) are especially common for people with borderline, narcissistic, and antisocial personality disorders. Although the presence of these disorders in relation to drug abuse and dependence has been recognized among researchers (Rounsaville, Kranzler, Ball, Tennen, Poling, et al., 1998), many practitioners are now beginning to call attention to the many chemically dependent patients who struggle with these so-called lesser co-occurring disorders.

People with certain personality disorders engage in impulsive, risky behavior and illegal or excess drug use, have frequent crises, exploit others, and are most often noncompliant with treatment. Once in treatment for their drug abuse or chemical dependence, these people readily abandon program services and are at great risk of relapse. It is also quite common for patients with a drug-use disorder to have both a major mental disorder such as depression or schizophrenia and a personality disorder—making for a difficult treatment experience. Unfortunately only people with co-occurring major mental health and drug-use disorders are considered high priority for treatment, whereas drug-dependent people with personality disorders are not considered a priority within the mental health system or eligible for third-party reimbursement.

Co-occurring drug-use disorders (DUDs) with other psychiatric disorders (OPDs) are very prevalent and associated with worse clinical and functional outcomes than either DUDs or OPDs alone (Busch, Weiss, & Najavits, 2005; Ritsher, Mckellar, Finney, Otlingam, & Moos, 2002). Many patients with these co-occurring disorders do not receive adequate treatment. Prevalence rates of co-occurring DUDs and OPDs vary depending upon the drugs and psychiatric disorders involved; for example, the National Comorbidity Survey (Kessler, Nelson, McGonagle, Edlund, Frank, et al., 1996) estimated that over 33% of patients with bipolar disorder would experience a DUD within the next 12 months, in comparison to almost 20% of those with major depression and 15% of those with anxiety disorder.

Case Study: Sam

Sam was a 37-year-old Vietnam combat veteran who had recently had a second DWI offense. The prospect of losing his driving license motivated him to reduce his alcohol use, as he needed to drive for his job. Sam completed a psychosocial history and drug-use evaluation. During his evaluation, it became apparent that his alcohol use and tolerance had grown increasingly since he began drinking at age 17. His history revealed a strong family background of alcohol problems by his father and paternal grandfather. His maternal family history was unclear. He described that he was consistently unable to maintain his alcohol use at a social drinking limit (two to three standard drinks per day). He was given the opportunity to control his use for 30 days and was allowed to drink daily, but could not exceed three standard drinks per day. He consciously tried to limit his alcohol use to the agreed-upon limit but exceeded his limit by several drinks, and he drank more than he intended many times during the 30-day period. He was allowed a second chance for another 30 days but again experienced problems limiting his use. In addition, his wife reported that when Sam was drinking he sometimes relived his Vietnam combat episodes, becoming terrified, hypervigilant, and imagining that Viet Cong soldiers were shooting at him. He often had terrible nightmares as well.

Sam was given a diagnosis of alcohol dependence and posttraumatic stress disorder. He agreed to enter an abstinence-based therapy group that met twice a week. After a medical evaluation he was placed on supervised use of disulfiram (Antabuse) at three times per week, and he began attending A.A. meetings one to two times per week. He was also referred for treatment of his traumatic experiences. After 6 months of complete abstinence from alcohol and other psychoactive drugs, his flashback episodes diminished, and he felt less troubled by his nightmares. Overall, he reported feeling much better, less tense, and less depressed. His wife reported that he was clearly more relaxed and much easier to live with.

Sam's case illustrates a clear co-occurring alcohol dependence and PTSD. It is difficult to tell how much his drug abstinence contributed to his well-being, compared to his therapy for PTSD. However, the treatments appeared to work, making Sam's prognosis excellent. Sam appeared to have a moderate form of alcohol dependence. We can assume his neurochemical dysregulation involved problems with the serotonin function of the mesolimbic system.

Case Study: Kathy

Kathy was 15 and had been in therapeutic foster care for the past year. She had used alcohol since age 10 and revealed a number of symptoms, including significant tolerance for alcohol, many episodes of intoxication, compulsive alcohol use, a return to use, and using in excess whenever the opportunity arose. She had also had numerous altercations with legal authorities when drinking. Her history revealed a history of rule deceitfulness, aggressive behavior, violations related to school attendance and curfew, promiscuity, and other risky behaviors. She would use any drugs that were available, especially sedatives. She revealed a chaotic family history of drug use, especially alcohol, by both parents as well as other relatives. Because of her young age, a diagnosis of alcohol dependence was deferred and a diagnosis of alcohol abuse and mixed drug abuse was given, along with a diagnosis of conduct disorder, adolescent onset.

This case is an illustration of multiple neurotransmitter dysregulations related to several co-occurring disorders. Kathy might respond to targeted individual therapy along with sessions of group therapy with peers. It would also be important to educate Kathy about the dangers of drug use and to provide role models that could help her live drug-free while learning new coping skills. Because she was still developing physically, emotionally, socially, and psychologically, Kathy's use of alcohol and other drugs at a young age probably enhanced her vulnerability to developing drug-use and mental health disorders, particularly axis II personality disorder. An antidepressant medication, properly prescribed by an addiction medicine specialist, might reduce her conduct disorder. Her prognosis would be fair, especially if she found good role models.

Chemical dependence and mental disorders are distinct from one another, and when simultaneously present in a patient, they influence and compound each other. Thus, these disorders cannot be readily separated, and integrated treatment may be the best approach.

A complete discussion of the treatment of co-occurring DUDs with OPD could consume an entire book in itself. Many chemically dependent patients have co-occurring OPDs, which makes their treatment for DUDs even more difficult. On the other hand, many users of drugs are self-medicating to reduce symptoms of OPDs or other discomforts, so when the drug use is treated, the OPDs or discomforts become the primary health concern of the individual. An excellent review of this topic has been provided by Busch and colleagues (2005).

The Promise of Chronic Care

Chronic care is an emerging and long overdue concept for chemical-dependence treatment. Also known as sustained recovery management (RM; White, 2005), this is a revolution within the areas of treatment and recovery support. RM has been discussed as a concept for several years (McLellan, Weinstein, Shen, Kendig, & Levine, 2005a; M. Flaherty, personal communication) and is beginning to become more fully developed, including "concurrent recovery monitoring," which is a way of evaluating recovery progress and making decisions about continuing care (McLellan, McKay, Forman, Cacciola, & Kempt, 2005b). RM is based upon our understanding, through genetic and neurobiological research, of chemical dependence as a chronic brain disease, as described in Chapter 1. It is logical that individuals with a brain disease (similar in basic nature to depression, panic disorder, epilepsy, and many others) should have lifelong monitoring (coupled with treatment as needed) once they have been diagnosed with the disease. Unlike long-term treatment for hypertension, for example, the more complex disease of chemical dependence will require (according to the model) posttreatment monitoring and support; long-term, stage-appropriate recovery education; peer-based recovery coaching; assertive linkage to communities of recovery; and, when needed, early reintervention (White, 2005). (Indeed, perhaps some forms of cancer could use the same recovery strategy.)

Of utmost importance is a question concerning whether our treatment infrastructure could handle a chronic-care model. Although most outpatient programs are longer than inpatient 30-day programs, there is a trend toward inpatient programs becoming longer-treatment models, many with at least telephone follow-up for many months. But many believe the model should be a medical recovery model (McLellan & Meyers, 2004), which when put into context with chronic care of other diseases means that the best outcome will be lifetime monitoring with care-on-demand. According to the N-SSATS Survey (Substance Abuse and Mental Health Services Administration, Office of Applied Studies, 2002) most of the over 13,000 separate treatment facilities in the United States do not employ medical personnel (perhaps in an effort to cut costs). Certainly insurance coverage for long-term treatment will have to be available, and just as with other diseases, intensive early treatment using the best we have to offer (including medications when indicated) will provide the most beneficial outcome in terms of reduced socioeconomic costs to the nation, reduced crime, happier families, and reduced mortality. Is it worth the investment? We need only look at the annual estimated cost to society of alcohol and other drug problems—$484 billion (Hanson & Li, 2003).

Chapter 9

The Power and Limitations of Addiction Research

PREVIOUS CHAPTERS HAVE PROVIDED the scientific basis for understanding the pharmacology of drugs, chemical dependence, and its treatment. But how do treatment professionals know with any confidence that this research story is sound and is the best interpretation of the available studies? Every day something new is published about "addiction," and every day we seem to hear conflicting stories about how to help people with chemical dependence. The "field of addiction and recovery" is already full of myths and misinformation. How do we know what to believe?

A friend of mine once told the story of how, in the old days, the skill of hunters was quantified by the number of animal skins hanging outside their cabins. In other words, if a man boasted of being a great hunter, the challenge was "Show me your skins!" Today, the challenge for great researchers and educators is "Show me your references!" If a person in search of an answer goes to the Internet today and types the word *addiction* into a search engine, literally tens of millions of hits will appear in less than three-tenths of a second. Narrowing the search to "addiction causes" leads to over one million hits in about the same time. Changing the search parameters to "addiction treatment" produces ten times more hits than "addiction causes" in half the time! Does this mean we know more about treatment than the causes of "addiction"? No—there are just more opinions about treatment (and more money to be made?) than on the causes of "addiction." With all of these sources of information on addiction science and treatment, how do we know what to believe? At the end of this chapter is a list of prominent myths about "addiction" and what the science tells us about those myths.

The Workings of Science

Once people learn about the workings of science, they understand the limits and power of research in any area, particularly addiction science. Many people think that "research" is simply writing a long review of the existing literature or observing animals or people in a naturalistic setting and publishing the observations. But the type of research that is helping us understand drug abuse and chemical dependence is much more controlled and rigorous than simple observation and theorizing. The power is in the rigorous collection of new data, in the statistical analysis, and in the checks-and-balance of peer review that is involved in writing the manuscript with appropriate conclusions. Good research is replicable (i.e., it can be repeated by other scientists), controlled, and based upon traditional rigor in thought and performance. Finally, acceptance of a particular theory is affected by the number of scientific papers available on it, the quality of the papers and how they were published, and by the "weight of the evidence" (whether solid facts are available, as opposed to a scientist's or educator's speculation about how the studies fit together). One of the practical conclusions about research is that no single study proves anything—rather, it is how the available studies fit together that is most important. I believe that given the likelihood that there will never be enough studies in addiction science to be totally convincing, the science that best matches the "voices of the afflicted" is most useful. And even though the "voices of the afflicted" might be wrong, they at least need to be heard and judged. Listening to the people who are living the problem is a great way to come up with hypotheses to test.

Types of Research

Each scientific discipline has its own style of research. *Biomedical research* measures in animals or humans the physiological changes accompanying a type of treatment. *Clinical research* is more "applied," with investigations in humans for benefit. *Psychosocial research* is carried out in human volunteers, with measures of psychological and environmental change. *Epidemiologic research* is carried out using surveys, both written and oral, under rigorous conditions.

Other types of research are described as *prospective* (preplanned), *retrospective* (investigation of past records), *basic* (research on animals or humans where application of the results is not immediately clear), and *applied* (results that can be used immediately). There are also *longitudinal* studies that take place over a long period of time, usually years. Scientists will often perform *controlled* types of research in which control conditions are added for the purpose of comparison with a "treated" condition. Controlled studies often use random assignment of subjects to conditions and may or may not involve placebo or other control strategies. In general, prospective longitudinal controlled studies using large numbers of subjects are more valuable and valid than retrospective uncontrolled studies.

Recently, the quality of research and the integrity of scientists have been questioned. For example, a report in the Journal of the American Medical Association (Ioannidis, 2005) stated that 16% of published studies were contradicted by later studies. In addition, another 16% of studies saw their findings weakened by subsequent discoveries. (Whether these studies involve a lack of integrity or faulty research was not addressed.) Although every professional field has its share of weak or shoddy work (even medicine and law), most published scientific studies are peer reviewed for quality control and represent merely steps along the path toward truth. It is reasonable for studies to contradict each other, as single findings are often not strong enough to form a solid, irrefutable conclusion. However, many studies over time will provide a clearer picture of whether a particular hypothesis has been proven or disproved.

Keeping Up With the Science

Obviously, keeping up with new findings can be a lot of work. Reading this book will help, but what about the future? Generally, people depend upon the news or popular magazines for new science information. This is fine for busy professionals who want to remain alert to emerging information and new ideas, but unfortunately news reporters are not scientists and they have a hard time staying away from science that is controversial or spectacular. News reporters are often biased and may not be aware of their bias. It is also the case that news reporters exaggerate scientific results or tell only one side of the story, as it is presumed that the public is disinterested in a scientific article that is not a "breakthrough" in some way. Reporters are also guilty of leaving out key details, qualifying comments, exceptions, and cautionary statements that are noted in a published study.

A helpful way to increase the chances of understanding contemporary addiction science findings is to have a basic understanding of how research works and when to get excited about new studies. Following is a basic definition of research validity.

Research Validity

Valid research is defined as being significant in its design and conclusions, capable of being replicated within the original environment as well as in other laboratories, and able to easily pass the scrutiny of other scientists who critically look at the investigations and their conclusions ("peer review"). In addition, validity is driven by sample size and length of the study. For example, a study of 10 or fewer subjects for 4 weeks would have a higher risk of chance and unknown confounding factors that could influence the results than would a study of 10,000 or more subjects over several years.

Very rarely should single original data scientific papers lead to changes in policy or treatment strategies. We have to keep in mind that individual studies, although exciting, do not reflect "truth" until they are reproduced in other laboratories, expanded upon, and validated. Research conclusions grow due to the "weight of the evidence"—by findings that build upon other findings. It makes sense to think that many studies with similar findings can accumulate knowledge to the point of being believable. A single study is always open to refutation unless subsequent studies come to the same conclusion. Too often people get excited about the results of individual studies, but the appropriate response when a study is first reported should only be "Hmm, that's interesting."

Examples of Research Validity Estimates

The following examples of research validity estimates (RVEs) demonstrate different levels of "believability" based upon available weight-of-the-evidence at the time the studies were published.

Low RVEs

These examples have almost no previous studies to support them. They could be considered pioneering, or pilot, or preliminary findings.

Example #1. Why do alcoholics crave chocolate during recovery? A study by Small, Zatorre, Dagher, Evans, and Jones-Gotman (2001) used positron emission tomography (PET) to study the response of brain areas to chocolate in hungry and sated (not hungry) self-proclaimed "chocoholics." They found that the "reward" value of chocolate appears in a part of the brain known as the orbitofrontal cortex (an area near the front of the brain that is affected by alcohol). They also found that different parts of the orbitofrontal cortex were activated depending on whether the person was hungry or not. This study suggests that the orbitofrontal cortex may be one of the brain areas that is common to the craving for alcohol and chocolate. The RVE of this study is low because this is the first study to suggest that alcohol and chocolate may affect the same brain area to produce craving. Does this study show proof that alcoholics crave chocolate and explain how it happens? No, because this study might be proven wrong by later studies, and the fact that two chemicals affect the same brain area does not prove cause-and-effect ("Hmm, that's interesting").

Example #2. Can marijuana be used to treat the symptoms of Parkinsonism? Preliminary animal studies and clinical anecdotes have suggested that cannabis (the active ingredient in marijuana) reduces the symptom of Parkinson's disease known as dyskinesia (difficulty in movement). In a placebo-controlled, randomized, crossover (i.e., well-designed) study, an oral extract of cannabis in either of two doses was given to each of 19 Parkinson patients (Carroll, Bain, Teare, Liu, Joint, et al., 2004). Although the cannabis was well-tolerated with few side effects, there was no beneficial outcome of the medication on dyskinesia. The RVE of this study is low, because this is the first study that did not support previous suggestions of a beneficial effect of cannabis on muscle movement ("Hmm, that's interesting").

Example #3. What is the cause of pathological gambling? In the introduction to this study (Reuter, Raedler, Rose, Hand, Glascher, et al., 2005), the researchers indicated that pathological gambling as diagnosed by *DSM* criteria has an estimated lifetime prevalence of 1.6%. In the study, 12 pathological gamblers and 12 matched control subjects were brain scanned using functional magnetic resonance imaging (fMRI) in association with a guessing task that provided a model of gambling. The researchers found reduced activation of the ventral striatum and ventromedial prefrontal cortex, suggesting increased "addiction" (as with compulsive, uncontrolled drug-using behavior) and impaired impulse control, respectively. They concluded that pathological gambling "is due to a reduced sensitivity of the mesolimbic reward system." The RVE of this study is low because this is the first study to show that pathological gambling is related to reduced activation of the reward pathway ("Hmm, that's interesting").

Example #4. Why do anesthesiologists apparently have a higher rate of "addiction" than other physicians? This study (McAuliffe, Gold, Bajpai, Merves, Frost-Pineda, et al., 2006) began with the observation that there is a disproportionate number of anesthesiologists in the medical profession who are dependent on opioids. These scientists measured the levels of the intravenous anesthetics fentanyl and propofol in operating room air, around the patients, and around the anesthesia equipment. They found greater amounts of aerosolized anesthetics in these areas (but not adjoining hallways) and concluded that anesthesiologists (especially those who are closest to the expirations of the patient) have an "unintended occupational exposure" to anesthetics during surgery, which may predispose them to chemical dependence. The RVE of this study is low because this is the first study to suggest the reason for the apparently higher rate of chemical dependence in physicians practicing this specialty ("Hmm, that's interesting").

Moderate RVEs

These two examples have some previous studies to support them.

Example #1. Does childhood behavior predict rates of alcoholism? Many studies have suggested that there is a "significant relationship" between childhood disruptive behavior and alcoholism as an adult. People generally believe there is an "addictive personality," suggesting that children's behavior, if properly recognized, can be predictive of "addiction" later in life. Kuperman and colleagues (2001) analyzed 54 adolescents enrolled in the Collaborative Study on the Genetics of Alcoholism (COGA; a large multisite study on the genetics of alcohol dependence). They found that three-fourths of the adolescents reported having attention deficit hyperactivity disorder (ADHD) or conduct disorder as children. The RVE of this study is moderate, because this article generally supports previous work on this topic. However, this is not a strong paper due to the facts that the number of subjects is small and much of the outcome is based upon self-report and recollection of childhood disorders by the subjects (That's *more* interesting).

Example #2. Does marijuana produce withdrawal symptoms? There is some disagreement about whether withdrawal symptoms can be seen clinically when people stop using marijuana. In addition, conflicting studies appear in the literature on marijuana withdrawal and its characteristics. This paper (Budney, Hughes, Moore, & Vandrey, 2004) described a literature review of 19 studies published between 1946 and 2003. The authors looked for signs of irritability, nervousness and anxiety, and restlessness in subjects who stopped smoking marijuana after various lengths of time. A majority of the studies indicated an abstinence effect ("withdrawal") of "substantial magnitude" with a severity of "clinical importance." Another problem with all of these studies is the common use of multiple drugs; therefore unknown or unaccounted for withdrawal from other drugs including alcohol, sedatives, and opioids must be clearly eliminated as a confounding factor of the study results. The RVE of this study is moderate because it is a report on a number of studies that, collectively, produce a stronger conclusion than any of them alone. However, it might be more valid if another team of scientists comes to a similar conclusion upon reviewing the same 19 studies (That's *more* interesting).

High RVEs

These two examples have many previous studies to support them.

Example #1. Should opioids such as methadone be used to treat heroin dependence? The use of methadone is very controversial, in spite of the overwhelming scientific evidence that such medications are useful. In a study by Johnson and colleagues (2000), the researchers asked whether methadone is the only useful opioid for treating heroin dependence. In this relatively large (220 subjects) blind study (the subjects did not know whether they were receiving an active or inactive medication), methadone, levo-alpha-acetylmethadol (LAAM; a long-acting form of methadone), and buprenorphine were given to the subjects every 1–3 days in different doses. All but the lowest dose of methadone reduced the use of heroin (one of the study's endpoints) and increased the time the subjects remained in the study, suggesting a reduced craving for illegal heroin. The RVE of this study is high, based upon the large number of positive studies that preceded this one and the fact that this study expanded upon already positive results (That's *really* interesting).

Example #2. Can naltrexone be used successfully in a medical setting to treat alcohol-dependent patients? Naltrexone has been shown in many studies to have various degrees of effectiveness in reducing relapse to alcohol dependence in patients undergoing behavioral treatment. In this study (O'Malley et al., 2003), 197 subjects received placebo or naltrexone plus primary care management (PCM; a medical-style model of treatment and follow-up) or cognitive behavioral therapy (CBT) for 10 weeks. In a study within the larger study, some of the patients received treatment for 24 weeks. Results showed that PCM plus naltrexone was more effective than CBT plus naltrexone for maintenance of improvement in abstinence from alcohol. The RVE of this study is high, based upon the large number of studies that preceded this one and the fact that this study showed even better outcome than most of the previous studies (That's *really* interesting).

How to Read Scientific Articles With a Critical Eye

Professionals who want to know the latest evidence-based information for purposes of educating clients and patients, establishing better treatment methods, or formulating policy in treatment centers should first realize that not all research provides "evidence." Some research is fallible, some research is simply a reexamination of conclusions previously published, and some research is not definitive (for example, epidemiological studies rarely address cause-and-effect and are designed to reveal the strength or weakness of relationships among study groups or factors).

Professionals further should be aware that they are themselves capable of seeing the strengths and weaknesses of research studies. In general, prospective, controlled studies with large numbers of study subjects from reputable laboratories are more powerful in producing valid evidence than retrospective studies with possible missing records, performed in an institution with limited tradition and experience.

How can a counselor, member of the clergy, attorney, criminal justice worker, or health professional keep up with such research? The best ways are (1) by subscribing to counseling newsletters that have science updates, (2) by periodically scanning valid and accurate research websites, and (3) devoting some time each week to reading and studying the latest research findings.

Useful Sources

Following are some recommended books that cover the basic pharmacology of drugs discussed in this book:

- Brick & Erickson, 1999
- Brick, 2004
- Brunton, Lazo, Parker, Buxton, & Blumenthal, 2006
- Kuhn, Swartzwelder, & Wilson, 2002
- Kuhn, Swartzwelder, & Wilson, 2003

Following are some recommended websites:

- University of Texas Addiction Science Research and Education Center (*www.utexas.edu/research/asrec*)
- National Institute on Drug Abuse (*www.drugabuse.gov*)
- National Institute on Alcohol Abuse and Alcoholism (*www.niaaa.nih.gov*)
- Join Together Online (*www.jointogether.org*)
- National Library of Medicine/National Institutes of Health publications website (*www.pubmed.gov*)

Nonscientists should be aware that the most accurate information about drugs and chemical dependence is found on academic websites, especially those of major universities and independent and national research centers around the world. Generally those websites are understandable to nonscientists and provide a good overview of the types of research (and current findings) carried out by those institutions. For more popular explanations of research findings, I recommend the U.S. federal websites of the National Institute on Drug Abuse (NIDA) and the National Institute on Alcohol Abuse and Alcoholism (NIAAA), although these are often not updated on a regular basis. There is downloadable information on both of these websites—even slide presentations that can be downloaded and used by educators. For a ready source of information about new research and policy announcements, the Join Together website provides a place to subscribe (at no cost) to a daily email newsletter (JT Direct). For access to original research articles on-line, with extensive search capability, the National Library of Medicine/National Institutes of Health (NLM/NIH) publications database (PubMed) is highly recommended. Entries in each of the preceding sources (JT Direct and PubMed) change daily.

Treatment professionals should also know that there is vast information in peer-reviewed, original-data and review articles. For a foundation of the research and the convergence of accumulated studies, the introduction of each publication can easily be read. The astute professional should be able to recognize how well past studies and present studies are converging. Merely reading the abstract of a new publication can give an overview of the findings, but other parts of each manuscript will probably need to be read to determine credibility and whether the finding is indeed "new."

Weight of the Evidence

The RVEs given earlier indicate that as studies of similar outcome accumulate, the validity and generalizability of the findings increase until they approach strong agreement (i.e., experts in the field tend to accept these findings as "facts" or "truth"). In other words, the weight of the evidence (and how fast it accumulates) determines whether an idea will be widely accepted. A single study is vulnerable to misinterpretation and refutation (others can prove it wrong), and requires replication before we can believe it and use the information in some application. Unfortunately, scientists and others often use single studies to drive an unproven hypothesis or (even worse) to justify a change in public policy or clinical practice. (One practitioner I know calls this "blindly falling in love with one's ideas," and it results in openly or covertly opposing any information that refutes your presumed-to-be-correct conclusions.) Certainly there are large, longitudinal studies that can be very convincing (such as the Framingham heart study), but interpretation of such data is usually in the hands of single investigators or investigative teams that may not look at all possible conclusions.

Consequences

Scientific findings are obviously not infallible, but good science accumulated over time should ideally drive policy and education of the public and health professionals about critical health issues such as drug disorders. When there is insufficient science, formal and informal educational programs tend to use anecdotal information, personal experience, emotional conclusions, biased conclusions, and innuendo to understand drug effect and "addiction" and form public policy. If we are looking for answers today, do we have to wait for the "weight of the evidence?" Of course not, as pressing issues often need quick action. People who use science for policy change and education must understand, however, that the more they use scientific findings that are inconclusive, the greater the chance they have of being wrong. At the very least, an educator or policy maker should understand what evidence they are using and the limitations of the evidence. Rather than pulling a scientific article that supports their position out of the literature to use as proof of their concept, it is best to become familiar with the literature and place the concept in perspective. Unfortunately, this takes time and effort, but it will make the messenger much more credible.

Perhaps a better idea, now being tested in the drug field, is to pair scientists with clinicians to form teams that can translate new research findings into clinical solutions. And, of course, excellent science communicated in understandable language to curious, motivated treatment professionals would be the best of all worlds.

Ten Representative Drug Myths

These myths help to demonstrate the existence of inaccurate or inappropriate information on drugs and "addiction" that prevail in the treatment field or in the minds of the public. More myths can be found on the website of the Addiction Science Research and Education Center of the University of Texas at Austin (*www.utexas.edu/research/asrec*).

Myth #1. "Abuse" is the best term to describe a destructive drug-use problem. As used in "substance abuse treatment centers," The Center for Substance Abuse Treatment, and "substance abuse disorders" (unfortunately, the term used in the *DSM*), the word *abuse* is an inappropriate term for several reasons. First, as White (2001, p. 4) has stated, "Of all the words that have entered the addiction/treatment vocabulary, 'abuse' is one of the most ill-chosen and . . . pernicious." He indicated that "abuse" has for centuries been the object of religious and moral censure. It has long implied the willful commission of a wrong and sinful act involving forbidden pleasure, and has been used to describe people with a violent character, such as child abusers and spouse abusers. Second, the word is technically incorrect. A person "abuses" someone or something, but the term *alcohol abuse* actually describes someone who is using alcohol in a damaging way, not someone who is damaging an object (i.e., alcohol). This is one of the reasons why scientists in Europe prefer the term "misuse," which better describes an inappropriate use of an object by a person. Third, the term *abuse* has become pervasive and meaningless with respect to drugs in our society. *Substance abuse* is now a catch-all term for any drug problem, without differentiation between voluntary use problems and uncontrolled use (illness) problems. As White (2001, p. 4) stated, "To refer to people who are addicted as alcohol, drug or substance abusers misstates the nature of their condition and calls for their social rejection, sequestration, and punishment."

Myth #2. THIQs are a cause of alcoholism. This old notion, first reported by Davis and Walsh (1970), asserts that synthetic alkaloids known as tetrahydroisoquinolines (THIQs) are formed in the brains of alcoholics, providing a biological basis for alcoholism. The early evidence for the existence of these chemicals came from analysis of postmortem brains of "alcoholics" and later observation of the presence of these plant alkaloids in animal and (later) human tissue. The 1970s and 1980s saw a proliferation of research studies attempting to (a) validate the role of acetaldehyde (metabolite of alcohol) in the formation of these chemicals in animals, (b) develop an accurate analytical method for THIQs in human tissues, and (c) demonstrate higher levels of THIQs in human alcoholics versus control subjects. Meanwhile, the theory caught the fancy of recovering alcoholics and a number of treatment professionals as providing a biological basis for why they lost control and for why they "felt powerless over alcohol." The theory became the first attractive demonstration of chemical imbalance in the brain that appeared to explain the nature of the disease, and there are still videotapes covering this topic in treatment centers throughout the world. However, in the late 1980s, scientists informally concluded that the theory was no longer attractive, based upon a weight-of-the-evidence conclusion that THIQs cannot be reliably found in human alcoholics and based upon the newer neurotransmitter theories described in Chapter 3. The best evidence for the decline in popularity of this notion is the lack of current research on the topic—only a handful of studies have been published in the past several years.

Myth #3. A person can overdose on marijuana and LSD. In fact, these two drugs have no known lethal dose in humans (Brick & Erickson, 1999). Driving and accidental deaths do occur under the influence of these drugs; however, the word *overdose* indicates a direct toxicological effect on the body causing death. Theoretically it would be possible to inject a huge dose of tetrahydrocannabinol (THC) or LSD into a person's vein and produce death, but these drugs are not administered in this manner, so lethal doses from usual use of the drugs are not known.

Myth #4. A person cannot overdose on alcohol. High school and college students often don't understand the dangers of alcohol. Alcohol is viewed either as not a drug or as a "safe drug" (a myth). The "no overdose" myth might be due to the general knowledge that "alcoholics" drink a lot of wine and often will consume an entire bottle of spirits. Young people do not understand the concept of tolerance and the fact that they do not have it. Not only is alcohol dependence-producing, but unlike marijuana and LSD, it can also be a killer. For example, one calculation of the lethal dose for a 150-pound alcohol-naïve male is generally a pint and a half of distilled spirits drunk within about an hour (Brick & Erickson, 1999). The cause of death is direct depression of the respiratory center in the brain stem or suffocating on inspired vomit while unconscious.

Myth #5. Therapeutic painkillers and stimulants (such as morphine and Ritalin) produce a high rate of addiction. The likelihood of becoming dependent on opioid painkillers, or stimulants used to treat ADHD, is really quite low. This myth derives from when people erroneously believe that "withdrawal" after abrupt cessation of a drug (resulting from "physiological dependence") is synonymous with "addiction." Many people given painkillers will experience physiological dependence, and once they are tapered off the drug (to prevent withdrawal) they never want or need the drug again. Also, some people on long-term opioid drugs for chronic pain, or on methadone or buprenorphine maintenance, become physiologically dependent on opioids, yet they are taking the drug as prescribed due to medical reliance. But physiological dependence and withdrawal are not the same as "addiction" or chemical dependence.

Because stimulants are sometimes traded or sold among adolescents, some people erroneously believe that the rate of "addiction" with these drugs is high. Actually, the "abuse" of stimulant drugs can be high, but when used therapeutically by a person who has been prescribed the drug, the rate of chemical dependence is quite low (Willens, Faraone, Biederman, & Gunawardene, 2003).

Myth #6. Progression to *the disease of addiction is the same thing as progression* of *the disease over time.* Progression *of* a disease means "to continue or get worse over time." This does occur with chemical dependence and is one of the characteristics of this chronic disease. However, progression *to* the disease suggests that people progress from social use to abuse of a drug to chemical dependence. Recent clinical evidence cited in Chapter 1 indicates that (1) some people become dependent very quickly and do not show progression to the disease, (2) some people stop at the "progressive step" of abuse, without continuing into chemical dependence, and (3) some people do progress to "addiction" but only after a long time. It is a fact, then, that progression to the disease in every case is an old concept not supported by science.

Myth #7. "Self-help" is an appropriate way to overcome the disease of addiction. Whether we're talking about "addiction" to alcohol or to other drugs, the term *self-help* connotes a person's overcoming the disease alone, perhaps through insight, revelation, or increased willpower to stop using (White, 2004). Thus, it is inappropriate to think of programs such as A.A. or N.A. as "self-help." These are not self-help groups; they are support programs or mutual-aid groups. Recovery in such groups involves the "utilization of resources and relationships beyond the self" (White, 2001). "Self-help" is an outdated concept that is no longer in keeping with the newest science of treatment and recovery.

Myth #8. The more educated people are about drugs, the less likely they are to become addicted. This idea that chemical dependence is preventable is an old one. Strong evidence concerning the brain mechanisms involved in chemical dependence (cited in Chapter 3) tells us that this disease can mainly be prevented by never using a mood-altering drug. If education-as-prevention could affect rates of chemical dependence, physicians, nurses, pharmacists, and pharmacologists would have a low rate of "addiction." Sadly, these health professionals have an incidence of chemical dependence that is at least as high as the general population.

Myth #9. "Crack babies" are a major clinical problem. There is no doubt that babies born of mothers who use crack do exist. However, such pregnant women often use other drugs (alcohol, nicotine, or marijuana), have poor prenatal care, and are undernourished. The baby born of a mother with such problems will have acute problems at birth. But *crack baby* is not a scientific term; it is a media term given by reporters doing a story on birth problems. Such babies, if they need a label, should be called "infants in distress," since the term *crack baby* is pejorative and likely to be a lifelong label.

Myth #10. Social drinking kills brain cells. People once thought that even one drink could kill thousands of brain cells. Alcohol *can* kill brain cells, but only after many years of heavy drinking. Anecdotally, there is an old study that involved giving alcohol daily to a dog for several weeks and then looking at damaged brain cells in the dog at autopsy. A calculation was made of the number of brain cells damaged, and this was extrapolated backwards to determine how many cells would be damaged with one drink. Obviously a single drink killing brain cells in this manner has nothing to do with humans drinking socially.

Myths in addiction science, medicine, and public understanding are severely damaging to the proper perception of people with chemical-dependence disease, to their acceptance by society, and to the resources available for treatment. The chances are that readers of this book have been (or will be) so severely affected by drug problems in their family or in society that they want to find ways to help those in need or those whom they love. An accurate understanding of what drugs do and what they don't do, as well as what "addiction" is and what it is not, is therefore critical in overcoming drug problems.

Chapter 10

Evidence-Based Research for the Future

NO BOOK ON THE SCIENCE OF ADDICTION would be complete without some speculation and prognostication about the future. It is pretty easy to look at current research areas and predict which ones will continue to grow and which are on a downward trend. However, research on alcohol and other drugs has always been dependent on several influences: availability of research grant funds, changing emphasis on hot topics based upon new breakthroughs in science, policy, and leadership, and specific interests of scientists in the field. Generally, research that is published is based upon the interests of scientists and the availability of research funds. In an ideal world, scientists who have interests and expertise in a specific area of research could submit research grants and easily get them funded. In a less than ideal world, scientists must force their research interests into pigeonholes created by funding agencies working with limited funds and deciding within themselves which types of studies should be supported.

The bulk of this chapter is devoted to the subject of brain imaging, which has undergone exciting new advances in recent years. I then raise some questions about where future research should focus, based upon the available technology, the state of the art in neuroscience and drug theory, and the discussions I have had with people in recovery, who hope that science can help them even more in the future.

Research Trends in Neurobiology and Related Fields

In the mid-2000s, there are some predominant research trends in the addiction science literature. Following is a partial listing of "hot topics" that are expected to provide strong conclusions over time, based on the facts that there is already a substantial amount of research in the area or they are of high priority in the scientific and granting communities.

- Continuing work on brain chemicals (neurotransmitters) involved in causation of chemical dependence, finding genes for the vulnerability to the disease (in both humans and animal models), epidemiological studies on who develops drug problems and how they receive help, fetal drug syndromes (especially alcohol), the effectiveness of combinations of medications and counseling, and clinical/research collaborations between scientists and practitioners
- Medical uses of marijuana
- Adolescent drinking and drug use and the effect of age of first use on chances of developing chemical dependence
- The exact mechanisms of transitions from social use of drugs to the disease of chemical dependence
- Potential medicines that affect the brain's endocannabinoids (naturally occurring cannabinoids)
- A better understanding and treatment of psychiatric and personality disorders that co-occur with drug problems
- Treatment outcome studies—demonstration of need for treatment, defining recovery, defining successful treatment
- "Translational research" involving the best ways to translate new research findings into clinical reality by providing practitioners with knowledge and skills to use research to provide better treatment outcomes for patients with dependence disease
- Brain-imaging studies on drug action and possible diagnostic uses of such technology

Areas of research that have declined in popularity or have not gained popularity with scientists include the following:

- Studies of THIQs (see Chapter 9)
- Studies on the effects of ethanol on nerve membranes

- Development of new rodent and primate models of drug preference or drug taking
- Studies of acetaldehyde effects in the brain (related to intoxication and hangover with alcohol)
- The search for alcohol antagonists (amethystic agents)
- Studies of hangovers and blackouts with alcohol and other drugs
- Studies on alternative methods of treating drug problems such as acupuncture, hypnosis, nutrition, and transcranial brain stimulation

Although these lists are not all-inclusive, they do demonstrate that there is an increasing number of varied studies in this area and that there are some barren areas in research, leading to a vision of what we can expect to see in the future scientific literature.

Brain Imaging

The drugs described in Chapters 5–7 can be expected to change brain function through effects on brain-cell transmission. Transmission might be changed by altering release rates of neurotransmitters, affecting the speed at which neurotransmitters are produced or broken down, or by how effectively the neurotransmitters activate their receptors. Brain imaging is a new technology that, combined with computers, is helping scientists measure such changes. The imaging tools we use today still cannot tell us everything we want to know about how the brain works, but they provide important clues on where to look for answers in the near future.

The brain scanning technologies of today are greatly improved over the old methods of electroencephalography (EEG) and X-ray computed tomography (CT). During brain scans, patients lie on a table that slowly moves through a doughnut-shaped scanner (detector), or the detector revolves around the head of the individual. Scans generally take only a few minutes, and unless the person is highly claustrophobic, the procedure is not uncomfortable, as there is no invasion of the brain and because the head is the only part of the body that is in the scanner. The output of the scanner goes directly to a computer that prints out a picture of what the scanner sees.

Use of Brain-Imaging in Chemical Dependence Diagnosis and Treatment

Recent brain-imaging studies provide bridges among behavior and brain chemistry and function. Beginning around the year 2000, a large number of studies looked at changes in brain function during manipulations of behavior, cognition, and emotions. Interesting studies including Furmark and colleagues (2002), Goldapple and colleagues (2004), Martin, Martin, Rai, Richardson, and Royall (2001), Paquette and colleagues (2003), and Penades and colleagues (2002) are consistently showing that psychotherapy and medications work similarly to change brain function in a positive direction to overcome psychiatric disorders. This provides evidence to counter those who believe that "addictions are behavioral problems because they are mainly treated behaviorally." Brain-imaging studies have provided us with evidence that "hypofrontality" (low activity of the frontal lobes) is related to the symptoms of obsessive-compulsive disorder (see Penades, Boget, Lomena, Mateos, Catalan, et al., 2002) and probably other brain diseases including chemical dependence. In addition, such technologies are being used to study the mechanisms of drug action on brain receptors, such as the effects of ecstasy on serotonin receptors (Buchert, Thomasius, Wilke, Petersen, Nebeling, et al., 2004). Studies are now planned or underway to identify the exact brain areas that are dysregulated during chemical dependence in humans. Once a brain area is found to "light up" in a brain scan of chemically dependent patients (compared to heavy drug abusers), the notion that "dependence is a brain disease" will become viable to those who still believe that this is a willpower or behavioral problem. Finally, treatment outcomes in the future will probably be followed by correlative changes in brain function as measured by brain imaging.

Positron Emission Tomography (PET)

This technology was developed soon after CT scans. PET was the first technology that could look beyond anatomy to infer changes in brain activity as mental acts were performed. In a typical PET study, patients are injected with water in which the oxygen molecule contains a radioactive "label" that sends out a low level of radiation for 15–20 minutes. The brain activity can thus be traced by monitoring blood as it flows through the brain, delivering the labeled oxygen to brain cells. The highest level of radioactivity indicates the site of the greatest blood flow and thus the greatest cellular activity at any given fraction of a second.

A typical PET study on cocaine users with some experience using the drug highlights multicolored scans showing different brain areas of different intensity, which is characteristic of PET scans. Because PET scans are usually done in pairs (one scan at one level of the brain and a second at another level of the brain), the likelihood of identifying changes in cell activity in different brain areas is enhanced.

In a study by Volkow (2004b), subjects were challenged by giving a dose of methylphenidate (Ritalin) or placebo (inactive injection). In one case, the subject was told he would receive placebo and then he was given placebo. This scan provided the baseline for the study. Then the subject was told he would receive methylphenidate but instead received placebo. The scan then showed the effects of anticipation of the active drug, which was seen as increased activity over placebo. In the next experiment, the subject was promised placebo but instead was given methylphenidate. That scan showed the effects of the drug without anticipation, and the activity was fairly low. Finally, the last experiment involved a promise of methylphenidate and the actual administration of methylphenidate, which produced the greatest change in color in most brain areas (greatest activation or change in function). In summary, this set of experiments illustrated not only the effects of methylphenidate on brain function but also the effects of drug anticipation. This study indicates that the psychological phenomenon of anticipation can be observed via a change in function as shown by brain imaging. Thus, psychology is based on neurochemistry, and it works both ways: Psychology and behavior influences neurochemistry, and neurochemistry influences behavior and psychology.

Functional Magnetic Resonance Imaging (fMRI)

MRI is similar to CT technology, but MRI probes the body with a combination of radio waves and a powerful magnetic field rather than X rays. MRI produces anatomical, not functional, images of the brain, so it is particularly good for showing specific brain areas and how those areas might be anatomically abnormal. Because oxygen-carrying red blood cells change magnetic fields, scientists have been able to use a series of MRI scans to monitor blood flow and oxygen consumption. Developed in the 1990s, fMRIs use computer technology to compare MRI images of the brain at rest and in the midst of an activity such as viewing a movie, thereby revealing areas of increasing and decreasing activity. The basic MRI brain scan is always black and white. In fMRI, colored areas on an MRI scan are the result of computer comparisons between control and "treated" brains (i.e., those without and with any intervention).

Using fMRI, Paquette and colleagues (2003) examined the effects of cognitive behavioral therapy (CBT) on reducing arachnophobia in female patients who were, at the beginning of the study, fearful of spiders. At the end of the therapy, brain areas that were previously active because of spider phobia had become normal. The computer was able to sort out the subjects' response to seeing spiders versus the response to butterflies (control), which added color ("functionality") to the MRI images. Thus, the study showed that CBT was able to change brain function successfully. Although not tested, therapeutic doses of an antianxiety medication would probably have the same effect.

Single Photon Emission Computerized Tomography (SPECT)

SPECT is a sophisticated nuclear medicine representation of cerebral blood flow and, indirectly, brain activity (metabolism). A small amount of a blood-labeling substance is injected into the arm vein of a subject, much like in the PET studies. This substance spreads evenly through the brain's circulation and reflects, through its regional concentration, the level of neuronal function in different brain areas. The SPECT "gamma" camera rotates around the head and detects exactly where the compound is located in different areas of the brain. Thus SPECT is able to differentiate areas of the brain that are active ("hot") and inactive ("cold")—and all levels in between. If brain function is extremely low or lost in a particular brain area, the SPECT picture shows a transparent portion where activity is not measurable. The picture looks as if the tissue has disappeared, but the tissue is actually still there—it simply doesn't have any measurable activity via SPECT. This technology is excellent for confirming brain-area involvement as it relates to reported symptoms, as in attention deficit hyperactivity disorder (ADHD), impulse control disorders, and Alzheimer's disease. This is also an important tool for tracking the effects of counseling and medications: As individuals get better, specific brain areas change accordingly. Medication dosage can also be adjusted, or new medications tried, based upon SPECT outcome studies. In addition, counseling and behavioral interventions could be evaluated to determine which ones produce positive changes and which patients are most likely to respond effectively to a given intervention. Unlike PET and MRI, SPECT images can be rotated in three dimensions and observed from the right, left, top, and bottom. In addition, internal brain structures can be observed.

SPECT, PET, and MRI are extremely valuable for studying the effectiveness and comparability of interactional behavioral therapy and pharmacotherapy (medications). Such pictures of the brain are now beginning to show function, with neurochemical changes as the foundation. If a patient presents to the clinician with certain symptoms (such as psychiatric symptoms or abnormal use of drugs), general brain areas involved in the experiencing of such symptoms can be visualized. This allows an outcome to be observed when medication doses are given (and then changed) or when counseling has a positive effect.

What Happens When Chemically Dependent Patients Get Better Through Interactive and Behavioral Counseling?

As discussed in previous chapters, chemical dependence is a chronic medical brain disease. It is clear that some people get better when they attend 12-step meetings and "work the steps"; others, when they participate in group, individual, or marital and family therapy; and still others, when they use anticraving medications. People don't get better without something changing. Thus, logic, evidence, and experience tell us that the treatments people receive cause brain function to change in a positive direction. Because medications and interactional and behavioral therapies are all beneficial, they probably have similar effects on the pathology of the condition—the dysregulated neurotransmitter systems of the mesolimbic dopamine system. The human brain-imaging studies are now confirming what animal research has shown us for decades: that strong emotions such as grief and anger, and cognitions such as new learning and new beliefs, alter brain function. With chemical dependence, just as in human depression and anxiety, counseling and medications do not correct (as in repair or fix) the brain dysregulation; instead, they "push the neurochemistry" back toward normal so that patients have a better chance of feeling better (less depressed, less anxious, less drug craving). There is also research to suggest that a combination of medications and psychotherapy are more effective than either one alone. This is because they have similar mechanisms and when used simultaneously, would be expected to have additive effects.

Recent Imaging Studies in Chemical Dependence

MRI studies on the brains of "alcoholics" clearly show a detrimental effect of chronic heavy alcohol consumption on brain anatomy and function.

Figure 10.1
Enlarged Ventricles in an Alcoholic Man Compared to a Nonalcoholic Man*

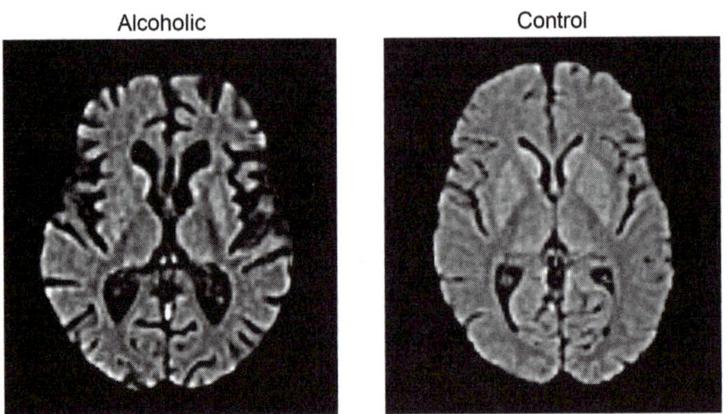

*Courtesy of A. Pfefferbaum, Stanford University.

Figure 10.1 illustrates the ventricles (inner brain cavities in which cerebrospinal fluid circulates) in alcoholic brains versus controls. The images, each of a 57-year-old man's brain, show how the ventricles are enlarged in the alcoholic's brain. Figure 10.2 shows the effects of prolonged alcohol consumption on the anatomy of the corpus collosum (the light comma-shaped structure in the middle of the brain that allows left- to-right-side brain communication. Data are described in Pfefferbaum, Lim, Desmond, & Sullivan, 1996). Many MRI brain scan studies

Figure 10.2
Thinning of the Corpus Callosum in an Alcoholic Compared to a Nonalcoholic*

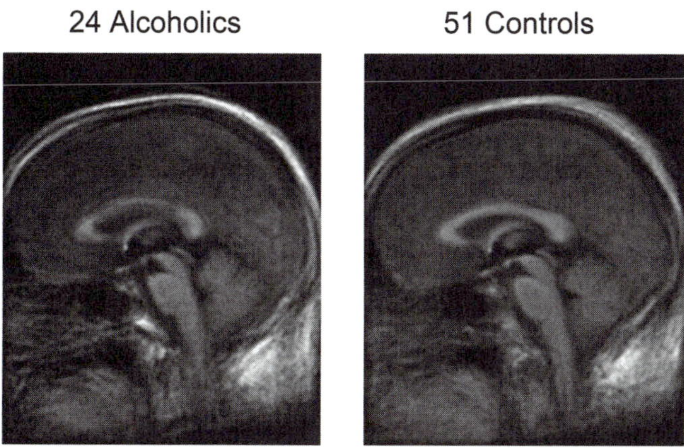

*Courtesy of A. Pfefferbaum, Stanford University.

dramatically show shrinkage of the gray matter, gyri, and sulci (grooves and fissures) in the brains of alcoholics (Sullivan, 2000). Other studies have shown that such shrinkage is reversible. For example, after about 1 month of sobriety, a group of 58 alcoholic men showed significant volume enlargement of cortical gray matter and shrinkage of cortical sulci and the lateral ventricles, compared to a control group of 58 age-matched men (Pfefferbaum, Sullivan, Mathalon, Shear, Rosenbloom, et al., 1995).

Available brain scans on drug abuse in scientific publications are generally quite technical and show only subtle changes. A classic PET study, however, clearly shows activation of two important limbic system structures (amygdala and anterior cingulate areas) of the brain in cocaine users shown cocaine videos and nature videos (Childress, Mozley, McElgin, Fitzgerald, Reivich, et al., 1999). The cocaine videos featured the simulated purchase, preparation, and smoking of crack cocaine. The nature videos featured a travelogue from public television. During the cocaine video, the cocaine users felt "craving" and showed an enhanced (though only unilaterally) blood flow in the two limbic areas. This suggested to the researchers that limbic activation is one component of cue-induced cocaine craving.

More recent brain-imaging studies on drug abuse and dependence have shown that increases in brain dopamine (DA) are associated with subjective reports of drug reinforcement, and that there are significant reductions in DRD2 (reward) receptors and DA release during withdrawal (Volkow, Fowler, Wang, & Goldstein, 2002; Volkow, Fowler, & Wang, 2003). In fact, DA imaging is perhaps the most frequent use of PET in drug-abuse research today. Other neurotransmitter systems of interest in drug-abuse research have also been probed using brain-imaging: opioid receptors (Schlaepfer, Strain, Greenberg, Preston, Lancaster, et al., 1998), glutamate (Bressan & Pilowsky, 2000), and GABA (Daglish & Nutt, 2003). Brain-imaging studies have already found a relationship between brain function, receptor activation, and glucose utilization (changes in blood flow) on the one hand and cognitive, behavioral, emotional, and brain structure on the other. This has led some authors to talk about the promise of brain imaging in understanding "the biochemistry of the mind" (Pietrini, 2003) and the brain function of murderers and other types of criminals (Raine, Buchsbaum, & LaCasse,1997). Brain-imaging as a research tool is still in its infancy, and of course it has its critics and supporters. Critics suggest that neuroimaging is nothing more than a modern-day version of phrenology (old science that assumed personality could be determined by the contours of the cranium and brain), is destined to fail, and is fundamentally uninformative. Supporters argue that although there are ethical questions (Friedrich, 2005), neuroimaging is in "a vibrant and healthy state of development" (Donaldson, 2004). In drug-abuse research, animal studies have clearly shown changes in brain neurotransmission with drug action and during the development of chemical dependence (it is not possible to directly measure neurotransmitter function in humans). Thus I believe that brain-imaging is a methodological locomotive that cannot be stopped. Nor should it be stopped—the proper use of this emerging technology will someday provide the exact answers to the causes of chemical dependence and provide a boost to therapeutic development (Schiffer, Lee, Brodie, & Dewey, 2005).

Questions to Be Answered in Future Studies

Because research on alcohol and drugs (and "addiction") had a late start—in the early 1970s—compared to research on, for example, cancer, heart disease, infectious diseases, diabetes, and polio, we are way behind in our knowledge of what causes chemical dependence and, to some extent, willful drug abuse. For a long time scientists thought they were studying a unitary (single) drug problem; thus, research on causes of drug problems fell behind what would be expected of disease research in the 1970s. The early studies (mostly on alcohol problems, with some interest in general mechanisms of other drug "addiction" and its treatment) focused on why people use and abuse alcohol, as well as on some very interesting etiological (causative) concepts. One of these concerned the role of acetaldehyde in "alcohol addiction," including the now defunct research interest on tetrahydroisoquinolines (THIQs) as a cause of "alcoholism." Other major emphases in the early days were how nutritional problems could cause "alcoholism" via metabolism and in the stomach ("the problem is 'in the belly' because people crave alcohol the same way they crave food") and in the liver ("alcoholics metabolize alcohol differently than nonalcoholics"). Although the latter studies gave us an enormous amount of good information on how alcohol is metabolized and how alcohol-induced liver problems come about, they did little to help with an understanding of the causes of "alcoholism," except by process of elimination. Another early idea that has fallen out of favor is the theory that alcohol "melts membranes" to cause intoxication (Goldstein, 1984).

Now that we have developed animal models of alcohol preference, intoxication, tolerance, and withdrawal (and to a lesser extent similar models with other drugs), we are poised to make a major leap in understanding how to use these models, along with new innovations in brain-imaging and genetic technologies. We now will be able to answer many of the following questions, if only the research funding can keep up with the innovation in technology and the pool of qualified investigators (many from other basic science and disease disciplines) who have already been trained and are awaiting the resources.

Following is my wish-list of questions to be answered by future "addiction" scientists. Many of these questions are based upon nonscientific reports from people with the disease. Answers to these will change the ways we think about treatment in the future.

Is there such a thing as the "instant addict"? Many people with drug problems report that they became "instantly addicted" the first time they used the drug. ("I knew I had a problem the first time I drank"; "I knew I had a problem the first time I used cocaine."). Is this a real phenomenon, or is it only a self-reported concern of people who do not understand the meaning of "addiction"?

Why do some people who drink or drug heavily become dependent whereas others don't? Do some people, but not everyone, really "have what it takes" to become dependent?

Why do some people with little drug exposure become dependent while others who drink or drug heavily do not become dependent? Is the answer mostly in the genes?

Why do so many people (even some scientists) resist calling chemical dependence a disease? (Remember that we are not talking about drug abuse.) Is the solution to addiction slowed by incomplete understanding of the science, by prejudice, stigma, and discrimination against "those people who hurt us," by our having a problem with people who cannot fight for themselves, by thoughts that those who have the disease are also breaking the law, by leftover concerns about the contribution of "willpower" to the "disease concept," or by our subconsciously wanting to punish those who are "not like us"? These, of course, are not questions that can be answered through biological studies—we need the help of our psychological/social/cultural colleagues.

Can brain-imaging help us understand and perhaps overcome stigma? With the emerging technology of brain imaging, it is now possible to examine the biological substrates (foundations) of established psychological/behavioral/cognitive human phenomena that are brain-based. If we can examine those phenomena, shouldn't it be possible to use brain-imaging and controlled conditions to examine the concept of stigma against "addicts"?

What is the relationship between recreational and therapeutic use of drugs? Almost everyone understands that a natural drug-free condition is optimum for human functioning, but how can we significantly reduce disease states? How can we significantly reduce the recreational use of drugs intended only for therapeutic use? Can drugs used recreationally also be used therapeutically (and if so, when and how much)? What is the proper balance of drug use and psychotherapy when making sick people feel better? Can these issues be studied scientifically?

What role does motivation play in treatment? Anecdotally it appears that problem drug users have a better outcome in formal treatment when they are highly motivated to get well because of the critical nature of their job (e.g., airline pilots have better treatment outcomes than retail workers). Is this really true or are clinicians simply treating more drug abusers than drug dependent patients? If it is true, how does "motivation to get better" affect treatment design, strategies for intervention, treatment modalities, and outcome measures?

What is the relationship between co-occurring mental disorders and clinical dependence, and how do we best treat individuals with these co-occurring disorders? Co-occurring axis I mental disorders interfere with the treatment of people with drug problems. Major unanswered questions include: How do mental disorders contribute to brain changes that increase production of chemical dependence? How does chemical dependence contribute to brain changes that increase risk of mental disorders? How do we properly integrate treatment of these disorders? Will people with co-occurring disorders respond better if treated in isolation from those who struggle only with chemical dependence?

What is the relationship between co-occurring personality disorders and chemical dependence, and how do we best treat individuals with these co-occurring disorders? Co-occurring axis II personality disorders often prevent people from seeking treatment and can exacerbate drinking and drugging problems. Key issues include the contribution of genetics and environment to the genesis of personality disorders, how that information helps us understand why such individuals use alcohol and other drugs, and how to help such people reduce the risk of relapse.

How can we develop objective assessment methods? Given the subjectivity of *DSM-IV* assessment criteria and experts' lack of agreement over their validity, addiction medicine badly needs objective assessment methods for differentiating between drug users at risk for chemical dependence and those who are overusing alcohol or other drugs for other reasons. Such diagnostic procedures might involve genetic markers or sophisticated brain imaging.

What is the nature of adolescent alcohol and drug use and how are adolescents with drug-use problems best treated? Drug use by adolescents often readily meets the criteria of abuse and in some cases of dependence, yet too often a diagnosis of dependence is given (possibly for purposes of insurance reimbursement). We need to know how the adolescent brain is affected by drugs and whether early use increases the risk of dependence. It is important to know if assessments are confusing excess use and abuse of drugs with chemical dependence. Also, do adolescents respond better to less restrictive treatment or to more involved treatment?

What is the relationship between brain trauma and drug use? Drug abuse and chemical dependence is common for many patients with traumatic head injury. Sometimes the drug problems are a precursor to the injury, but they can also develop as a postinjury outcome. It would be valuable to know whether the injured brain becomes more sensitized to psychoactive drugs after trauma. If it does, we should try to determine how trauma alters brain chemistry to cause this result. Other key goals would be to find which pharmacotherapeutic agents might help curtail the effects of traumatic brain injury and reduce drug abuse. Finally, what are the best psychotherapeutic measures for chemically dependent people with brain injury?

Should treatment be gender-specific? Compared to men, women respond to and are affected differently by many drugs. Also, a history of psychological and physical trauma is a common theme for women with chemical-use problems. Is the subsequent use of drugs one of choice—a coping mechanism in response to the trauma? Or does such trauma increase the incidence of chemical dependence? Does trauma alter brain chemistry, specifically neurotransmission in the MDS? How should pharmacotherapy and behavioral treatment for chemically dependent women be modified to increase effectiveness?

How should we approach pain management for recovering chemically-dependent people? This is an important issue that requires much more attention, study, and better guidelines for the medical community. Given that people are in recovery from a large number of different drugs, what should the prescribed regimen for reducing major pain in these individuals be? Is there a way to block the likelihood of new dependence on opioid painkillers, as well as relapse on a drug of choice (and convince the recovering person that this can be done)?

Answers to all of the above questions would go a long way in reducing the consequences of drug problems and chemical dependence in society. It is clear, however, that this will take an enormous investment in human and financial resources. Given what science has done so far with limited resources (compared to that for the other, "good" diseases), the future is bright for greater knowledge of drug problems and the science of addiction.

Appendix A

Alcohol Concepts Affecting Neurobiology and Treatment

BASIC KNOWLEDGE IS ESSENTIAL FOR UNDERSTANDING the entire picture of drug addiction, its prevention, and treatment. Neurobiological principles are based upon accurate information about alcohol. Alcohol is a legal drug that has tremendous social impact, both positively and negatively—and its abuse by adolescents and adults is related to the development of alcohol dependence.

The following items are intended to supplement the material in the main chapters. They have been adapted from the website of the University of Texas at Austin's Addiction Science Research and Education Center (*www.utexas.edu/research/asrec*). The website folder "Alcohol Facts to Share with Others" contains over 300 of these items. These items were chosen as "important for chemical-dependency counselors and other treatment professionals" by a panel of individuals associated with the Addiction Technology Transfer Centers, funded by the federal Center for Substance Abuse Treatment.

Basic Alcohol Pharmacology

- The main metabolizing (breakdown) enzyme for alcohol is known as *alcohol dehydrogenase*. This produces a compound called acetaldehyde, which is in turn broken down by aldehyde dehydrogenase. Genes for expression of acetaldehyde dehydrogenase are mutated in individuals in the Asian population, which leads to "flushing" and other negative effects that might protect those individuals from becoming alcohol-dependent.

- Is alcohol hydrophilic or lipophilic? The root *philic* relates to attraction, and *hydro* and *lipo* relate to water and fat, respectively. So, is alcohol more attracted to water or fat in the body? Actually, alcohol has an attraction to both, but more so to water than to fat. Thus alcohol concentrates readily in any body tissue with high amounts of water (blood, blood in the brain, urine, sweat, heart, etc.). Although alcohol readily concentrates in fat in the body, it leaves it very quickly as BACs drop, so there is no long-term storage of alcohol in the body.
- Some beverages are "lite" such as some beers and wines, (containing lower concentrations of ethanol), whereas others are "light" (in color), such as white wine, vodka, gin, and tequila. There is some evidence that light beverages produce fewer hangovers than darker beverages like red wine, bourbon, and scotch. There is no evidence that people become dependent on spirits more readily than on beer or wine. Spirits, however, are more likely to produce death in overdose situations.
- Can alcohol be taken in a vapor form? An expensive new alcohol-without-liquid (AWOL) device vaporizes alcoholic beverages to provide a new way to take alcohol. Long ago, scientists gave rodents alcohol in vapor chambers to produce high stable BACs for experimentation. The new AWOL device is scary, however, because vapor/BAC correlations have not been done for humans, as they have with oral alcohol intake. Thus it is not possible to predict BACs for drink/driving purposes, and new drug-administration forms (remember crack, black tar heroin) tend to be overused and abused. Reaching lethal BACs with such devices should be rather easy. The upside? None. Companies selling such devices will make money, but for what purpose? Is snorting alcohol better than a good beer or a fine wine?
- There's a popular drink in Holland and Belgium called *jenever* ("the Dutch National Drink"). It is a 38–50% distilled spirit, with over a

hundred different flavors, which is consumed chilled, straight, or in various mixed drinks. It is similar to gin in other countries. Like other liquors, caution is advised because it is a smooth beverage and the effects are often felt after too much has been consumed.

- What are "alcopops"? Also known as malternatives, these are new hard lemonades and fruit-flavored malt beverages that are appealing to teenagers, some sources say. They have an alcohol content from 4–8%. There is some evidence that such beverages increase the amount consumed at each sitting, based upon their masking of the taste of hard alcohol, which might lead to more intoxication. Research on the level of use and consequences of these beverages is needed to make a determination of their value and dangers.

Epidemiology and Demographics

- Alcohol is the drug used most often by high school seniors. Even though such students cannot legally buy alcohol, over 90% of them have tried alcohol and almost one-third report that they have had more than five drinks at one time in the past 2 weeks. (National Institute on Alcohol Abuse and Alcoholism, 2006b.)
- About one-half to two-thirds of boating accidents are alcohol-related. I believe that advertisements by the alcohol industry suggesting a "fun" relationship between alcohol and boating are irresponsible. Although there is no direct evidence that alcohol advertising directly increases boating accidents, one could ask the question, "What is the value of such advertising, especially when the rate of alcohol-related boating accidents is so high?"

Effects of Alcohol on the Brain

- "Blackouts," contrary to public knowledge, are not a diagnostic criterion for alcohol dependence (alcoholism). Blackouts are memory lapses caused by heavy alcohol use (and sometimes moderate alcohol use), where the individual does not pass out but rather appears to act relatively normal during drinking. However, the next day, events that occurred during portions of the drinking period cannot be remembered. Blackouts probably occur because the function of the hippocampus, the part of the brain that registers memory, is depressed by alcohol. Whether the memories never get "registered" or whether they become registered but cannot be retrieved has not been determined. Anecdotal information suggests that the memories are never registered, because hypnosis cannot retrieve them.

- Blackouts after heavy drinking can be experienced by anyone, not just alcohol-dependent ("alcoholic") individuals. Many college students typically drink so much at one time that blackouts are frequent in this population. In any given group of heavy drinkers, some will experience blackouts and some won't. This is due to biological variability—different people have different sensitivities to the effects of alcohol.
- Alcohol is a very poor drug for reducing a person's anxiety or depression. These mental symptoms are caused by an inappropriate response to life events, often have biological origins, and in many cases the causes are unknown. Drinking alcohol to reduce such symptoms can actually make them worse. Therefore the best treatment for these symptoms is medication prescribed by a doctor, and psychotherapy. In most cases, the depressive symptoms due to alcohol abuse or dependence will abate and disappear after a period of time. Prolonged depression (more than a month post abstinence) often requires antidepressant medication or psychotherapy.
- Alcohol causes shrinkage of brain tissue in people after long-term use of large amounts, according to new brain-imaging studies. The shrinkage is due to the loss of brain cells, and the research is mixed with respect to recovery from this loss of brain cells. When people stop drinking, the shrinkage reverses itself, but it is still not clear whether this reversal parallels improved cognition or whether the damage is permanent. More research is needed.
- Once a person's brain cells are damaged by alcohol, can the brain repair itself if the person becomes abstinent? Brain-scan studies suggest that brain anatomy begins to return to normal within 6 months of abstinence. However, cognitive function does not always return when the brain scans appear normal. More studies are being carried out to identify which parts of the brain are repaired first.

Appendix A

Prevention of Alcohol Problems

- One of the most widely used screening tests for problem drinking is the CAGE:

  Have you ever felt the need to Cut down on your drinking?
  Have you ever felt Annoyed by someone's criticizing your drinking?
  Have you ever felt Guilty about your drinking?
  Have you ever felt the need for an Eye-opener (a drink at the beginning of the day)?

  In the newer CUGE (modification of CAGE) questionnaire, the A is replaced by "Have you ever driven a vehicle Under the influence of alcohol?" "Yes" answers to one or two of these questions suggests problem drinking and that more assessment of the individual is needed by a qualified professional.
- A recent trend is for more emergency-room doctors to be screening patients for alcohol problems. This follows a lot of good research indicating that people showing up in emergency rooms are not only involved in alcohol-related incidents, but also that at the time of injury they are more amendable to intervention about drinking problems. Society needs more opportunities such as this for physicians to be involved in reducing alcohol abuse and dependence.
- Do alcohol ads promote underage drinking and binge drinking? Available research suggests "yes," but this is a difficult phenomenon to study. With so many influences on youth, there may not be a direct causal effect of advertising on drinking. How do we know that the family, life stressors, or risk-taking behavior of underage people don't promote drinking? To say that an advertisement promotes binge drinking is pretty difficult. On the other hand, if the ads have no influence, why are they there? The alcohol industry may be truly attempting to promote brand sales and loyalty, but does this have to be done where American youth can see such ads?
- How does increasing the price of alcoholic beverages affect alcohol consumption? Keeping in mind that there are two alcohol problems, willful *abuse* and pathological *dependence* ("alcoholism"), increasing the difficulty in obtaining alcohol has been shown to reduce alcohol abuse but not alcohol dependence. People who really don't need to

drink will cut back on alcohol consumption (or give it up altogether), whereas people with the disease will use alcohol any way they can get it.

- Can reducing the number of liquor outlets reduce accidental deaths? Of course. There is plenty of research to suggest that this reasonable approach can have a positive outcome (Gruenewald, Freisthler, Remer, LaScala, & Treno, 2006). The question is, does this work at the community level? And how does a community make this happen? Recent interesting research suggests that comprehensive, community-wide efforts in this area are effective. The next question becomes, how can the government help communities across the nation implement such programs?

Alcohol and Genetics

- Why is there a genetic basis for alcohol dependence? The genetics of alcohol problems have been studied for over 20 years, and such studies have clearly shown that many of the causes of alcohol dependence are related to the genetic tendency to develop the disease. Family, twin, and adoption studies implicate the hereditary nature of, and tendency for, alcohol dependence.
- Is alcohol dependence a genetic disease? Yes, with qualifications. Genetics studies performed over the past 20–25 years have clearly shown that the *tendency* to become alcohol-dependent ("alcoholic") is inherited. In other words, genetic vulnerability coupled with unknown environmental factors, plus exposure to alcohol, is the cause of most types of alcohol dependence. Science has yet to fully understand the transmission of genetic vulnerability and the specific environmental factors that trigger the disease.
- Geneticists estimate that about 60% of the causes of alcohol dependence are due to genes that lead to increased "vulnerability" to alcoholism. These genes probably affect some physiological component of the brain (probably neurotransmitter receptors) that is associated with the production of "impaired control," the hallmark of alcohol dependence.
- How are genes related to alcohol dependence? Genes form proteins in the brain. In the brain's neurotransmitter systems, proteins and

enzymes (specialized proteins) are involved in the manufacture, release, and metabolism of chemicals that allow brain cells to communicate with one another. When such communication is disrupted between nerve cells in the "pleasure pathway," dependence on alcohol (impaired control over drinking) can occur. This disruption is probably caused by abnormal gene regulation of protein function.

- New research has found that genes for two neurotransmitter receptors are probably involved in the causes of alcohol dependence. These two receptors, GABA-A, and a form of the gene that codes for the serotonin transporter (SERT, also known as 5-HTT), may produce abnormalities in the mesolimbic dopamine system that cause people to be unable to stop drinking. Other neurotransmitter receptors have also been implicated.
- A recent study (Bowirrat & Oscar-Berman, 2005) indicates that people with a variant of the DRD2 gene (a gene associated with dopamine function in the brain) may be more prone to receive pleasure from drinking. The implication is that people with this gene might drink more than people without the variant. Does this mean the gene variant may be the cause of alcohol dependence? No, because this gene merely relates to the pleasure associated with drinking, which is not the same as the genetic cause of alcohol dependence.
- Can we find individual genes that cause alcohol dependence ("alcoholism")? The concept that a single or multiple genes cause a disease is much more complex than we expected. The latest research on genomics is telling us that the interplay of several genes probably affects the risk of developing the disease. Some gene sequences greatly enhance the risk of becoming alcohol-dependent, whereas other sequences enhance the risk only somewhat. Other sequences may lower the risk of developing the disease.
- What about a genetic test for alcohol dependence? Presently, the only available tests are paper-and-pencil tests and biomarkers. Paper-and-pencil tests involve asking questions of people who are drinking too much or too often and using their answers to determine whether they have the disease. These are not medical tests. Presently available blood or urine biomarker tests cannot determine who has alcohol

dependence, only whether a person has been drinking recently. Thus a genetic test would be an excellent medical test, and some of these are under development. However, we lack the basic knowledge on all the genes involved in alcohol dependence for such a test to be available right now.

Alcohol Abuse and the Disease of Alcohol Dependence

- The estimated incidence of alcohol-dependent people ("alcoholics") in the United States is about 4% of the population, or roughly 11 million Americans. Another way of looking at this incidence is that roughly 10–15% of those who drink alcohol are or will become alcohol-dependent.
- Alcohol shares with some other chemicals the distinction of being the oldest "addicting" drugs in the history of the world. Although no one knows for sure, alcohol may be older than marijuana and opium. There are records of Egyptian use of alcohol, and certainly the lore of alcohol's use as an intoxicant is as old as recorded history. This has led some to suggest that man's exposure to alcohol over the ages caused a brain susceptibility to alcohol dependence. There is no evidence for this.
- Where in the brain does "craving" for alcohol arise? No one knows for sure, but one paper (Pelchat, 2002) suggests that craving (desire, urge) for alcohol arises in the orbitofrontal cortex, a part of the brain behind the forehead. This may be the major site of craving, or it could be only one of several brain areas involved in this sensation.
- Does alcohol abuse lead to alcohol dependence ("alcoholism")? Although it appears that many people progress from social drinking to alcohol abuse (misuse) to alcohol dependence, obviously not everyone who drinks heavily develops an alcohol problem. Evidence is beginning to emerge that abuse and dependence are two separate conditions. For example, one study (Schuckit, Smith, Danko, Bucholz, Reich, et al., 2001) of alcohol abusers and dependent drinkers found that only about 3% of abusers had become dependent after 5 years.
- Does everyone who is dependent on alcohol have a history of alcohol abuse? Anecdotal evidence indicates that some people become alcohol-dependent very early (there are 8-year-old alcoholics), and

sometimes with their very first drink. If this is true, scientists must find out why and how some people become dependent with first exposure to the drug. The answer will probably be found in genetics studies.

- Why are so many Native Americans alcoholic? They may not be. We see more drinking among Native Americans than the general American population, but this doesn't mean they're alcoholic. Remember that *alcoholism* is a broad, overused term that (to some people) means the same as problem drinking. But the better term for alcoholic today is *alcohol dependent*, and new research is indicating that some American tribes have a low rate of alcohol dependence, whereas other tribes have a higher rate of alcohol dependence. To broadly state that all Native Americans have a high rate of alcohol dependence is probably wrong.
- Alcohol dependence is just like other medical diseases. Some people "have what it takes" to get the disease, and other people don't. "Having what it takes" involves having a genetic tendency, plus other (as yet) unknown factors. (Remember, we're not talking about voluntary alcohol *abuse*, as in college student drinking.)
- There are early-onset and late-onset forms of alcohol dependence. The early-onset form (before the age of 25) is more severe, more closely associated with genetic causes, and involves more male than female sufferers. This is called type II or type B. Type I or type A is late-onset alcohol dependence, and it is probably driven more by sensitivity to alcohol and its effects in producing dependence. There is also a "very early-onset" alcohol dependence, where people seem to become "hooked" with the very first drink (although there is almost no research on this type).
- New brain-scan research is showing that alcohol affects decision-making and judgment (the so-called executive functions of the brain) by reducing activity in the frontal lobes, where such functions reside. Interestingly, it appears that preexisting (or alcohol-induced) impaired function of these same brain areas leads to the disease of alcohol dependence, making it impossible for the person to exert conscious will over drinking behaviors.
- Is there a relationship between attention deficit hyperactivity disorder (ADHD) and alcohol dependence? Yes, but it is unlikely that ADHD

is a cause of alcohol dependence. ADHD might be a factor in early reasons to use alcohol or use it in excess. One study (Willens, Faraone, Biederman, & Gunawardene, 2003) has shown that ADHD often precedes the onset of alcohol dependence, but only in less than about 30% of alcohol-dependent patients. However, people with ADHD often have an earlier onset of alcohol dependence, compared to those without ADHD.

- People who are-alcohol dependent lack control over their drinking. An analogy is a patient with type I diabetes who cannot control the levels of insulin. Disagree? Talk to an alcohol-dependent patient who has unsuccessfully tried to stop drinking, has received the best treatment available, cannot stop drinking even with support in A.A., and has tried the latest anticraving medications, without success.
- Evidence of stigma against alcohol-dependent people is all around us. It ranges from treatment centers' having difficulty locating facilities in new neighborhoods ("not in my backyard") to high-ranking administrators' and policy makers' stating that "alcoholism is nature's way of killing off the weak people." History is too often forgotten—similar stigma existed for polio, leprosy, epilepsy, and tuberculosis over 50 years ago. Even today, there is stigma and prejudice against mentally ill people in general, and addicts in particular.
- Which is more "addictive"—alcohol or marijuana? According to available figures, about 10–15% of people who drink will become dependent on alcohol. The same source indicates that about 9% of people who smoke marijuana on a regular basis will become dependent on the drug. Both of these drugs are less "addicting" than others such as cocaine (about 17%), heroin (about 23%), and nicotine (about 32%). But "addiction" is not the only factor in the use of these drugs—intoxication outcomes, lethality, and social consequences are also important.
- Is a person who drinks in the morning an alcoholic? Although most experts agree that an "eye-opener" in the morning is a sign of alcoholism, this is not always true. What about the person who enjoys a Bloody Mary or Screwdriver in the morning while on vacation? What about the "graveyard shift" laborer who gets off work at 7 a.m. and has a drink before going home to sleep for the day? What about a Mimosa the first morning of the honeymoon? Taken alone, these

instances do not indicate alcohol dependence. Combined with other signs and symptoms of heavy drinking, these drinking episodes might be much more meaningful.

- One of the biggest problems with alcohol dependence is a lack of recognition of alcohol problems and intervention in patients by physicians. Alcohol dependence is neglected in the education of U.S. physicians and other health professionals as well. But when physicians, who have great opportunities to affect patients' drinking habits (or refer to treatment if necessary), are not trained about the effects of alcohol, public health suffers. It has been clearly documented that for every dollar spent on treatment of alcohol dependence, seven healthcare dollars are saved. (Then why not treat alcohol dependent patients and cover their treatment costs with insurance?)

Treatment of Alcohol Dependence

- Why not just punish alcoholics? Science has clearly shown that punishment is not the answer to alcohol dependence. Punishment does tend to reduce alcohol drinking (as in multiple DWIs), but only in those who still have control over their drinking (alcohol abusers). Those with the disease of alcoholism need empathy and treatment, for they have a brain disease that makes them unable to stop drinking without professional help or a 12-step program. At the same time, people with alcohol dependence often do need to be mandated into treatment, which may include threat of loss of employment, incarceration, or imposed consequences if they fail to comply.
- There is a complex interaction between drinking alcohol and smoking cigarettes. During treatment for alcohol dependence, it is difficult to obtain approval from patients to stop smoking as well. It's almost as if the addictive process for alcohol and nicotine is not affected by alcohol treatment. The continuance of the addictive process is best illustrated by a person who continues smoking after giving up alcohol.
- A comment overheard regarding benzodiazepines (e.g., Valium, Xanax) used for alcohol withdrawal: "Unlike anticonvulsants, benzodiazepines have the potential to trigger relapse, and the interaction of benzodiazepine and alcohol can be fatal." This mistaken

impression is held by many who don't understand the way benzodiazepines block potentially lethal withdrawal seizures during alcohol-dependence treatment. Benzodiazepines are given carefully while alcohol levels are declining (not increasing), and giving these drugs therapeutically for a short period of time produces little likelihood of dependence. Then they are discontinued, so they have no potential to produce relapse, because the person is under treatment. Experience has shown that most patients never want to continue to use benzodiazepines because of their exposure to them during detoxification.

- "Sweat patches" are now being studied clinically to aid in tracking sobriety in recovering alcoholics and as indicators of compliance to treatment. These patches are similar to large Band-Aids and can be placed on the skin and left for several days. They pick up and hold alcohol in the sweat released through the skin. Although they are not sufficiently accurate to be an indicator of blood alcohol concentrations, they are helpful in determining whether a person has consumed alcohol in the past several days.

Appendix B

Drug Concepts Affecting Neurobiology and Treatment

BASIC PHARMACOLOGICAL KNOWLEDGE IS ESSENTIAL for understanding the entire picture of drug addiction and its treatment. Neurobiological principles are based upon accurate information about drugs (including alcohol, covered in Appendix A). Licit (legal) and illicit (illegal) drugs have enormous social impact, especially related to crime, long-term toxicity in the drug-using individual, psychological and family problems associated with drug use, and the development of chemical dependence in those susceptible to the disease.

The following items are intended to supplement the material in the main chapters. They have been adapted from the website of the University of Texas at Austin's Addiction Science Research and Education Center (*www.utexas.edu/research/asrec*). The website folder "Drug Facts to Share with Others" contains over 300 of these items. These items were chosen as "important for chemical-dependency counselors and other treatment professionals" by a panel of individuals associated with the Addiction Technology Transfer Centers, funded by the federal Center for Substance Abuse Treatment.

Terminology

- What are the differences among the terms *sedative*, *tranquilizer*, *anxiolytic*, and *neuroleptic*? They are all related. The word *sedative* is a general, older term for anything that calms people down. *Tranquilizer* is also an older term for a drug that reduces anxiety ("minor" tranquilizer) or psychotic symptoms ("major" tranquilizer). These terms have mostly been replaced by *anxiolytics* (anxiety-reducers) and *neuroleptics* (antischizophrenic drugs).

- What is "dope"? We hear the pejorative terms *smoking dope*, *dope fiends*, and *using dope*. Obviously, *dope* is an unscientific term for illegal drugs, including marijuana, heroin, and perhaps all other illegal drugs. The term obviously does not apply to alcohol and nicotine. Reducing the use of the term will help to reduce the stigma associated with public misunderstanding of what these drugs do to the brain.
- Heroin and methadone are called *opioid agonists* because they cause activation of the opioid receptor, which leads to analgesia, euphoria, and, in some people, dependence on these drugs. New drugs are being developed to treat heroin dependence. One interesting drug, buprenorphine, is a "partial agonist," which means that its opioid-receptor activating effects level off at a certain dose. This limited excitatory action has been shown to be effective in helping heroin addicts break free of their dependence on heroin.
- *Substance abuse* is a poor term when applied to treatment centers and some government agencies. (*Substance abuse* is willful use of drugs and not a focus of clinical treatment.) The name "substance abuse treatment center," is inaccurate in light of the new definition of *addiction.* A better term is "dependence treatment centers." (This is especially true for treatment of sex and gambling disorders, which are not "substances.")

Basic Drug Pharmacology

- Part of the variability in response to drugs from person to person is due to "set" and "setting." (The "set" is the expectation of the drug's effect by the user, along with the user's mood, state of mind, and alertness at the time of drug use. The "setting" is the environment in which the drug is taken.) An example of this is that people will get higher smoking marijuana if they have a positive attitude about it than if they were raised to believe that marijuana is harmful. Also, a person will generally get a better response using a drug with other people than using it alone.

- A basic pharmacological concept is that potent drugs (such as LSD or Xanax) require fewer molecules to produce a therapeutic or toxic effect in people than less potent drugs (such as Soma or ethanol). Nonpharmacologists often confuse "potency" (amount of action on a cell, receptor, or tissue produced by a fixed amount of drug) with "dose" (the amount of drug to produce an effect). People can change doses of a drug but they cannot change the potency of a drug.
- All drugs affecting the brain have a common *general* mechanism of action. That is, they all affect nerve cells (neurons) in some way. Some brain-affecting drugs reduce nerve cell function, whereas others increase it. But it isn't that simple. When a person falls asleep, some parts of the brain continue to function and are refreshed by the reduced activity of the body. In a similar manner, some brain areas are "disinhibited" when a depressant drug such as heroin is working. The result is an energized feeling.
- Illegal drugs (as well as nicotine) are administered into the body by different routes: orally (by mouth), smoking (to the lungs via the trachea from the mouth), the nasal membranes ("snorting"), by vein (intravenously), under the skin (subcutaneously), into a muscle (intramuscularly), by artery (injection into a major neck artery, for example), into the rectum (rectally, as by suppository), and under the tongue (sublingually). Chemically dependent people often have tried every site of administration imaginable. Sometimes the act of preparing and administering the drug is more exciting than the drug itself (often seen with cocaine use).
- Can drugs other than alcohol cause "blackouts"? Although the alcohol-induced blackout is most well-known, other drugs can cause it too. A blackout is nothing more than a brief period of drug-induced short-term amnesia. Thus, some anesthetics used for surgery cause blackouts, but the term is not used with the therapeutic use of drugs because short-term amnesia of the surgical event is a desired outcome. Other drugs that cause intense intoxication, such as opioids (powerful analgesics such as morphine), most barbiturates, cocaine, LSD, ecstasy, and some benzodiazepines can also cause blackouts.

- How do blackouts occur? Blackouts are an apparent result of depression of activity in the part of the brain known as the hippocampus. The function of this brain area concerns cognitive learning and memory. It is known to be very sensitive to the effects of central nervous system depressant drugs such as alcohol, opioids, anesthetics, and even some stimulants such as cocaine. The rest of the brain is not as sensitive to such drugs, so that an intoxicated person may appear fine—until the next day when certain events of the night before are not remembered.
- Neurotransmitters are chemicals released at the ends of nerve cells (neurons) that help signals pass from nerve cell to nerve cell, thereby making the brain capable of behavior, thought, and emotions. There are over 50 specially identified neurotransmitters in the brain and probably hundreds more that are only now being discovered. Drug effects on brain cells are generally associated with specific actions on certain neurotransmitters. For example, scientists believe that the effects of heroin are exerted through chemicals called endorphins; cocaine, through dopamine; and benzodiazepines (such as Xanax), through gamma aminobutyric acid (GABA).
- All drugs that affect the brain act at the cellular (that is, nerve cell) level. Nerve cells talk to one another through chemicals called neurotransmitters. Neurotransmitters are made, destroyed, and cause a "connection" between nerve cells through their release during electrical firing of individual nerve cells. Most drugs that affect the brain (to cause either unwanted or therapeutic effects) act by changing the actions of neurotransmitters.
- There are several neurotransmitters in the brain that appear to be related to chemical dependence ("addiction"): dopamine, serotonin, endorphins, GABA, glutamate, acetylcholine, and endocannabinoids. It appears that dysregulation of one or more of these chemicals in the brain's pleasure pathway determines the primary drug upon which a person becomes dependent. For example, we might assume that cocaine dependence is related to dopamine dysregulation. Another match-up includes heroin and endorphins. Finally, nicotine dependence might be related to dysregulation of nicotine receptors (acetylcholine system).

- Many, but not all, abused drugs are "receptor agonists." An "agonist" (such as heroin) activates a receptor in the brain to produce its effects. An "antagonist" (such as naloxone, Narcan) occupies a receptor site and prevents an agonist from activating the receptor. Thus, when a person overdoses on heroin, Narcan (in sufficient doses) is capable of taking the place of heroin at the receptor and reversing the heroin effects. This is why Narcan is a lifesaving drug in heroin overdose situations. Because Narcan does not activate the opioid receptors, it is not "addicting."
- "Addicting" drugs act at the cellular (nerve cell) level by activating receptors that help to propagate certain types of signals from cell to cell. When a drug enters the brain, it floods the nerve cells and eventually reaches the synaptic area (spaces between nerve cells) where the cells "talk to each other" by way of chemicals. Receptors for drugs and neurochemicals are very specific, being sensitive to only one or a few chemicals.

Drug Use and Abuse

- There are an enormous number of chemicals in the world. Why do people use some to get "high"? Perhaps the normal human desire is to feel better, and when normal everyday activities fail to satisfy people, they use drugs to feel better. Some people have said, "People use drugs because the drugs work, they work fast, and are easier for coping with life than learning more effective methods."
- People "abuse" many drugs. A few that we're hearing about these days include Ritalin (see the previous item), Vicodin (often used by health professionals and people who begin using it for rational therapeutic reasons such as back pain), club drugs (GHB, rohypnol, ketamine, and others that are taken because of peer group acceptance), Ultram (tramadol, a nontraditional opioidlike analgesic that is abused by health professionals), and codeine (a mild opioid antitussive, or anti-cough, medication). Club drugs and codeine, especially, have been taken with other drugs such as alcohol, which makes the complications of their abuse even more problematic. Some of these drugs have a large dependence potential whereas some have a low dependence potential.

- People are confused by the legal availability of alcohol and nicotine, two highly toxic drugs when used in excess, and the illegality of drugs such as marijuana. In addition, some Native Americans in religious ceremonies can use some drugs such as mescaline and other psychedelics legally, and some potentially dangerous drugs (opium, coca leaves) are legal in some parts of the world. No drugs, however, are legal for Americans under the age of 18, except "medicines" prescribed by physicians or by other healthcare providers. These medicines, however, include abusable drug categories such as amphetamines, opioid analgesics, and the antianxiety and sleep-inducing benzodiazepines.
- It is pretty clear that the reason people with schizophrenia smoke cigarettes is that they are self-medicating with nicotine. A recent study (Salokangas, Honkonen, Stengard, Koivisto, & Hietala, 2006) showed that schizophrenics are up to three times more likely to smoke as nonschizophrenics. One of the reasons they smoke appears to be that nicotine increases attention and short-term memory. This makes sense when we look at old research showing that nicotine can enhance memory in animals. Nicotine also has a sedating effect and elevates mood, so such use is understandable, since depression is very common in such patients.
- Which is a worse drug problem in the United States—marijuana or methamphetamine? Federal emphasis is on prevention of marijuana use in adolescents, yet emergency rooms are seeing more and more methamphetamine users. It is well known that marijuana use is more prevalent than methamphetamine use, but the dangers associated with methamphetamine use are much higher and more dramatic.
- Drug-use histories in the United States show us that most drugs have cycles in their use. We have had, in the past, "epidemics" of LSD, cocaine, crack, methamphetamine, ecstasy, and many others. Exceptions to these epidemics are continued high use of alcohol, marijuana, and cigarettes (nicotine). Bottom line: Do we want to have an epidemic-reactive policy or a policy against all drugs, regardless of their danger (or lack thereof) to the public?
- Using dextromethorphan along with decongestants can dramatically increase blood pressure. Both of these drugs are found in cough medicines, but in usual therapeutic doses they are usually not a problem.

It is when people trying to get "high" abuse cough medicines that problems can arise. There are reports that young people are buying cough medicines to abuse them. Cough medicines are not without danger, especially in people sensitive to these ingredients.

- Does the use of one drug, such as marijuana, lead to the use of other drugs, such as heroin, amphetamines, or cocaine? Some studies suggest this happens, even in animals. But this phenomenon is difficult to measure, especially in humans. Do people who use marijuana "progress" to heroin because of the effects of marijuana on the brain? Or do people who use marijuana have greater risk-taking behaviors that include the use of "stronger" drugs? It will take a while to sort out the cause-and-effect aspects of this question.
- Why are OxyContin and cocaine "legal" if they both produce massive chemical dependence? Both of these drugs have federally accepted therapeutic uses: OxyContin for pain relief, and cocaine as an anesthetic for eye surgery. As long as the distribution (sale) of these drugs is regulated, they are deemed to have more positive medical effects than detrimental effects. Practically, both are excellent drugs, if we could just control their distribution in society. Where society breaks down is in its ability to regulate the illegal use or abuse of these medications.
- A recent news story talked about a hurricane placing an "added strain on people who may have been walking the line between moderate use and addiction." What does this mean? The description suggests, and is partially erroneous, that stress can increase a person's drug use from moderate use to addiction. We know that stress *can* prompt people to use a drug or increase use of a drug; however, increasing the amount of drug use cannot be presumed to lead to dependence. It would be more accurate to state, "More drug use may lead to more drug-related problems."
- Some people use medications but are neither willful "abusers" nor "dependent" as defined by psychiatric assessment criteria. They consciously believe that they are better off when taking a drug every day to make their lives more comfortable (for example, they sleep better with a mild hypnotic drug or they relieve mild to moderate pain with regular use of nonopioid analgesics such as ibuprofen). This unlabeled class of drug users was formerly called *habitual* drug

users but now might be called *comfort seekers*. More research is needed on this class of drug users.

Drug Toxicity and Mortality

- Do drugs destroy brain cells? The only drugs for which there is solid evidence on this is alcohol and inhalants, but there are some animal studies on ecstasy (MDMA, a psychedelic drug), and some brain-imaging studies on methamphetamine (a powerful stimulant). Alcohol destroys brain cells ("neurotoxicity") only in large, prolonged doses. But with ecstasy (MDMA), the ends of the serotonin nerve cells are simply gone (as seen in animal studies). Not only is the serotonin gone, but all the other cell components of the nerve terminal have disappeared.
- Small doses of MDMA apparently produce little or no damage to nerve cells, moderate doses produce damage but some of the serotonin system is still functional, and large doses can completely destroy the nerve terminals. ("Small," moderate," and "large" doses are relative terms; they vary from person to person.) Methamphetamine studies in animals suggest that this drug can also permanently damage nerve cells.
- Which drugs can cause death in overdoses? Most people understand that people can overdose on heroin (cause is respiratory depression), cocaine (stroke or heartbeat abnormalities), alcohol (respiratory depression or drowning on vomit), barbiturates (respiratory depression), and amphetamines (convulsions). However, there are two drugs for which the lethal dose is not known: marijuana and LSD. This does not mean that these drugs should be legalized, however, for they both have harmful mood-altering effects.
- The three most dangerous drugs or drug classes with respect to negative effects on organ systems are (in descending order): inhalants, nicotine, and alcohol. Inhalants are poisons in every sense of the word—taking them in through the mouth and nose can not only cause instant death (for example, as in airway freezing with aerosols), but also heartbeat irregularities, breathing stoppage, and (with long-term use) kidney, heart, liver, and brain damage. Nicotine is well-known for its ability to produce lung cancer and heart disease with long-term use, and alcohol produces liver cirrhosis, heart disease,

brain changes, gastrointestinal problems, pancreatitis, and many other effects in long-term heavy drinkers.

- Although we know there is an association between smoking and strokes, recently the association appears to continue even after a person quits smoking. It appears that the more cigarettes smokers consume in their lifetime, the thicker their arteries will be, regardless of how long they are abstinent. "Thicker arteries" suggests greater atherosclerosis. This conclusion is based upon recent MRI scans of former smokers.
- Although there is incomplete evidence on the amount of harm produced by drugs on the developing fetus, it appears that most drugs (other than alcohol) taken by a mother produce only temporary effects on the fetus. Of course, any harm to the fetus is a serious issue, and most nonscientists do not understand that withdrawal from drugs in a newborn is not life-threatening unless there are other complications. In addition, small birth weight, premature births, and other major concerns are rare and reversible over time.
- Some advocates of child welfare have indicated they would like to criminalize drug use by pregnant women. Although this idea appears to have merit on the surface regarding safety of the newborn, it is not science-based. First, it does not recognize that some women who are using drugs need treatment to become abstinent during pregnancy (i.e., they have the disease of chemical dependence). Second, it includes all illicit drugs—marijuana, LSD, methamphetamine, and others—implying that all of these drugs when ingested by the mother will be dangerous to the fetus. None of these drugs is as dangerous to the fetus as alcohol.

Treatment of Drug Abuse and Dependence

- New anticraving medications are becoming available for the treatment of chemical dependence. Some of them are older drugs that are now being used for this new purpose; others are new drugs designed specifically as abstinence-enhancing drugs that will supplement existing behavioral treatments ("talk therapy").
- Abstinence-enhancing and anticraving pharmacotherapies include bupropion (Zyban, for nicotine dependence), naltrexone (ReVia, for

alcohol dependence), and methadone (Dolophine, for heroin dependence). To date, there are no effective pharmacotherapies for treating dependence associated with cocaine, marijuana, benzodiazepines, amphetamines, and miscellaneous drugs (PCP, ketamine, rohypnol).

- The use of methadone to treat heroin and other opioid dependence is highly effective because the drug reduces the craving for heroin, "stabilizes" the neurotransmitter dysregulation in the brain associated with heroin craving, and gets the person out of the crime-related activities associated with the acquisition of heroin. However, many people mistakenly think that methadone treatment is only "replacing one addicting drug with another." People who believe in strict or absolute abstinence-based treatment disagree with the use of methadone. However, methadone treatment saves lives.
- Pharmacotherapy (pharmaceutical treatment) of chemical dependence falls into four general categories: (1) drugs that reduce withdrawal severity (for example, nicotine patches and gum for nicotine, clonidine for heroin), (2) drugs that reduce craving that leads to drug seeking or relapse (for example, bupropion, Zyban, and naltrexone for alcohol), (3) drugs that block or impede a desired effect (such as naltrexone for heroin), and (4) drugs that address co-occurring or related psychiatric illness (such as antidepressants for cocaine).
- The big challenge in developing medications to treat chemical dependency is to achieve high potency, great specificity, and no significant side effects. This means that new medications must be effective in low doses (e.g., in the 1–4 mg/dose range), must target only the brain areas involved in dependence (e.g., various parts of the medial forebrain bundle, where addiction occurs), and have effects that do not "spill over" into other areas of the body such as peripheral systems, where side effects would be produced.
- Vaccines are now being developed for the treatment of several drug dependencies: cocaine, nicotine, and methamphetamine. These "polyclonal" and "monoclonal" antibodies have been developed to bind with the parent drug to prevent the drug from reaching the brain or from attaching to the brain receptor that produces the drug effect. Thus, an animal or person who is given one of these vaccines will not feel the effects of the drug. Will these be highly useful in addiction treatment? We must wait for the clinical trials to be completed.

- We often hear the term *compliance to treatment*. How does this relate to addiction treatment? "Compliance" has to do with the regularity with which people continue treatment over time. It is a common medical problem for patients to become less compliant with treatment when they feel better, or when treatment is difficult to obtain. However, recent research suggests that alcoholics and other chemically dependent people are as compliant with their treatment as are people with less stigmatized diseases such as diabetes, high blood pressure, and asthma (McLellan et al., 2000).
- We hear a lot about "methadone maintenance," which is a controversial treatment for heroin dependence. But what about "nicotine maintenance," where people stop smoking cigarettes but continue to use nicotine in the form of patches or gum? These people believe that they are reducing their risk of lung cancer or heart disease because they are no longer exposing themselves to carbon monoxide, tars, and other harmful effects of cigarette smoke. But nicotine itself is highly toxic, and long-term exposure to it over many years will probably have lethal effects. However, it is better than continued smoking.
- What is LAAM? This is an acronym for the chemical name of a drug similar to methadone. It differs from methadone in that it lasts longer when given to heroin-dependent patients, and it only needs to be given every 3 days instead of daily. However, this drug is no longer on the market due to cardiac irregularities associated with its use, and therefore it is only of historical interest.
- What is buprenorphine (Buprenex)? This drug is a powerful analgesic. Recently, the Food and Drug Administration approved buprenorphine for the treatment of heroin dependence (under the brand names Subutex and Suboxone). It is unique because, unlike methadone, it has a "partial agonist" effect, which means that its therapeutic effect plateaus at certain doses. Thus, it is less likely to be abused by opioid addicts in treatment (that is, they are less likely to get "high" on it during slips in recovery). It can be given sublingually (under the tongue) for quick action. Unlike methadone, which must be administered by an approved clinic, it can be prescribed by any properly trained physician in an outpatient setting.
- "Rapid detox" of heroin users is very controversial. The procedure involves injecting patients with a cocktail of antiopioid medications

under sedation and promises detoxification within 24 hours rather than the days of agony suffered by patients who go "cold-turkey." A recent clinical study from Columbia University (Collins, Kleber, Whittington, & Heitler, 2005) found that the 3-month success rate for rapid detox was no better than for two other, more traditional detoxification methods lasting 36–48 hours in inpatient or (even longer in) outpatient treatment. Further, deaths have occurred with rapid detox and the procedure is quite expensive.

- The new era of endocannabinoid pharmacology (development of medications that affect the naturally occurring marijuanalike chemicals in the brain) is as exciting as the 1980s era of endorphin pharmacology (which produced medications that affect the morphinelike chemicals in the brain). The new drug rimonabant is the frontrunner of medications that antagonize brain endocannabinoids. Rimonabant is effective in reducing food hunger and is a smoking cessation aid. It is also being tested for its possible anticraving effects for other drugs such as alcohol and cocaine.
- Scientists are always looking for new medications to treat people with chemical dependence. A group of neurotransmitters called hypocretin/orexin peptides has been tied to reward and pleasure for many decades and could be involved in chemical dependence. If the true involvement of this potential neurotransmitter can be confirmed and expanded upon, it might provide another chemical system in the brain that is vulnerable to medication. So far, studies on orexin have involved reward-seeking for morphine, cocaine, and food by animals. Scientists were able to initiate and reduce craving to these substances by introducing and blocking orexin.
- Web-based treatment has hit the Internet. The treatment includes two dozen counseling sessions in a 3-month period and a year of aftercare. The Getgoing.com program advertises that it is covered by most major insurance companies and is backed by a guarantee. It will take a while to determine whether such a program increases treatment in those who really need it. One of the obvious weaknesses of the program is that it is based upon anonymous group therapy, and it is not apparent whether it targets chemically dependent people or

merely anyone who has a drug problem. In other words, it does not appear to be evidence-based in its strategies and outcomes.

Drug Screening

- "Doping" can be a big problem in athletes. Although drug screens can pick up most illegal drugs in an athlete's urine, some newer growth-enhancing steroids cannot be detected. Drug screens will always lag behind newly discovered drugs, because the need to excel in some sports outweighs the risk of getting caught and punished.
- If an adolescent is brought to an emergency room with a first-time seizure, there should be a drug screen to determine if cocaine was involved. Cocaine and other stimulants such as methamphetamine can cause seizures if the dose is too high or if the person is very sensitive to the effects of such drugs.
- Most drug screens are only preliminary and qualitative (meaning they can tell whether patients have a drug in their urine or blood, above a certain low level). If a positive result is seen in the qualitative screen, a quantitative screen is run to identify the exact drug in the tissue, as well as the exact amount of the drug, which provides an idea as to how much of the drug was consumed.

Glossary

(Some genetic terms are from *Alcohol Research & Health*, 2002)

Abuse – A type of drug overuse. This is a condition in which individuals consciously and voluntarily overuse drugs, causing danger to themselves or others. Drug abuse can be diagnosed or assessed using clinical and medical criteria. (Compare with *dependence*.)
Acetaldehyde – The primary metabolite (breakdown product) of ethanol (beverage alcohol).
Acetylcholine – An excitatory neurotransmitter in the brain and peripheral nervous system that acts through activation of nicotine- or muscarine-type receptors to produce a pharmacological effect. Acetylcholine is involved in memory and muscle movement, among other actions in the nervous system.
Action potential – The electrical impulse that travels from a nerve cell body (soma) toward another neuron.
Active transport – The carrier of a molecule from the outside to the inside of a cell, via a system that uses energy for the process. (Used in this particular context for neurotransmitter molecules that have been released from a nerve cell.)

Addiction – The general term for a condition of drug use or habitual activity that is beyond voluntary control. The term has been used erroneously to describe any activity or practice (such as "addiction to chocolate") that a person may not wish to stop or feels he or she cannot stop.
Adenosine receptors – Binding sites for the neurotransmitter/neuromodulator adenosine. they are the main site of action of caffeine.
Agonist – A drug that activates a neuronal receptor to produce a pharmacological effect.
Alcoholic – A person who is alcohol-dependent (scientific definition) or who attends Alcoholics Anonymous (broader definition).
Alcoholics Anonymous – A program of 12 steps to sobriety that are studied and practiced by individuals who wish to stop drinking because of the negative effects of alcohol in their lives and who maintain anonymity about their recovery except to others in the program.
Alcoholism – The general term for a condition of alcohol overuse that is beyond voluntary control. *Alcohol dependence* is the more accurate diagnostic term for clinical and research purposes. In some contexts (as in Alcoholics Anonymous groups) the term is used to describe anyone who wants to achieve abstinence through the 12-step program.
Allele – One of two or more variants of a gene or other DNA sequences. Different alleles of a gene generally serve the same function (e.g., code for a protein that affects eye color) but may produce different phenotypes (e.g., blue eyes or brown eyes). Some alleles may be defective and produce a protein that has no function or an abnormal function.
Allostasis – The process of achieving stability through change; the pathological process during which homeostasis is lost, causing the set point for drug action to gradually move away from "normal." In the context of this book, one of the main theories for neuroadaptation due to long-term drug exposure.
Amygdala – A brain area associated with the mesolimbic dopamine system that stores emotional memories and thus is involved in emotional behavior.
Anandamide – The first cannabinoid agonist (activator) discovered; activates the cannabinoid receptors.
Anhedonia – The inability to experience pleasure.
Antagonist – A drug that blocks the activation of a receptor, thereby blocking or reversing the effects of an agonist (activator) of the receptor.
Anxiolytic – An agent that reduces anxiety.

Autoreceptor – A site on a neuron that binds the neurotransmitter released by that neuron, which then regulates the neuron's activity.
Axon – The "sending" fiber of a nerve cell that transmits an electrical impulse toward the next neuron.
Benzodiazepines – The class of chemicals that includes medications for the treatment of anxiety, seizures, and different types of insomnia.
Beverage unit (of alcohol) – The standard unit of alcohol by which measures of beer, wine, and spirits are equated. Each beverage unit contains about 14 grams of absolute (99.5% by weight) ethanol (beverage alcohol).
Blackout – A period of amnesia for a portion of a drinking or drugging binge; can be caused by alcohol, marijuana, and other depressant drugs.
Blood alcohol concentration (BAC) – The concentration of alcohol in blood in terms of grams of alcohol per 100 milliliters of blood (g%), or milligrams of alcohol per deciliter of blood (mg/dl).
Candidate gene – A gene that has been implicated in causing or contributing to a particular phenotype (e.g., a disease).
Cannabinoids – Organic chemicals present in *Cannabis sativa*, the plant from which marijuana is extracted. These chemicals have a variety of pharmacologic properties.
Cannabinoid (CB) receptor – The binding site for the active ingredient in marijuana, tetrahydrocannabinol (THC). CB receptors come in two general types: CB1, which activate cannabinoid receptors in the sentral nervous system, and CB2, which activate cannabinoid receptors in the nervous systems outside the central nervous system.
Chemical – A broad class of substances (including drugs) that may or may not produce noticeable effects in the body.
Chromosome – A microscopic rod-shaped structure composed of double-stranded DNA and proteins; can be visualized during a certain phase of the cell cycle and is generally found within the cell nucleus. Chromosomes are often regarded as representing the entire genome of an organism.
Cloning – The production of multiple exact copies of a single gene or other segment of DNA to obtain enough material for further study. Also applied to the production of complete, genetically identical animals.
Club drug – A drug used at informal "clubs," called *raves* or *rave parties*. Club drugs include LSD, ecstasy, methamphetamine, rohypnol, GHB, and ketamine.

Codon – A sequence of three consecutive nucleotide base subunits in an mRNA molecule that together represent the genetic code for a particular amino acid.
Corticotropin releasing factor (CRF) – A pituitary hormone released during stress; used as a biochemical measure of stress.
Craving – The urge or desire to continue taking a drug or carrying out an activity. In the drug-research arena, the word *craving* does not have a solid scientific meaning. It is also difficult to measure. When patients are asked to describe drug craving, scientists receive widely different answers. Thus, the words *urge* or *desire* are often more meaningful. Craving is *not* the same as dependence.
Cross-dependence – A situation in which a person who is dependent on one drug is also dependent on another drug or drugs.
Cross-tolerance – A situation in which a person who is tolerant to a drug is also tolerant to another drug in the same chemical class or a closely related class of drugs.
Dendrite – The "receiving" portion of a nerve cell that picks up and transmits an impulse from a previous neuron.
Dependence – A type of drug overuse. This is a more scientific and clinically accurate term for **addiction**. It describes the brain disease associated with impaired control over drug use. (Compare with *abuse*.)
DNA (deoxyribonucleic acid) – The molecule that carries the genetic code in all organisms except some viruses.
Dopamine – A monoamine neurotransmitter involved in pleasure, muscle control, motivation, and emotional response through its actions in the brain.
Dopamine transporter (DAT) – The presynaptic binding site for dopamine, where dopamine is taken back into the presynaptic area and becomes part of the reusable or nonreusable pool of dopamine involved in transmitting the signal to the next cell. The DAT process removes dopamine from the synapse and prepares the system for refiring.
Drug – Any chemical other than food or water that produces a therapeutic or nontherapeutic pharmacological action (effect) in the body.
Dysregulation – A problem with control of the rate or manner in which a process progresses or a product is formed; most simply, the process is not working normally.
Ecstasy – A methamphetaminelike drug that is highly abused. It is also known as MDMA or methylenedioxy-methamphetamine.

Endocannabinoids – Naturally occurring (in the brain) cannabinoids, known for activating CB receptors.

Endogenous – Originating or produced within the organism or one of its parts (as opposed to exogenous, something introduced into the body).

Endorphins – Naturally occurring (in the body) morphinelike substances, that include beta-endorphin, enkephalins, and dynorphins.

Enzyme – A substance (usually a protein) that speeds up, or catalyzes, a specific biochemical reaction without being itself permanently altered or consumed.

Euphoria – A sense of well-being; with drugs, often described as a "high."

First messenger – With respect to nerve transmission of impulses, the first change in signal in the system; in this case, a neurotransmitter.

GABA – Gamma aminobutyric acid, the primary inhibitory neurotransmitter in the brain, involved in mechanisms of anxiety and sleep, among others.

GABA receptor – A receptor for the amino acid GABA, which when activated causes reduced firing of nerve cells. This is one of the sites of action of alcohol and benzodiazepine medications.

Gene – A combination of DNA segments that together constitute a unit capable of expressing one or more functional gene products.

Gene expression – The process of converting the genetic information encoded in DNA into a final gene product (i.e., a protein or any of several types of RNA).

Gene mapping – Determination of the positions of genes on a chromosome relative to one another.

Genetic code – The way in which the information carried by the DNA molecules determines the arrangement of amino acids in the proteins synthesized by the cells.

Genome – The total genetic material of an organism or species.

Genotype – The genetic makeup of an individual organism; determined by the specific alleles of each gene carried by the individual. Differences in alleles among individuals interact with environmental influences to account for the differences in phenotype observed among those individuals.

GHB – Gamma-hydroxybutyrate, a club drug that is a metabolite of the natural neurotransmitter GABA.

Glia – Support (structural) cells for neurons in the central nervous system.
Glutamate – The primary excitatory neurotransmitter in the brain; involved in the mechanism of intoxication caused by alcohol and perhaps other drugs.
Glutamate receptor – The binding site for the amino acid glutamic acid (glutamate). Activation of this receptor produces increased nerve cell firing.
Half-life – The time it takes for a drug to fall to one-half of its concentration in the blood. A second half-life leads to a loss of one-half of the remaining concentration, and so on, until the drug can no longer be measured in the blood.
Hallucination – A perception of something (such as a visual image or a sensation of sound) with no external cause, usually arising as a disorder of the nervous system (as in psychosis) or in response to a drug (for example, LSD).
Hangover – A period of discomfort occurring several hours after the overuse of a drug, often related to overdrinking by alcohol abusers or dependent individuals, but also occurring with any drug that causes a "morning-after" array of uncomfortable symptoms.
Hypnotic – An agent that causes sleep.
Impulse-control disorders – Mental disorders characterized by an inability to resist impulses, urges, or temptations to do something that harms the patient or others.
Instinctual – Relating to an enduring disposition or tendency of an organism to act in an organized and biologically adaptive manner characteristic of its species.
Ion channels – Protein-lined sites in nerve cells through which physiological ions pass to aid in the transmission of nerve impulses.
Ketamine – An anesthetic that has properties causing a person to be out-of-touch with the environment while appearing to be "awake" (a dissociative state); a club drug.
Knockout – The deletion or deactivation of a gene in a mouse or other laboratory animal in all cells, including the germ cells, to create a line of animals that are incapable of producing the gene product.
Ligand – A molecule that binds to a macromolecule (e.g., a ligand binding to a receptor).

Lipid solubility – The ability of a drug or its metabolites to dissolve in body fat.

Magnetic resonance imaging (MRI) – A brain-imaging method in which body structure (in this case, the brain) is scanned using powerful magnets to measure tissue density, resulting in black-and-white photographs of the structure's anatomy. *Functional MRI* (*fMRI*) is an investigational type of scan that computer-analyzes structural differences in treated versus control subjects or conditions, resulting in an MRI picture with differences indicated in color.

MDMA – See *ecstasy*.

Medial forebrain bundle – Another term for the mesolimbic dopamine system.

Mesolimbic dopamine system (MDS) – The reward pathway of the brain, consisting of two primary functional areas, the ventral tegmental area and the nucleus accumbens. The MDS is also called the medial forebrain bundle.

mRNA (messenger RNA) – A type of ribonucleic acid that relays the coding information for proteins from the DNA in the nucleus to the ribosomes in the cytoplasm, where actual protein synthesis occurs.

Mutation – A heritable change in the DNA nucleotide sequence that can potentially result in a change in the function of one or more genes.

Neuroadaptation – The process of gradual change in nervous-system (or individual-nerve-cell) function, leading to an elevated or depressed response to a drug or chemical. The change occurs because of an effect of the drug or chemical on nerve cell function, such as at the receptors themselves.

Neuron – A nerve cell in the brain, spinal cord, or peripheral nervous system.

Neurotransmitter – The chemical released between nerve cells to affect transmission from one nerve cell to the next.

Nicotine receptor – A binding site for the neurotransmitter acetylcholine. Activation of this binding site by acetylcholine or nicotine leads to increased cell firing in the autonomic nervous system or certain brain sites.

NMDA receptor – The n-methyl-d-aspartate receptor, one of the proposed sites of action of alcohol. This is an excitatory receptor, which when activated causes increased nerve-cell firing.

Norepinephrine – A monoamine neurotransmitter in the brain; involved in arousal, dreaming, and mood.
Nucleus accumbens (NAcc) – The primary dopamine-releasing portion of the mesolimbic dopamine system.
Peptide – A compound of two or more amino acids in which peptide bonds are present, leading to products such as hormones, secretory agents, and established or potential neurotransmitters.
Pharmacogenomics – The study of the effect of an individual's genotype on the body's potential response to medications.
Phenotype – The observable structural or functional characteristics of an individual organism that result from the interaction of its genotype with environmental factors.
Physiological (physical) dependence – The process of adaptation (usually neuroadaptation) to a drug or chemical, generally when given over a long period of time, resulting in withdrawal upon cessation of the drug's use or when a specific antagonist to the drug is given. Not the same as *dependence*.
Pleasure pathway – A popular term for the mesolimbic dopamine system.
Pleasure neurotransmitter – Dopamine.
Polymorphism – The presence of two or more alleles of a gene or other DNA sequence in a population. A variant allele that occurs in less than 1% of the population is considered a mutation.
Positron emission tomography (PET) – A colorful type of brain imaging that measures blood flow or radioactively labeled components (receptors, etc.) in brain areas, directly relating to the activity of cells (neurons) in the brain areas.
Postsynaptic tissue – The part of a nerve cell that receives neurotransmitter input on its receptors for communication of an impulse (signal) from a previous neuron.
Prefrontal cortex or lobes – The forward (anterior) portion of the frontal lobe of the brain.
Presynaptic ending – The part of a nerve cell that releases neurotransmitters for communication of an impulse (signal) to the next neuron.
Protein – A large molecule composed of one or more chains of amino acids in a specific order.
Protein synthesis – The production or manufacture of proteins during the gene-translation process.

Proteomics – The large-scale analysis of the structure and function of proteins as well as of protein-protein interactions.
Psychostimulant – A chemical with mood-elevating properties.
Quantitative trait locus (QTL) – A polymorphic site on a chromosome containing alleles that differentially influence the expression of a quantitative trait (which is a phenotypic trait that varies along a continuum within a population).
Rebound hyperexcitability – Signs and symptoms of excitation (tremors, seizures, excess nervous system activity) after a prolonged period of depressant drug use; caused by systems of the body attempting to become normal after being depressed but unable to prevent overstimulation. Also known as *withdrawal.*
Receptor – The "binding site" on neurons where neurotransmitters attach and transfer a signal from one nerve to another or within a single neuron. Binding to a receptor causes a change in the cell that leads to a change in sensitivity of the neuron to a stimulus.
Reliance – The therapeutic use of medications in cases where the medication is needed to reduce symptoms of an illness. (Compare with *dependence.*)
REM sleep – The most restful state of sleep; characterized by rapid eye movement under the eyelids.
Reticular activating system (RAS) – The brain's alerting system, found in the brain stem between the brain and spinal cord.
Ribosomes – Cytoplasmic structures composed of rRNA and proteins; where proteins are assembled from amino acids during translation.
Rohypnol – A benzodiazepine club drug, illegal in the United States.
rRNA (ribosomal RNA) – A type of RNA that forms structural and functional components of ribosomes; binds to both mRNA and tRNA to ensure the correct order of amino acids in a protein during translation.
Second messenger – With respect to nerve transmission of an impulse, the second in the chain of messengers that transmits a signal through the system; in this case, the postsynaptic chemicals that are modified by the binding of a neurotransmitter to a receptor.
Selective serotonin reuptake inhibitor (SSRI) – A chemical that blocks the uptake of serotonin from the synapse back into the presynaptic tissue. The result is a greater concentration of serotonin in the synapse, which is beneficial in overcoming clinical depression of the type that

involves a deficiency of serotonin. Thus SSRIs are usually antidepressant medications.

Sequencing – Determining the order of bases in a DNA or RNA segment or of amino acids in a protein.

Serotonin – A major neurotransmitter in the central and peripheral nervous systems; an indole amine also known as 5-hydroxytryptamine (5-HT); involved in the brain in emotional disorders such as depression, suicide, impulsive behavior, and aggression.

Serotonin transporter (SERT) – The presynaptic binding site for serotonin, where serotonin is taken back into the presynaptic area and becomes part of the reusable or nonreusable pool of serotonin involved in transmitting the signal to the next cell. The SERT process removes serotonin from the synapse and prepares the system for refiring.

Single photon emission computerized tomography (SPECT) – A brain scan resulting from analysis of an organ (in this case, the brain) that has been treated with a radiolabeled chemical, allowing specific brain areas to "light up" based upon their volume of blood flow. Thus, "hot" brain areas (high blood flow) can be differentiated from "cold" brain areas (low blood flow), giving an overall picture of the differences in activity of nerve cells throughout the entire brain.

Substance – A weak term that has been used to describe all chemicals or drugs that are abused by people. The more specific term *chemical* or *drug* should be substituted for the word.

Substance abuse – A general term that relates to all drug problems and in some cases erroneously to the treatment of chemical dependence (as in "substance abuse treatment centers" and Center for Substance Abuse Treatment). The term, scientifically and clinically, should be abandoned.

Synapse – The end of one nerve cell where it releases neurotransmitters and the beginning of the next nerve cell to which an impulse is transmitted, plus the space (synaptic cleft) in between.

Synaptic cleft – The space between nerve cells where neurotransmitters are released to increase or slow a nerve impulse.

Synaptic plasticity – The ability of synapses (including structural and chemical components) to remain adaptable, changing in function (sometimes permanently) with prolonged stimulation or exposure to drugs or chemicals.

Tachyphylaxis – Rapid appearance of progressive decrease in response to a given dose after repetitive administration of a pharmacologically active chemical; also, "very rapid tolerance."
Teratogenic – A condition of abnormal prenatal development, or (teratogen) an agent that causes such a condition.
Tetrahydrocannabinol (THC) – The active ingredient in cannabis (marijuana).
Tolerance – A neuroadaptive or metabolic change causing chemicals to be given in greater and greater doses to produce the same effect they had initially.
Transcription – The process by which the genetic information contained in a linear sequence of DNA nucleotides is converted into an exactly complementary sequence of mRNA nucleotides; the first stage of gene expression. (Not the same as gene expression.)
Translation – The process by which the genetic information encoded by a specific mRNA is converted into a corresponding sequence of amino acids.
tRNA (transfer RNA) – A type of RNA molecule that carries a specific amino acid and matches it to its corresponding codon on an mRNA during translation.
Twelve-step program – A program of group interaction in which the 12-step program of Wilson and Smith ("Big Book" of Alcoholics Anonymous) is followed to gain abstinence.
Ventral tegmental area – The "beginning" of the mesolimbic dopamine system, in the center of the brain, where there are located receptors for a number of drugs that stimulate the system.
Withdrawal syndrome – The signs and symptoms that arise when the use of a drug is abruptly stopped or when a specific antagonist to the drug is given. The withdrawal syndrome is an indication of the body's adaptation to the drug, which is also known as *physiological dependence*.

References

Agarwal, D. P. (2002). Cardioprotective effects of light–moderate consumption of alcohol: A review of putative mechanisms. *Alcohol & Alcoholism, 37*, 409–415.

Alcohol Research & Health. (2002). Concepts and terms in genetic research–A Primer. *26*, 165–171.

Allen, J. P. & Wilson, V. B. (Eds.). (2003). Assessing alcohol problems: A guide for clinicians and researchers. Bethesda, Maryland: National Institute on Alcohol Abuse and Alcoholism, National Institute of Health Publication 03–3745.

American Psychiatric Association. (1987). *Diagnostic and Statistical Manual of Mental Disorders* (3rd rev. ed.). Washington, DC: Author.

American Psychiatric Association. (2000). *Diagnostic and Statistical Manual of Mental Disorders*, (4th rev. ed.). Washington, DC: Author.

Amodio, D. M., & Frith, C. D. (2006). Meeting of minds: The medial frontal cortex and social cognition. *Nature, 7*, 268–277.

Anton, R. F., O'Malley, S. S., Ciraulo, D. A., Cisler, R. A., Couper, D., Donovan, D. M., et al., for the COMBINE Group. (2006). Combined pharmacotherapies and behavioral interventions for alcohol dependence. The COMBINE study: A randomized controlled trial. *Journal of the American Medical Association, 295*, 2003–2017.

Anthony, J. C., Warner, L. A., & Kessler, R. C. (1994). Comparative epidemiology of dependence on tobacco, alcohol, controlled substances, and inhalants: Basic findings from the national comorbidity survey. *Experimental & Clinical Psychopharmacology, 2*, 244–268.

Arnst, C. (2005, April 11). Can alcoholism be treated? *Business Week*, 96–97.

Asbridge, M., Poulin, C., & Donato, A., (2005). Motor vehicle collision risk and driving under the influence of cannabis: Evidence from adolescents in Atlantic Canada. *Accident Analysis & Prevention, 37*, 1025–1034.

Berrettini, W. H., Ferraro, T. M., Alexander, R. C., Buchberg, A. M. & Vogel, W. H. (1994). Quantitative trait loci mapping of three loci controlling morphine preference using inbred mouse strains. *Natural Genetics, 7*, 54–58.

Bice, P. J., Foroud, T., Carr, L. G., Zhang, L., Liu, L., Grahame, N. J., et al. (2006). Identification of QTLs influencing alcohol preference in the high alcohol preferring (HAP) and low alcohol preferring (LAP) mouse lines. *Behavior Genetics, 36*, 248–260.

Biederman, J., Wilens, T., Mick, E., Spencer, T., & Faraone, S. V. (1999). Pharmacotherapy of attention-deficit/hyperactivity disorder reduces risk for substance use disorder. *Pediatrics, 104*, 1–5.

Bierut, L. J., Saccone, N. L., Rice, J. P., Goate, A., Foroud, T., Edenberg, H., et al. (2002). Defining alcohol-related phenotypes in humans. *Alcohol Research & Health, 26*, 208–214.

Blomqvist, O., Gelernter, J., & Kranzler, H. R. (2000). Family-based study of DRD2 alleles in alcohol and drug dependence. *American Journal of Medical Genetics, 96*, 659–664.

Bonese, K. F., Wainer, B. H., Fitch, F. W., Rothberg, R. M., & Schuster, C. R. (1974). Changes in heroin self-administration by a rhesus monkey after morphine immunization. *Nature, 252*, 708–710.

Bowirrat, A., & Oscar-Berman, M. (2005). Relationship between dopaminergic neurotransmission, alcoholism, and Reward Deficiency syndrome. *American Journal of Medical Genetics Part B, 132B*, 29–37.

Breslau, N., David, G. C., & Schultz, L. R. (2003). Posttraumatic stress disorder and the incidence of nicotine, alcohol, and other drug disorders in persons who have experienced trauma. *Archives of General Psychiatry, 60*, 289–294.

Bressan, R. A., & Pilowsky, L. S. (2000). Imaging the glutamatergic system in vivo: Relevance to schizophrenia. *European Journal of Nuclear Medicine, 27*, 1723–1731.

Brick, J., (Ed.). (2004). *Handbook of the Medical Consequences of Alcohol and Drug Abuse*. New York: Haworth.

Brick, J., & Erickson, C. K. (1999). *Drugs, the Brain, and Behavior: The Pharmacology of Abuse and Dependence*. Binghamton, NY: Haworth.

Brunton, L. L., Lazo, J. S., Parker, K. L., Buxton, I. L. O., & Blumenthal, D. (Eds.). (2006). *Goodman & Gilman's The Pharmacological Basis of Therapeutics* (11th Ed.) New York: McGraw-Hill.

Buchert, R., Thomasius, R., Wilke, F., Petersen, K., Nebeling, B., Obrocki, J., et al. (2004). A voxel–based PET investigation of the long–term effects of "ecstasy" consumption on brain serotonin transporters. *American Journal of Psychiatry, 161*, 1181–1189.

Budney, A. J., & Higgins, S. T. (1998). *National Institute on Drug Abuse Therapy Manuals for Drug Addiction, Manual 2. A Community Reinforcement Plus Vouchers Approach: Treating Cocaine Addiction.* Rockville, Maryland. National Institute on Drug Abuse, National Institute of Health Publication 98–4309.

Budney, A. J., Hughes, J. R., Moore, B. A., & Vandrey, R. (2004). Review of the validity and significance of cannabis withdrawal syndrome. *American Journal of Psychiatry, 161*, 1967–1977.

Busch, A. B., Weiss, R. D., & Najavits, L. M. (2005). Co-occurring substance use disorders and other psychiatric disorders. In R. J. Frances, S. I. Miller, & A. H. Mack, (Eds.), *Clinical Textbook of Addictive Disorders* (3rd ed., pp. 271–302), New York: Guilford.

Cami, J., & Farre, M. (2003). Drug addiction. *New England Journal of Medicine, 349*, 975–86.

Campbell, W. G. (2003). Addiction: A disease of volition caused by a cognitive impairment. *The Canadian Journal of Psychiatry, 48*, 669–674.

Carlson, K. R., Saulnier-Dyer, C. M., & Moolten, M. J. (1996). Selective breeding for oral opioid acceptance or rejection in rats. *Pharmacology Biochemistry & Behavior, 53*, 871–876.

Carr, L. G., Habetter K., Spence, J., Ritochotte, A., Liu, L., Lumeng, L., et al. (2003). Analyses of quantitative trait loci contributing to alcohol preference in HAD1/LAD1 and HAD2/LAD2 rats. *Alcoholism: Clinical & Experimental Research, 27*, 1710–1717.

Carroll, C. B., Bain, P. G., Teare, L., Liu, X., Joint, C., Wroath, C., et al. (2004). Cannabis for dyskinesia in Parkinson disease. *Neurology, 63*, 1245–1250.

Chambers, R. A., Taylor, J. R., & Potenza, M. N. (2003). Developmental neurocircuitry of motivation in adolescence: A critical period of addiction vulnerability. *American Journal of Psychiatry, 160*, 1041–1052.

Childress, A. R., Mozley, P. D., McElgin, W., Fitzgerald, J., Reivich, M., & O'Brien, C. P. (1999). Limbic activation during cue-induced cocaine craving. *American Journal of Psychiatry, 156*, 11–18.

Chklovskii, D. B., Mel, B. W., & Svoboda, K. (2004). Cortical rewiring and information storage. *Nature, 431*, 782–788.

Cloninger, C. R., Bohman, M., & Sigvardsson, S. (1981). Inheritance of alcohol abuse. Cross-fostering analysis of adopted men. *Archives of General Psychiatry, 38*, 861–868.

Cloninger, C. R, Sigvardsson, S., Gilligan, S. B., von Knorring, A. L., Reich, T., & Bohman, M. (1988). Genetic heterogeneity and the classification of alcoholism. *Advances in Alcohol & Substance Abuse, 7*, 3–16.

Collins, E. D., Kleber, H .D., Whittington, R. A., & Heitler, N. E. (2005). Anesthesia-assisted vs. buprenorphine- or clonidine-assisted heroin detoxification and naltrexone induction. *Journal of the American Medical Association, 294*, 903–913.

Compton, P., & Athanasos, P. (2003). Chronic pain, substance abuse and addiction. *Nursing Clinics of North America, 38*, 525–537.

Dackis, C. A., Kampman, K. M., Lynch, K. G., Pettinati, H. M., & O'Brien, C. P. (2005). A double-blind, placebo-controlled trial of modafinil for cocaine dependence. *Neuropsychopharmacology, 30*, 205–211.

Dackis, C., & O'Brien, C. (2005). Neurobiology of addiction: Treatment and public policy ramifications. *Nature Neuroscience, 8*, 1431–1436.

Daglish, M. R. C., & Nutt, D. J. (2003). Brain imaging studies in human addicts. *European Neuropsychopharmacology, 13*, 453–458.

D'Aquila, P. S., Peana, A. T., Tanda, O., & Serra G. (2002). Different sensitivity to the motor-stimulating effect of amphetamine in Sardinian alcohol-preferring and non-preferring rats. *European Journal of Pharmacology, 435*, 67–71.

Dani, J. A., & Harris, R. A. (2005). Nicotine addiction and comorbidity with alcohol abuse and mental illness. *Nature Neuroscience, 8*, 1465–1470.

Dasgupta, N., Kramer, E. D., Zalman, M., Carino, S., Smith, M. Y., Haddox, J. D., et al. (2006). Association between non–medical and prescriptive usage of opioids. *Drug & Alcohol Dependence, 82*, 135–142.

Davis, V. E., & Walsh, J. J. (1970). Alcohol, amines, and alkaloids: A possible biochemical basis for alcohol addiction. *Science, 167*, 1005–1007.

Deroche-Gamonet, V., Belin, D., & Piazza, P. V. (2004). Evidence for addiction-like behavior in the rat. *Science, 305*, 1014–1017.

Dick, D. M., Edenberg, H. J., Xuei, X., Goate, A., Hesselbrock, V. Schuckit, M., et al. (2005). No association of the GABAA receptor genes on chromosome 5 with alcoholism in the collaborative study on the genetics of alcoholism sample. *American Journal of Medical Genetics Part B, 132B*, 24–28.

Dick, D. M., & Foroud, T. (2002). Genetic strategies to detect genes involved in alcoholism and alcohol-related traits. *Alcohol Research & Health, 26*, 172–174.

Domino, E. F. (2003). The Pharmacology of NMDA antagonists: Psychotomimetics and dissociative anesthetics. In A. W. Graham, T. K. Schultz, M. F., Mayo-Smith, R. K. Ries, & B. B. Wilford, (Eds.), *Principles of Addiction Medicine* (pp. 287–294). Chevy Chase, Maryland: American Society of Addiction Medicine, Inc.

Donaldson, D. I. (2004). Parsing brain activity with fMRI and mixed designs: What kind of a state is neuroimaging in? *Trends in Neurosciences, 27*, 442–444.

Doyon, W. M., York, J. W., Diaz, L. M., Samson, H. H., Czachowski, C. L. & Gonzales, R. A. (2003). Dopamine activity in the nucleus accumbens during consummatory phases of oral ethanol self-administration. *Alcoholism: Clinical & Experimental Research, 27*, 1573–1582.

Edenberg, H. J., Dick, D. M., Xuei, X., Tian, H., Almasy, L., Bauer, L. O., et al. (2004). Variations in GABRA2, encoding the alpha 2 subunit of the GABAA receptor, are associated with alcohol dependence and with brain oscillations. *American Journal of Human Genetics, 74*, 705–714.

Edenberg, H. J., & Kranzler, H. R. (2005). The contribution of genetics to addiction therapy approaches. *Pharmacology & Therapeutics 108*, 86–93.

Ehlers, C. L., Gilder, D. A., Wall, T. L., Phillips, E., Feiler, H., & Wilhelmsen, K. C. (2004). Genomic screen for loci associated with alcohol dependence in Mission Indians. *American Journal of Medical Genetics Part B, 129B*, 110–115.

Erickson, C. K., Javors, M. A., & Morgan, W. W. (1990). Drug dependence: Defining the issues. In C. K. Erickson, M. A. Javors, W. W. Morgan, & B. Stimmel (Eds.) *Addiction Potential of Abused Drugs & Drug Classes*. New York: The Haworth Press.

Erickson, C. K. (1995). Voice of the victims: There is a difference between alcohol abuse and alcoholism. *Alcoholism: Clinical & Experimental Research, 19*, 533–534.

Erickson, C. K. (2003). Addiction is a disease. *Addiction Today*, Jan/Feb, 17–19.

Erickson, C. K., & Wilcox, R. E. (2001). Neurobiological causes of addiction. *Journal of Social Work & Practice on Addictions, 1*, 7–22.

Eriksson, K. (1968). Genetic selection for voluntary alcohol consumption in the albino rat. *Science, 159*, 739–741.

Everitt, B. J., & Robbins, T. W. (2005). Neural systems of reinforcement for drug addiction: From actions to habits to compulsion. *Nature Neuroscience, 8*, 1481–1489.

Farah, M. J. (2002). Emerging ethical issues in neuroscience. *Nature Neuroscience, 5*, 1123–1124.

Feeney, G. F., Conner, J. P., Young, R. M., Tucker, J., & McPherson, A. (2006). Combined acamprosate and naltrexone, with cognitive behavioural therapy is superior to either medication alone for alcohol abstinence: A single centres' experience with pharmacotherapy. *Alcohol & Alcoholism, 41*, 321–327.

Feighner, J. P., Robins, E., Guze, S. B., Woodruff, R. A., Winokur, G., & Munoz, R. (1972). Diagnostic criteria for use in psychiatric research. *Archives of General Psychiatry, 26*, 57–63.

Feinn, R., Nellissery, M., & Kranzler, H. R. (2005). Meta-analysis of the association of a functional serotonin transporter promoter polymorphism with alcohol dependence. *American Journal of Medical Genetics Part B, 133B*, 79–84.

Fingarette, H. (1970). The perils of Powell: In search of a factual foundation for the "disease concept of alcoholism." *Harvard Law Review, 83*, 793–812.

Friedrich, M. J. (2005). Neuroscience becomes image conscious as brain scans raise ethical issues. *Journal of the American Medical Association, 294*, 781–783.

Fuller, R. K., & Hiller-Sturmhöfel, S. (1999). Alcoholism treatment in the United States. *Alcohol Research & Health, 23*, 69–77.

Furmark, T., Tillfors, M., Marteinsdottir, I., Fischer, H., Pissiota, A., Langstrom, B., et al. (2002). Common changes in cerebral blood flow in patients with social phobia treated with citalopram or cognitive–behavioral therapy. *Archives of General Psychiatry, 59*, 425–433.

Garbutt, J. C., Kranzler, H. R., O'Malley, S. S., Gastfriend, D. R., Pettinati, H. M., Silverman, B. L., et al., for the Vivitrex Group. (2005). Efficacy and tolerability of long–acting injectable naltrexone for alcohol dependence. *Journal of the American Medical Association, 293*, 1617–1625.

Garrett, B. E., & Griffiths, R. R. (1997). The role of dopamine in the behavioral effects of caffeine in animals and humans. *Pharmacology Biochemistry & Behavior 57*, 533–541.

Gendreau, P. L., & Vitaro, F., (2005). The unbearable lightness of "light" cigarettes: A comparison of smoke yields in sex varieties of Canadian "light" cigarettes. *Canadian Journal of Public Health, 96*, 167–172.

Gianoulakis, D., Krishnan, B., & Thavundayil, J. (1996). Enhanced sensitivity of pituitary beta-endorphin to ethanol in subjects at high risk of alcoholism. *Archives of General Psychiatry, 53*, 250–257.

Goldapple, K., Segal, Z., Garson, C., Lau, M., Bieling, P., Kennedy, S., et al. (2004). Modulation of cortical–limbic pathways in major depression: Treatment–specific cognitive behavior therapy. *Archives of General Psychiatry, 61*, 34–41.

Goldman, D., Oroszi, G., & Ducci, F. (2005). The genetics of addictions: Uncovering the genes. *Nature Reviews Genetics, 6*, 521–532.

Goldstein, A., & Kalant, H. (1990). Drug policy: Striking the right balance. *Science, 249*, 1513–1521.

Goldstein, D. B. (1984). The effects of drugs on membrane fluidity. *Annual Review of Pharmacology and Toxicology, 24*, 43–64.

Grant, B. F., & Dawson, D. A. (1997). Age at onset of alcohol use and its association with DSM-IV alcohol abuse and dependence: Results from the National Longitudinal Alcohol Epidemiologic Survey. *Journal of Substance Abuse, 9*, 103–110.

Grant, B. F., Hasin, D. S., Chou, P., Stinson, F. S., & Dawson, D. A. (2004). Nicotine dependence and psychiatric disorders in the United States. *Archives of General Psychiatry, 61*, 1107–1115.

Grant, B. F., Harford, T. C., Muthen, B. O., Yi, H., Hasin, D.S., & Stinson, F. S. (In press). *DSM–IV* alcohol dependence and abuse: Further evidence of validity in the general population. *Drug & Alcohol Dependence.*

Grant, J. E., & Kim, S. W. (2002). Effectiveness of pharmacotherapy for pathological gambling: A chart review. *Annals of Clinical Psychiatry, 14*, 155–161.

Grant, J. E., Potenza, M. N., Hollander, E., Cunningham-Williams, R., Nurminen, T., Smits, G., et al. (2006). Multicenter investigation of the opioid antagonist nalmefene in the treatment of pathological gambling. *American Journal of Psychiatry, 163*, 303–312.

Gray, M. T. (2005). The shifting sands of self: A framework for the experience of self in addiction. *Nursing Philosophy, 6*, 119–130.

Griffiths, R. R., & Mumford, G. K. (1995). Caffeine – A drug of abuse. In F. E. Bloom, & D. J. Kupfer (Eds.) *Psychopharmacology: The Fourth Generation of Progress* (1669–1713). New York: Raven Press.

Gruenewald, P. J., Freisthler, B., Remer, L., Lascala, E. A., & Treno, A. (2006). Ecological models of alcohol outlets and violent assaults: Crime potentials and geospatial analysis. *Addiction, 101*, 666–677.

Gutstein, H. B. & Akil, H. (2001). Opioid analgesics. In J. G. Hardman, L. E. Limbird, & A. G. Gilman (Eds.), *Goodman & Gillman's The Pharmacological Basis of Therapeutics, Tenth Edition* (pp. 569–579) New York: McGraw-Hill.

Hanson, G. R., & Li, T. -K. (2003). Public health implications of excessive alcohol consumption. *Journal of the American Medical Association, 289*, 1031–1032.

Hart, C. L. (2005). Increasing treatment options for cannabis dependence: A review of potential pharmacotherapies. *Drug & Alcohol Dependence, 80*, 147–149.

Hasin, D. (2003). Classification of alcohol use disorders. *Alcohol Research & Health, 27*, 5–15.

Hasin, D. S., Hatzenbueler, M., Smith, S., & Grant, B. F. (2005). Co–occurring DSM–IV drug abuse in DSM–IV drug dependence: Results from the National Epidemiologic Survey on alcohol and related conditions. *Drug & Alcohol Dependence, 80*, 117–123.

Hill, S. Y., Shen, S., Zezza, N., Hoffman, E. K., Perline, M., & Allan, W. (2004). A genome side search for alcoholism susceptibility genes. *American Journal of Medical Genetics Part B, 128B*, 102–113.

Hjelmstad, G. O. (2004). Dopamine excites nucleus accumbens neurons through the differential modulation of glutamate and GABA release. *Journal of Neuroscience, 24*, 8621–8628.

Hollander, E., Pallanti, S., Allen, A., Sood, E., & Rossi, N. B. (2005). Does sustained-release lithium reduce impulsive gambling and affective instability versus placebo in pathological gamblers with bipolar spectrum disorders? *American Journal of Psychiatry, 162*, 137–145.

Hyman, S. E. (2005). Addiction: A disease of learning and memory. *American Journal of Psychiatry, 162*, 1414–22.

The ICD-10 Classification of Mental & Behavioural Disorders. (1992). Geneva, Switzerland: World Health Organization.

Ioannidis, J. P. A., (2005). Contradicted and initially stronger effects in highly cited clinical research. *Journal of the American Medical Association, 294*, 218–228.

Jackim, L. W. (2005, October). Entering the diagnostic debate. *Behavioral Healthcare Tomorrow*, 12–16.

Johnson, B. A. (2005). Recent advances in the development of treatments for alcohol and cocaine dependence: Focus on topiramate and other modulators of GABA or glutamate function. *Central Nervous System Drugs, 19*, 873–896.

Johnson, B. A. (2004). Progress in the development of topiramate for treating alcohol dependence: From a hypothesis to a proof-of-concept study. *Alcoholism: Clinical & Experimental Research, 28*, 1137–1144.

Johnson, B. A., Ait-Daoud, N., Akhtar, F. Z., & Ma, J. Z. (2004). Oral topiramate reduces the consequences of drinking and improves the quality of life of alcohol-dependent individuals. *Archives of General Psychiatry, 61*, 905–912.

Johnson, R. E., Chutuape, M. A., Strain, E. C., Walsh, S. L. Stitzer, M. L., & Bigelow, G. E. (2000). A comparison of levomethadyl acetate, buprenorphine, and methadone for opioid dependence. *New England Journal of Medicine, 343*, 1290–1297.

Jones, D. C., Duvauchelle, C., Ikegami, A., Olsen, C. M., Lau, S. S., de la Torre, R., & Monks, T. J. (2005). Serotonergic neurotoxic metabolites of ecstasy identified in rat brain. *Journal of Pharmacology & Experimental Therapeutics, 313*, 422–431.

Jorenby, D. E., Hays, J. T., Rigotti, N. A., Azoulay, S., Watsky, E. J., Williams, K. E., et al. Varenicline Phase 3 Study Group. (2006). Efficacy of varenicline, an alpha4beta2 nicotinic acetylcholine receptor partial agonist, vs placebo or sustained–release bupropion for smoking cessation: a randomized controlled trial. *Journal of the American Medical Association, 296*, 94–95.

Juliano, L. M., & Griffiths, R. R. (2004). A critical review of caffeine withdrawal: Empirical validation of symptoms and signs, incidence, severity, and associated features. *Psychopharmacology 176*, 1-29.

Kalivas, P. W., & Volkow, N. D. (2005). The neural basis of addiction: A pathology of motivation and choice. *American Journal of Psychiatry, 162*, 1403–1413.

Kamens, H. M., Burkhart-Kasch, S., McKinnon, C. S., Li, N., Reed, C., & Phillips, T. J. (2005). Sensitivity to psychostimulants in mice bred for high and low stimulation to methamphetamine. *Genes, Brain & Behavior, 4*, 110–125.

Kessler, R. C., Nelson, C. B., McGonagle, K. A., Edlund, M. J., Frank, R. G., & Leaf, P. J. (1996). The epidemiology of co–occurring addictive and mental disorders: Implications for prevention and service utilization. *American Journal of Orthopsychiatry, 66*, 17–31.

Kiefer, F. & Mann, K. (2005). New achievements and pharmacotherapeutic approaches in the treatment of alcohol dependence. *European Journal of Pharmacology, 526*, 163–171.

Kiefer, F., & Wiedemann, K. (2004). Combined therapy: What does acamprosate and naltrexone combination tell us? *Alcohol & Alcoholism, 39*, 542–547.

Kiianmaa, K., Nurmi, M., & Sinclair, J. D. (1994). Genetically determined influences on voluntary ethanol consumption: Extracellular levels of ethanol and monoamines in the nucleus accumbens of the alcohol preferring AA and alcohol avoiding ANA rate lines. *Alcohol & Alcoholism, Supplement 2*, 73–78.

Koch, A. L., Arfken, C. L., & Schuster, C. R. (2006). Characteristics of U.S. substance abuse treatment facilities adopting buprenorphine in its initial stage of availability. *Drug & Alcohol Dependence, 83*, 274–278.

Koob G. F. (1992). Drugs of abuse: Anatomy, pharmacology, and function of reward pathways. *Trends in Pharmacological Science, 13*, 177–184.

Koob, G. F. (2003). Alcoholism: Allostasis and beyond. *Alcoholism: Clinical and Experimental Research, 27*, 232–243.

Koob, G. F., & Le Moal, M. (1997). Drug abuse: Hedonic homeostatic dysregulation. *Science, 278*, 52–8.

Koob, G. F., & Le Moal, M. (2001). Drug addiction, dysregulation of reward, and allostasis. *Neuropsychopharmacology, 24*, 97–129.

Koob, G. F., Ahmed, S. H., Boutrel, B., Chen, S. A., Kenny, P. J., Markou, A., O'Dell, L., Parsons, L. H., & Sanna, P. P. (2004). Neurobiological mechanisms in the transition from drug use to drug dependence. *Neuroscience & Behavioral Reviews, 27*, 739–749.

Krampke, H., Stawicki, S., Wagner, R., Bartels, C., Aust, C., Ruther, E., Poser, W., & Ehrenreich, H. (2006). Follow–up of 180 alcoholic patients for up to 7 years after outpatient treatment: Impact of alcohol deterrents on outcome. *Alcoholism: Clinical & Experimental Research, 30*, 86–95.

Kranzler, H. R., Koob, G., Gastfriend, D. R., Swift, R. M., & Willenbring, M. L. (2006). Advances in the pharmacotherapy of alcoholism: Challenging misconceptions. *Alcoholism: Clinical & Experimental Research, 30*, 272–281.

Kuhn, C., Swartzwelder, S., & Wilson, W. (2002). *Just Say Know.* New York: Norton.

Kuhn, C., Swartzwelder, S., & Wilson, W. (2003). *Buzzed.* New York: Norton.

Kuperman, S., Schlosser, S. S., Kramer, J. R., Bucholz, K., Hesselbrock, V., Reich, T., et al. (2001). Developmental sequence from disruptive behavior diagnosis to adolescent alcohol dependence. *American Journal of Psychiatry, 158*, 2022–2026.

Kurtz, E. (1979). *Not-God: A History of Alcoholics Anonymous.* San Francisco,: Harper & Row.

Lawson, K. A., Wilcox, R. E., Littlefield, J. H., Pituch, K. A., & Erickson, C. K. (2004). Educating professionals to promote addiction science research: Demographics of knowledge and belief changes. *Substance Use & Misuse, 39*, 1237–1260.

Le Foll, B., & Goldberg, S. R. (2005). Cannabinoid CB1 receptor antagonists as promising new medications for drug dependence. *Journal of Pharmacology & Experimental Therapeutics, 312*, 875–883.

Lerman, C., Patterson, F., & Berrettini, W. (2005). Treating tobacco dependence: State of the science and new directions. *Journal of Clinical Oncology, 23*, 311–323.

Leshner, A. I. (1997). Addiction is a brain disease. *Science, 278*, 45–47.

Lewis, D. C. (2005). Untitled letter on "crack" and "meth" babies, on behalf of 92 signees. www.csdp.org/news/news/Meth_Letter.pdf

Lewis, D. C. (1991). Comparison of alcoholism and other medical diseases: An Internist's view. *Psychiatric Annals, 21*, 256–265.

Linden, D. E. J. (2006). How psychotherapy changes the brain – the contribution of functional neuroimaging. *Molecular Psychiatry, 11*, 528–538.

Litten, R. Z., Fertig, J., Mattson, M. E., & Egli, M. (2005). Development of medications for alcohol use disorders: Recent advances and ongoing challenges. *Expert Opinion on Emerging Drugs, 10*, 323–343.

Luik, J. C. (1996). "I can't help myself": Addiction as ideology. *Human Psychopharmacology 11*, S21–S32.

Maldonado, R., Valverde, O., & Berrendero, F. (2006). Involvement of the endocannabinoid system in drug addiction. *Trends in Neuroscience, 29*, 225–232.

Mann, K., Lehert, P., & Morgan, M. Y. (2004). The efficacy of acamprosate in maintaining abstinence in alcohol-dependent individuals: Results of a meta-analysis. *Alcoholism: Clinical & Experimental Research, 28*, 51–63.

Martin, S. D., Martin, E., Rai, S. S., Richardson, M. A., & Royall, R. (2001). Brain blood flow changes in depressed patients treated with interpersonal psychotherapy or venlafaxine hydrochloride. *Archives of General Psychiatry, 58*, 641–648.

Mayer, P. & Höllt, V. (2005). Genetic disposition to addictive disorders: Current knowledge and future perspectives. *Current Opinion in Pharmacology, 5*, 4–8.

McAuliffe, P. F., Gold, M. S., Bajpai, L., Merves, M. L., Frost–Pineda, K., Pomm, R. M., et al. (2006). Second–hand exposure to aerosolized intravenous anesthetics propofol and fentanyl may cause sensitization and subsequent opiate addiction among anesthesiologists and surgeons. *Medical Hypotheses, 66*, 874–882.

McLellan, A. T., Lewis, D. C., O'Brien, C. P., & Kleber, H. D. (2000). Drug dependence, a chronic medical illness. *Journal of the American Medical Association, 284*, 1689–1695.

McLellan, A. T., Luborsky, L., O'Brien, C. P., & Woody, G. E. (1980). An improved diagnostic instrument for substance abuse patients: The Addiction Severity Index. *Journal of Nervous & Mental Diseases, 168*, 26–33.

McLellan, A. T., & Meyers, K. (2004). Contemporary addiction treatment: A review of systems problems for adults and adolescents. *Biological Psychiatry, 56*, 764–770.

McLellan, A. T., Weinstein, R. L., Shen, Q., Kendig, C., & Levine, M. (2005a). Improving continuity of care in a public addiction treatment system with clinical case management. *American Journal of Addiction, 14*, 426–440.

McLellan, A. T., McKay, J. R., Forman, R., Cacciola, J., & Kempt, J. (2005b). Reconsidering the evaluation of addiction treatment: From retrospective follow–up to concurrent recovery monitoring. *Addiction, 100*, 227–458.

McNeece, C. A., & DiNitto, D. M. (2005). *Chemical dependency: A systems approach*. Boston: Pearson Education, Allyn & Bacon.

Melamede, R. (2005). Cannabis and tobacco smoke are not equally carcinogenic. *Harm Reduction Journal, 2*, 21–26.

Melendez, R. I., Rodd–Henricks, Z. A., Engleman, E. A., Li, T. K., McBride, W. J., & Murphy, J. M. (2002). Microdialysis of dopamine in the nucleus accumbens of alcohol–preferring (P) rats during anticipation and operant self–administration of ethanol. *Alcoholism: Clinical & Experimental Research, 26*, 318–325.

Meyerhoff, D. J., Bode, C., Nixon, S. J., de Bruin, E. A., Bode, J. C., Seitz, H. K. (2005). Health risks of chronic moderate and heavy alcohol consumption. How much is too much? *Alcoholism: Clinical & Experimental Research, 29*, 1334–1340.

Miller, W. R. (2005). Motivational enhancement therapy. In M. Hersen, & J. Rosqvist (Eds.), *Encyclopedia of Behavior Modification and Cognitive Behavior Therapy. Vol 1. Adult Clinical Applications* (pp. 379–383). Thousand Oaks, California: Sage.

Mooney, M. E. & Sofuoglu, M. (2006). Bupropion for the treatment of nicotine withdrawal and craving. *Expert Review of Neurotherapeutics, 6*, 965–981.

Moos, R. H., & Moos, B. S. (2005). Paths of entry into Alcoholics Anonymous: Consequences for participation and remission. *Alcoholism: Clinical & Experimental Research, 29*, 1858–1868.

Mukamal, K. J., Conigrave, K. M., Mittleman, M. A., Camargo, C. A. Jr., Stampfer, M. J. Willett, W. C., et al. (2003). Roles of drinking pattern and type of alcohol consumed in coronary heart disease in men. *New England Journal of Medicine, 348*, 109–118.

National Institute on Alcohol Abuse and Alcoholism (NIAAA). (2006a). Frequently Asked Questions (FAQs), www.niaaa.nih.gov/FAQs/General–English/FAQ1.htm

National Institute on Alcohol Abuse and Alcoholism (NIAAA). (2006b). Trends in the prevalence of alcohol use among high school seniors. Monitoring the Future Study, 1975–2003, www.niaaa.nih.gov/Resources/DatabaseResources/QuickFacts/AlcoholConsumption/dkpat10.htm

National Institute on Drug Abuse (NIDA). (2006). Selected Prescription Drugs with Potential for Abuse, www.nida.nih.gov/DrugPages/PrescripDrugsChart.html

Nehlig, A. (1999). Are we dependent upon coffee and caffeine? A review on human and animal data. *Neuroscience & Behavioral Reviews, 23*, 563–576.

Nelson, T. F., Naimi, T. S., Brewer, R. D., & Wechsler, H. (2005). The state sets the rate: The relationship among state-specific college binge drinking, state binge drinking rates, and selected state alcohol control policies. *American Journal of Public Health, 95*, 441–446.

No Health Gain from Mild, Light Cigarettes, Join Together Website, May 16, 2005. www.jointogether.org/new/research/summaries/2005

Nutt, D., & Lingford-Hughes, A. (2004). Infecting the brain to stop addiction? *Proceedings of the National Academy of Science, 101*, 11193–11194.

O'Brien, M. S., & Anthony, J. C. (2005). Risk of becoming cocaine dependent: Epidemiological estimates for the United States, 2000–2001. *Neuropsychopharmacology, 30*, 1006–1018.

O'Brien, C. P., & Gardner, E. L. (2005). Critical assessment of how to study addiction and its treatment: Human and non–human animals models. *Pharmacology & Therapeutics, 108*, 18–58.

O'Brien, C. P., Volkow, N., & Li, T. K. (2006). What's in a word? Addiction versus dependence in DSM–V (Editorial). *American Journal of Psychiatry, 163*, 765–766.

Odegaard, S., Peller, A., & Shaffer, H. J. (2005). Addiction as syndrome. *Paradigm, 10*, 12–13 & 22.

O'Malley, S. S., Rounsaville, B. J., Farren, C., Namkoong, K., Wu, R., Robinson, J., et al. (2003). Initial and maintenance naltrexone treatment for alcohol dependence using primary care vs. specialty care. *Archives of Internal Medicine, 163*, 1695–1704.

Oslin, D. W., Slaymaker, V. J., Blow, F. C., Owen, P. L., Colleran, C. (2005). Treatment outcomes for alcohol dependence among middle aged and older adults. *Addictive Behaviors, 30*, 1431–1436.

Papgeorgiou, C., Rabavilas, A., Liappas, I., & Stefanis, C. (2003). Do obsessive-compulsive patients and abstinent heroin addicts share a common psychophysiological mechanism? *Neuropsychobiology, 47*, 1–11.

Paquette, V., Levesque, J., Mensour, B., Leroux, J. -M., Beaudoin, G., Bourgouin, P., et al. (2003). Change the mind and you change the brain: Effects of cognitive-behavioral therapy on the neural correlates of spider phobia. *NeuroImage, 18*, 401–409.

Parsey, R. V., Hastings, R. S, Oquendo, M. A., Huang, Y.–Y., Simpson, N., Arcement, J., et al. (2006). Lower serotonin transporter binding potential in the human brain during major depressive episodes. *American Journal of Psychiatry, 163*, 52–58.

Pelchat, M. L. (2002). Of human bondage: Food craving, obsession, compulsion, and addiction. *Physiology & Behavior, 76*, 347–352.

Penades, R., Boget, T., Lomena, F., Mateos, J. J., Catalan, R., Gasto, C., et al. (2002). Could the hypofrontality pattern in schizophrenia be modified through neuropsychological rehabilitation? *Acta Psychiatrica Scandinavica, 105*, 202–208.

Pentel, P., & Malin, D. (2002). A vaccine for nicotine dependence: Targeting the drug rather than the brain. *Respiratory Research, 69*, 193–197.

Pertwee, R. G. (2006). Cannabinoid pharmacology: The first 66 years. *British Journal of Pharmacology, 147*, S163–S171.

Peters, K. D., & Wood, R. I. (2004). Androgen dependence in hamsters: Overdose, tolerance, and potential opioidergic mechanisms. *Neuroscience, 130*, 971–981.

Pfefferbaum, A., Lim, K. O., Desmond, J., & Sullivan, E. V. (1996). Thinning of the corpus callosum in older alcoholic men: A magnetic resonance imaging study. *Alcoholism: Clinical & Experimental Research, 20*, 752–757.

Pfefferbaum, A., Sullivan, E. V., Mathalon, D. H., Shear, P. K., Rosenbloom, M. J., & Lim, K. O. (1995). Longitudinal changes in magnetic resonance imaging brain volumes in abstaining and relapsed alcoholics. *Alcoholism: Clinical & Experimental Research, 19*, 1177–1191.

Phillips, T. (2002). Animal models for the genetic study of human alcohol phenotypes. *Alcohol Research & Health, 26*, 202–207.

Pietrini, P. (2003). Toward a biochemistry of mind? *American Journal of Psychiatry, 160*, 1907–1908.

Porjesz, B., Almasy, L., Edenberg, H.J., Wang, K., Chorlian, D. B., Foroud, T., et al. (2002). Linkage disequilibrium between the beta frequency of the human EEG and a GABAA receptor gene locus. *Proceedings of the National Academy of Sciences of the USA, 99*, 3729–3733.

Portenoy, R. K., Lussier, D., Kirsh, K. L., & Passik, S. D. (2005). Pain and addiction. In R. J. Frances, S. I. Miller, & A. H. Mack (Eds.), *Clinical Textbook of Addictive Disorders*, (3rd ed., pp. 367–395). New York: Guilford.

Pryce, G., & Baker, D. (2005). Emerging properties of cannabinoid medicines in management of multiple sclerosis. *Trends in Neurosciences, 28*, 272–276.

Raine, A., Buchsbaum, M., & LaCasse, L. (1997). Brain abnormalities in murderers indicated by positron emission tomography. *Biological Psychiatry, 42*, 495–508.

Randall, C. L., & Lester, D. (1975). Social modification of alcohol consumption in inbred mice. *Science, 189*, 149–151.

Ray, O., & Ksir, C. (2004). *Drugs, Society, and Human Behavior.* New York: McGraw-Hill.

Reich, T., Edenberg, H. J., Goate, A., Williams, J. T., Rice, J. P., Van Eerdewegh, P., et al. (1998). A genome–wide search for genes affecting the risk for alcohol dependence. *American Journal of Medical Genetics (Neuropsychiatric Genetics), 81*, 207–215.

Reuter, J., Raedler, T., Rose, M., Hand, I., Glascher, J., & Buchel, C., (2005). Pathological gambling is linked to reduced activation of the mesolimbic reward system. *Nature Neuroscience, 8*, 147–148.

Rhodes, J. S. & Crabbe, J. C. (2005). Gene expression inducted by drugs of abuse. *Current Opinion in Pharmacology, 5*, 26–33.

Ridenour, T. A., Maldonado–Molina, M., Compton, W. M., Spitznagel, E. L., & Cottler, L. B. (2005). Factors associated with the transition from abuse to dependence among substance abusers: Implications for a measure of addictive liability. *Drug & Alcohol Dependence, 80*, 1–14.

Rigotti, N. A. (2002). Treatment of tobacco use and dependence. *New England Journal of Medicine, 346*, 506–512.

Ritsher, J. B., McKellar, J. D., Finney, J. W., Otlingam, P. G., & Moos, R. H. (2002). Psychiatric comorbidity, continuing care and mutual help as predictors of five-year remission from substance use disorders. *Journal of Studies on Alcohol, 63*, 709–715.

Robbins, T. W. (2002). ADHD and addiction. *Nature Medicine, 8*, 24–25.

Robinson, T. E. (2004). Addicted rats. *Science, 305*, 951–953.

Robinson, T .E., & Berridge K.C. (1993). The neural basis of drug craving: An incentive-sensitization theory of addiction. *Brain Research Review, 18*, 247–291.

Robinson, T. E., & Berridge, K. C. (2000). The psychology and neurobiology of addiction: An incentive-sensitization view. *Addiction, 95*, S91–S117.

Robinson, T. E., & Berridge, K. C. (2003). Addiction. *Annual Reviews in Psychology, 54*, 25–53.

Robinson, T. E., & Kolb, B. (1997). Persistent structural modifications in nucleus accumbens and prefrontal cortex neurons produced by previous experience with amphetamine. *Journal of Neuroscience, 17*, 8491–8497.

Rounsaville, B. J., Kranzler, H. R., Ball, S., Tennen, H., Poling, J., & Triffleman, E. (1998). Personality disorders in substance abusers: Relation to substance use. *Journal of Nervous and Mental Disease, 186*, 87–95.

Saitz, R. (2005). Unhealthy alcohol use. *New England Journal of Medicine, 352*, 596–606.

Salokangas, R. K., Honkonen, T., Stengard, E., Koivisto, A. M., & Hietala, J. (2006). Cigarette smoking in long–term schizophrenia. *European Psychiatry, 21*, 219–223.

Samaha, A.-N. & Robison, T. E. (2005). Why does the rapid delivery of drugs to the brain promote addiction? *Trends in Pharmacological Sciences, 26*, 82–87.

Savage, S. R., Joranson, D. E., Covington, E. C., Schnoll, S. H., Heit, H. A., & Gilson, A. M. (2003). Definitions related to the medical use of opioids: Evolution towards universal agreement. *Journal of Pain Symptom Management, 26*, 655–667.

Sawyer, S. M., & Fardy, H. J. (2003). Bridging the gap between doctors' and patients' expectations of asthma management. *Journal of Asthma, 40*, 131–138.

Saxe, R. (2006). Why and how to study Theory of Mind with fMRI. *Brain Research, 1079*, 57–65.

Schiffer, W. K., Lee, D. E., Brodie, J. D., & Dewey. S. L. (2005). Imagining addiction with PET: Is insight in sight? *Drug Discovery Today, 10*, 547–62.

Schlaepfer, T. E., Strain, E.C., Greenberg, B. D., Preston K. L., Lancaster, E., Bigelow, G. E., et al. (1998). Site of opioid action in the human brain: Mu and kappa agonists' subjective and cerebral blood flow effects. *American Journal of Psychiatry, 155*, 470–473.

Schuckit, M.A. (2000). Biological phenotypes associated with individuals at high risk for developing alcohol-related disorders. Part 2. *Addiction Biology, 5*, 23-36.

Schuckit, M. A., Edenberg, H. J., Kalmijn, J., Flury, L., Smith, T. L., Reich, T., et al. (2001). A genome–wide search for genes that relate to a low level of response to alcohol. *Alcoholism: Clinical & Experimental Research, 25*, 323–329.

Schuckit, M. A., Smith, T. L., Danko, G. P., Bucholz, K. K., Reich, T., & Bierut, L. (2001). Five-year clinical course associated with DSM-IV alcohol abuse or dependence in a large group of men and women. *Archives of General Psychiatry, 158*, 1084–1090.

Schultz, W., Dayan, P., Montague, P. R. (1997). A neural substrate of prediction and reward. *Science, 275*, 1593–1599.

Schwartz, R. P., Jaffe, J. H., Highfield, D. A., Callaman, J. M., O'grady, K. E. (In press). A randomized controlled trial of interim methadone maintenance: 10–month follow–up. *Drug & Alcohol Dependence.*

Shaffer, H. J., LaPlante, D. A., LaBrie, R. A., Kidman, R. C., Donato, A., & Stanton, M. V. (2004). Toward a syndrome model of addiction: Multiple manifestations, common etiology. *Harvard Review of Psychiatry, 12*, 367–374.

Slutske, W. S. (2006). Natural recovery and treatment-seeking in pathological gambling: Results of two U.S. national surveys. *American Journal of Psychiatry, 163*, 297–302.

Small, D. M., Zatorre, R. J., Dagher, A., Evans, A. C., & Jones-Gotman, M. (2001). Changes in brain activity related to eating chocolate. *Brain, 124*, 1720–1733.

Smith, A. P. (1996). Caffeine dependence: An alternative view. *Nature Medicine* 2, 494.

Smith, D. G., Learn, J. E., McBride, W. J., Lumeng, L., Li, T. K., & Murphy, J. M. (2001). Alcohol-naïve alcohol-preferring (P) rats exhibit higher local cerebral glucose utilization than alcohol-nonpreferring (NP) and Wistar rats. *Alcoholism: Clinical & Experimental Research, 25*, 1309–1316.

Sofuoglu, M., & Kosten, T. R. (2005). Novel approaches to the treatment of cocaine addiction. *Central Nervous System Drugs, 19*, 13–25.

Sorensen, J. L., & Guydish, J. R. (1991). Adopting effective interventions. In J. L. Sorensen, L. A. Wermuth, D. R. Gibson, K. H. Choi, J. R. Guydish, & S. L. Batki (Eds.), *Preventing AIDS in Drug Users & Their Sexual Partners* (pp. 153–67). New York: Guilford.

Spanagel, R., & Heilig, M. (2005). Addiction and its brain science. *Addiction, 100*, 1813–1822.

Stepney, R. (1996). The concept of addiction: Its use and abuse in the media and science. *Human Psychopharmacology, 11*, S15–S20.

Sterling, P., & Eyer, J. (1988). Allostasis: A new paradigm to explain arousal pathology. In S. Fisher, & J. Reason (Eds.), *Handbook of Life Stress, Cognition and Health* (pp. 629–649). Chichester, UK: Wiley.

Strathdee, S.A., Picketts, E.P., Huettner, S., Cornelius, L., Bishai, D., Havens, J. R., et al. (2006). Facilitating entry into drug treatment among injection drug users referred from a needle exchange program: Results from a community–based behavioral intervention trial. *Drug & Alcohol Dependence, 83*, 225–232.

Substance Abuse and Mental Health Services Administration, Office of Applied Studies. (2002). *Data on Substance Abuse Treatment Facilities. DASIS Series: S–16*. National Survey of Substance Abuse Treatment Services (N–SSATS). Rockville, Maryland: Substance Abuse and Mental Health Services Administration.

Sullivan, E. V. (2000). Human brain vulnerability to alcoholism: Evidence from neuroimaging studies. In A. Noronha, M. Eckardt, & K. Warren (Eds.), *Review of NIAAA's Neuroscience and Behavioral Research Portfolio* (NIAAA Research Monograph No. 34, pp. 473–508). Bethesda, Maryland: National Institutes of Health.

Supreme Court of the United States (1988). Traynor v. Turnage, Administrator, Veteran's Administration, et al.

Tamminga, C. A., & Nestler, E. J. (2006). Pathological gambling: Focusing on the addiction, not the activity. *American Journal of Psychiatry, 163*, 180–181.

Terry, P, & Wright, K. A., (2005). Self–reported driving behaviour and attitudes towards driving under the influence of cannabis among three different user groups in England. *Addictive Behavior, 30*, 619–626.

Vanderschuren, L. J., & Everitt, B. J. (2004). Drug seeking becomes compulsive after prolonged cocaine self-administration. *Science, 305*, 1017–1019.

Vanderschuren, L. J., & Kalivas, P. W. (2000). Alterations in dopaminergic and glutamatergic transmission in the induction and expression of behavioral sensitization: A critical review of preclinical studies. *Psychopharmacology, 151*, 99–120.

Vandrey, R., Budney, A. J., Kamon, J. L., & Stanger, C. (2005). Cannabis withdrawal in adolescent treatment seekers. *Drug & Alcohol Dependence, 78*, 205–210.

Vanyukov, M. M., Moss, H. B., Kaplan, B. B., Kirillova, G. P., & Tarter, R. E. (2000). Antisociality, substance dependence, and the DRD5 gene: A preliminary study. *American Journal of Medical Genetics, 96*, 654–658.

Verdoux, H., & Tournier, M. (2004). Cannabis use and risk of psychosis: An etiological link? *Epidemiologia e Psichiatria Sociale, 13*, 113–119.

Verhaak, P. F., Kerssens, J. J., Dekker, J., Sorbi, M. J., & Bensing, J. M. (1998). Prevalence of chronic benign pain disorder among adults: A review of the literature. *Pain, 36*, 363–366.

Vocci, F., & Ling, W. (2005). Medications development: Successes and challenges. *Pharmacology & Therapeutics, 108*, 94–108.

Volkow, N.D. (2004a). The reality of comorbidity: Depression and drug abuse. *Biological Psychiatry, 56*, 714–717.

Volkow, N. D. (2004b). Expectation and brain function in drug abuse. *American Journal of Psychiatry, 161*, 621.

Volkow, N. D., Fowler, J. S., & Wang, G. -J. (2003). The addicted human brain: Insights from imaging studies. *Journal of Clinical Investigation, 111*, 1444–1451.

Volkow, N. D., Fowler, J. S., Wang, G. -J., & Goldstein, R. Z. (2002). Role of dopamine, the frontal cortex and memory circuits in drug addiction: Insight from imaging studies. *Neurobiology of Learning & Memory, 78*, 610–624.

Volkow, N. D., & Li, T. -K. (2005a). The neuroscience of addiction. *Nature Neuroscience, 8*, 1429–1430.

Volkow, N. D., & Li, T. -K. (2005b). Drugs and alcohol: Treating and preventing abuse, addiction and their medical consequences. *Pharmacology & Therapeutics, 108*, 3–17.

Wagner, F. A., & Anthony, J.C. (2002). From first drug use to drug dependence: Developmental periods of risk for dependence upon marijuana, cocaine, and alcohol. *Neuropsychopharmacology, 26*, 479–488.

Walitzer, K. S., & Connors, G. J. (1999). Treating problem drinking. *Alcohol Research & Health, 23*, 138–143.

Wallace, J. (1990). Controlled drinking, treatment effectiveness, and the disease model of addiction: A commentary on the ideological wishes of Stanton Peele. *Journal of Psychoactive Drugs, 22*, 261–284.

Wamboldt, M. Z., Weintraub, P., Krafchick, D., & Wamboldt, R. S. (1996). Psychiatric family history in adolescents with severe asthma. *Journal of the American Academy of Child & Adolescent Psychiatry, 35*, 1042–1049.

Wellman, P. J., Bellinger, L. L., Cepeda–Benito, A., Susabda, A., Ho, D. H., et al. (2005). Meal patterns and body weight after nicotine in male rats as a function of chow or high–fat diet. *Pharmacology Biochemistry & Behavior, 82*, 627–634.

White, W. L. (1998). *Slaying the dragon*. Bloomington, IL: Chestnut Health Systems/Lighthouse Institute.

White, W. L. (2005 September). Recovery management: What if we really believe that addiction was a chronic disorder? *Greater Lakes Addiction Technology Transfer Center Bulletin*, 1–7.

White, W. (2001). The rhetoric of recovery advocacy: An essay on the power of language. Posted at http://www.facesandvoicesofrecovery.org/pdf/rhetoric_of_advocacy.pdf

White, W., Kurtz, E., & Acker, C. (2001). Combined Addiction Disease Chronologies of William White, MA, Ernest Kurtz, PhD, and Caroline Acker, PhD, 1966–1972. *Behavioral Health Recovery Management* website. Retrieved November 2006 from http://www.bhrm.org/papers/add.papers.htm

Wilcox, R. E., & Erickson, C. K. (2004). Prevention of relapse to addiction: Information for the practitioner. *Journal of Texas Medicine, 100*, 51–61.

Wilcox, R. E., Gonzales, R. A., & Erickson, C. K. In D. Toft (Ed.), (1995). *Understanding Addiction.* Addiction Science Research & Education Center, University of Texas, Austin. [three booklets].

Willens, T .E., Faraone, S. V., Biederman, J., & Gunawardene, S. (2003). Does stimulant therapy of attention-deficit/hyperactivity disorder beget later substance abuse? A meta-analytic review of the literature. *Journal of Pediatrics, 111*, 179–185.

Wilson, W. A., & Kuhn, C. M. (2005). How addiction hijacks our reward system. *Cerebrum, 7*, 53–66.

World Health Organization. (1992). *The ICD–10 Classification of Mental and Behavioural Disorders.* Geneva, Switzerland: World Health Organization.

Index

Index